Dennis A. Mahony

The Prisoner of State

Dennis A. Mahony

The Prisoner of State

ISBN/EAN: 9783744757881

Printed in Europe, USA, Canada, Australia, Japan

Cover: Foto ©Suzi / pixelio.de

More available books at **www.hansebooks.com**

THE

PRISONER OF STATE.

BY D. A. MAHONY.

'It is important that the habits of thinking in a free country should inspire caution in those entrusted with its administration, to confine themselves within their respective spheres, avoiding, in the exercise of the powers of one department to encroach upon another. The spirit of encroachment tends to consolidate the powers of all the departments in one, and thus to create, whatever be the form of Government, a real Despotism."—WASHINGTON.

"Cling to the Constitution, as the shipwrecked mariner clings to the last plank, when night and the tempest close around him."—DANIEL WEBSTER.

New-York:
CARLETON, PUBLISHER, 413 BROADWAY.
M DCCC LXIII.

TO

EDWIN M. STANTON,

SECRETARY OF WAR, U. S. A.

Sir,—Having considered for some time to whom it was most appropriate to dedicate a work describing the kidnapping of American freeman by arbitrary power, and their incarceration, without trial or the judgment of any court in Military Prisons, no one has occurred to my mind who has so well earned the unenviable distinction as yourself of having your name connected imperishably with the infamy of the acts of outrage, tyranny and despotism which the book, I hereby dedicate to you, will publish to the American People.

You it was, sir, who after setting at liberty the victims immured in Forts Lafayette and McHenry by your predecessors in tyranny, Messrs. Cameron and Seward, and after causing the great heart of the People to leap with joy and swell with gratification at this, one of the first of your official acts, and exult in hope that by you, the Constitution of our country, violated and abrogated by your predecessors in infamy, would be restored—you it was, who, after thus exciting emotions in the American People that they should again be governed by the Constitution of their country and not by the will of a partisan, united in your person and committed by your acts the treacherous tyranny of Seward and the arbitrary despotism of Cameron. To you, then, far beyond and above all others of the monsters which have been begotten by the demon of fanaticism which is causing our country to be desolated, belongs the distinction of connecting your name with this work, not only to live in the memory of the deeds which you have caused to be committed, but to be kept forever present in the American mind whenever it recurs in time to come to that period in American history when the Constitution of the United States was first abrogated, when the Government of the Union was subverted, and when the rights and liberties of the American People were trampled like dust beneath the feet of a person clothed in a little brief authority which is used to subvert and destroy that which it should preserve, protect and defend, and who uses as the heel of his despotism, you, Edwin M. Stanton.

In this character which you have assumed towards the American People be handed down in this work, and by your evil deeds to posterity, and receive as your just reward the execrations and maledictions of those present and future whom you have been the means of depriving of their inheritance of personal rights and political liberty.

I am, sir, one of the many hundred victims of the despotism of the arbitrary power of which you have become the willing, servile and pensioned tyrant.

D. A. MAHONY.

CONTENTS.

	PAGE
Introduction	9
Assumption of Arbitrary Power—Increase of the regular army by Proclamation—Extending the period of volunteer enlistments beyond the period prescribed by law	29
Conflict between Chief Justice Taney and the President on the assumption of arbitrary power—Opinion of Chief Justice Taney and other Jurists on the suspension of the *Habeas Corpus*—Historical authorities on the same question.	46
Other authorities and proofs to show that the rightful power is not in the President to suspend the privileges of the writ of *Habeas Corpus*, or to arrest a citizen otherwise than as prescribed by law.	75
Conflict with Missouri—Capture of Camp Jackson—Massacre in St. Louis—Missouri driven into rebellion	89
Suppression of the Maryland Legislature—Arrest of the members	98
Usurpation of Legislative powers by the President—Creation of a Judicial Tribunal with civil jurisdiction in New Orleans	106
Orders of the War Department on which American freemen were kidnapped and imprisoned—Suspension of the *Habeas Corpus*	110

CONTENTS.

	PAGE
Kidnapping of D. A. Mahony—Incidents connected with it, and on the way to Washington—Meeting with Mr. Sheward a fellow-prisoner—Introduction to and description of the Capitol	117
Visits of friends	167
Address of D. A. Mahony to the citizens of the Third Congressional District, Iowa	172
Effect of the Address on the tyrants and their satellites	206
My Journal in the Old Capitol	208
Incidents in the Old Capitol—How free citizens became transformed into servile soldiers	246
Application for trial—no trial granted	247
Statement of Judge Mason for Mahony and Sheward	248
A proposition to take bonds for the release of prisoners	254
Military commission for the trial of political offenders	255
My first Sunday in the Old Capitol—The Gospel according to Jeff Davis, and according to Abe Lincoln	257
How the prisoners were fed	261
Belle Boyd—Defeat of General Banks attributed to her strategy—Arrested and taken to the Old Capitol—Subjected to solitary confinement,—Makes the acquaintance of a Confederate officer—Romantic sequel	268
Writing on the wall	280
No. 10, and its occupants	282
No. 16, and its inmates	287
Prison amusements and recreation	289
Introducing a new prisoner	295
A compassionate contraband shares his bread with a victim of despotism	300
Murder of two prisoners in the Old Capitol—Jesse W. Wharton and Harry Stewart	301
Arrest of sympathizing females, and their subjection to insult and outrage	305

CONTENTS.

vii

	PAGE
Espionage in the prison	308
The Guard-house in the Old Capitol	311
Carelessness or culpable recklessness of the guards	315
Martial Law used as a cover to official corruption	319
A Chapter on Letters	325
Nellie Grey came near getting us in trouble	331
Kidnapping of the Editors and Proprietors of the Harrisburg Patriot and Union	333
Statement of the arrest of Joseph C. Wright, of Milford, N. J.	337
Statement of the Kidnapping of John Apple, of Philadelphia	340
Arrest of Aquila R. Allen, John H. Wise and their incarceration in the Old Capitol by order of General Wadsworth, Military Governor of Washington	344
Case of Dr. Bundy	349
Dr. A. B. Hewitt and John W. Smith, or the Wandering Jew	354
Kidnapping of Hon. Andrew D. Duff, one of the Circuit Judges of Illinois, with some other gentlemen	359
Narrative of the arrests of J. Blanchard	365
The Kidnapping of the Rev. Judson D. Benedict—Christ's Sermon on the Mount regarded as treasonable—Mr. Benedict brought before U. S. Judge Hall, of Buffalo, on a writ of *Habeas Corpus*—Discharged from custody by the Judge, no one appearing against him—Kidnapped again, and taken to the Old Capitol	368
Kidnapping and imprisonment of Geo. W. Wilson, of Upper Marlboro, Md	379
The case of Dr. Ellis, a Medical Director in the Army	385
The other victims in O. C. P	391
Another appeal for a hearing, or to be released	392
Prisoners' health affected—Physician's Certificate	397

CONTENTS.

PAGE

Conditions of Release of some of the Political Prisoners. 399
Released at last 404
Duplicity of the Secretary of War—Public order for the release of Prisoners of State—Private order to disregard the one publicly promulgated 406
Conclusion 411

INTRODUCTION.

The extraordinary and unprecedented course of the Executive Department of the Federal Government, in suspending, or rather in violating the Constitution of the United States, under the plea of military necessity,—the arrest without legal warrant, and the incarceration of citizens of the United States in forts and other military prisons without judicial trial or the judgment of any court, has become a part of the history of this country, and, in the opinion of many, a reproach upon Americans as a sovereign and free people.

In separating from the mother country, and setting up as a nation by themselves, the American people acted upon the principle that government was an institution deriving all its authority and power from the governed, and that, contrary to the principles which had theretofore been almost universally recognized as fundamental in European governments, the right to govern was in the people themselves, and not in any single person, family or dynasty. This principle of self-government was not only incorporated in the Constitution of the United States, the fundamental compact of government among the American people, but it was expressly stipulated in that compact that certain natural rights of the people individually, as well as collectively, should be reserved by them, and that certain other rights, called political, because appertaining to their government polity, should be enjoyed by them, and exercised without restraint or hindrance. It needs but to refer the reader to the Constitution of the United States to call attention to those provisions of that compact which specially reserve to the people in their individuality certain rights. Among these is the right of what is called free speech, and a free press; the right of trial by jury when a person is accused of crime, and a conviction sought; the right of what is called the writ of *habeas corpus*, a personal right wrung by force from the tyrant rulers of Great Britain, and which was carefully transplanted into the American system of Government, and until the accession to power of the Lincoln Administration, guarded with the most vigilant and zealous care by the American people.

These personal rights of the American people having been ruthlessly violated by Executive power, assumed arbitrarily, as the writer of this believes, and exercised despotically towards a number, not less than hundreds of American citizens, who have been immured in forts, fortresses and other military prisons for exercising their constitutional rights of free speech and a free press, it is due to truth and justice that as much as possible of the testimony be gathered and preserved which will show to future ages how Constitutional Government was subverted in the United States of America, and how, in a few months, the American people, from being the freest politically, the most prosperous in wealth, and the most progressive in the civilized and enlighted arts and sciences, became the most abject subjects of despotism, the most acquiescent serfs of arbitrary power; nay, the advocates of the principle which was repudiated by their Revolutionary fathers that the rights and liberties of the people were at such disposal of any ruler as to violate and sacrifice them at his will and pleasure. Having been made one of the victims of this new American doctrine that all power is centered in the Executive head of the Federal Government, the writer of these pages proposes to furnish such portion of the history of the arbitrary arrests and imprisonment of American citizens by the Lincoln Administration, as he has experienced in his own person, and as have come under his observation.

Before proceeding to this task, it might be well for me to put the reader in possession of some facts which, though of rather a personal nature, are nevertheless pertinent to the issue between the Executive head of the Government and the victims of his arbitrary assumption of power.

The pretexts for most of the arrests and imprisonment of those, who, like myself, were incarcerated in the Old Capitol at Washington were that we were disloyal to the Government, that we had discouraged enlistments, and that we had become, as it was officially expressed, dangerous persons. In speaking for myself to these imputations, and in disproving, as I mean to do, not only every charge of the kind which I have understood to be made against me, but others which might with as much truth and justice have been alleged, I am sure that in general terms I state the relations towards the Government of every one of those who have been my fellow-victims of arbitrary power, not only in the Old Capitol, but in the several other Bastiles which have become a characteristic and peculiar institution of the Lincoln Administration. I shall not put the reader off with mere assertions or assumptions of what I said or did, but quote for my own vindication from the Dubuque *Herald*, a newspaper of which I was the sole editor, so far as expressions of opinion on political subjects are concerned, from the first of May, 1860, to the fourteenth day of August, 1862, the date of my arrest by order of the War Department. I pray the reader not to turn away impatiently or hastily from this proof, because it is not only the expression of the sentiments of a mere individual, but that of a large portion, if not a majority of the American people; and it is also the issue of fact and principle on which the Executive head of the Federal Government has assumed and exercised the power to arrest me for disloyalty to the Constitution and infidelity to my country; and so far as other victims of this arbitrary power have coincided with me in opinion and have expressed their sentiments the same pretext for their arrest and imprisonment. I confess myself to the reader that I was one of those who, ever since I learned the nature and object of Abolitionism, both as a political and philanthropic ism, dreaded its ultimate effects upon the people and government of the United States. Politically, it was an antagonism to the Constitution; philanthropically, it was a hostile element of power in the body politic, to what had been conceded in the institution of the Government to the people of the Slave States. The success of this party could have no other effect than a change in the system of Government which had been established by the Constitution. It was, from its very conception, and before it had a tangible being rebellious to the Constitution, treating that compact as a covenant with death, and the Union of the States and people brought together as one Nation by that compact as a league with hell. With its first breath, Abolitionism repudiated the Constitution, and appealed from its obligations to the higher law. Therefore it was that I was one of those who resisted by such means as a newspaper afforded me an opportunity to do, the acquisition of the authority and power of the Federal Government by this party.

Apprehending the evil effects to the country of investing this Abolition party with the authority and power of the Federal Government, I expressed the following sentiments on the 11th of October, 1860, in an article appealing to the people to resist its efforts for the acquisition of power:

"The white people of the United States at large are inheritors in common with us, and with each other of the bequests of our fathers. A portion of these have formed themselves into a party to deprive their co-heirs of their rights. This party finding itself numerically strong, refuses to submit to the obligations which they regard as onerous, imposed as a condition of the enjoyment of national prosperity, personal security, freedom in the pursuit of happiness and the many other blessings secured to us as a nation by the wisdom, and toil, and sacrifice of our fathers. Need we say to you who they are and what the party is that thus arrogates to themselves more than their share of the common inheritance? that thus wilfully refuse to comply with the obligations imposed upon their posterity by the parents of the government as a condition upon which alone heirship was conferred? It is needless for us to recite to you facts which have become familiar to you all. The Republican party, as you are well aware, aims to deprive a portion of the people of fifteen States of their just rights as bestowed upon them by the same ancestral will which makes the whole people co-heirs with each other in all the privileges conferred upon us by our fathers. * * * The Republican party, led by Seward, Lincoln, Hale, Giddings, and other unscrupulous men, have devised a scheme which, if successful, will deprive the people of fifteen States of the Union of their inheritance; and instead of being the equals of their co-heirs, as was designed by their common ancestors, they will be brought under subjection to their brethren unless they have the will and power to resist."

These were my sentiments on the 11th of October, 1860. How unfortunately correct was the opinion I entertained of the Republican party and its leaders, including the then candidate of the Abolitionists and Republicans for the Presidency.

When the result of the Presidential election of 1860 became known, and it began to be evident that the people of the South regarded the success of the Abolitionists as a manifestation of hostility on the part of the people of the North to the Constitutional rights of the South, and when the question of secession became a subject of consideration, the writer of this took early and decided ground against secession, both as a remedy for the evils and injuries the South complained of, and as the Constitutional right of separate States feeling themselves aggrieved at the acts of their sister States; at the same time recognizing to the fullest extent the right of an aggrieved people to resort to force to obtain redress of their grievances, a right in the abstract belonging, it is almost universally conceded, to every people. The argument founded on the refusal of the Convention which formed the Federal Constitution to grant the power of coercion to the Federal Government over a State in rebellion against the Federal authority, did not affect my judgment to favor the right of secession, for opposed to the argument founded upon the action of the Convention on the propositions to confer the powers of coercion in the Federal authority was the absence in the Constitution of any specially reserved right in a State to secede at will from the Union. Hence I came to the conclusion, and so expressed myself as early as the 12th of November, 1860, that "The Constitution makes no provision for secession. A government is not a corporation whose existence is limited by a fixed period of time, nor does it provide means for its own dissolution. The Constitution of the United States provides that it may be amended, and prescribes how this may be done, but it does not, as it exists now, contemplate its own destruction, nor a dissolution of the government of which it is the living evidence. Constitutionally there can be no such thing as secession of a State from the Union."

In the same article I continued, " But it does not follow that because a State cannot secede Constitutionally, it is obliged under all circumstances to remain in the Union. There is a natural right, which is reserved to all men, and which cannot be given to any government, and no goverment can take it away. It is the natural right of a people to form a government for their mutual protection, for the promotion of their mutual welfare, and for such other purposes as they may deem most conducive to their mutual happiness and prosperity; but, if for any cause the government so formed should become inimical to the rights and interests of the people. instead of affording protection to their persons and property and securing their happiness and prosperity, to attain which it was established, it is the natural right of the people to change the government, regardless of Constitutions. For be it borne in mind, the Constitution is an agreement made among the people that the government formed by it is to be just such a government as it prescribes; that when it recognizes a right to exist, it must protect the person in the enjoyment of that right, and when it imposes a reciprocal duty upon a portion of the people, as the condition of union with the other portion, the performance of that duty it will have enforced. When a government fails in any of these essential respects, it is not the government the people intended it to be, and it is their right to modify or abolish it. So, if the rights of the people of the United States, as recognized by the Constitution, are not secured to them by the government, and the people of any State have no other means to redress their grievances, except by separating themselves from their oppressors, it is their undoubted natural right to do so."

These sentiments became the subject of violent vituperation in the Abolition and Republican press of the North-west, and led to the conclusion, rashly and unjustly drawn by my revilers, that I was a secessionist. In reply to an attack of one of the Iowa Abolition papers on my position and sentiments, as set forth in the foregoing extract, I endeavored to illustrate my sentiments by the following argument, which appeared in an article in the Dubuque Herald, of the date of December 22nd, 1860:

"When one section asserts a right, and the other denies its existence, and opposes its exercise, there must be some way to settle the dispute. If the South cannot decide for itself what are its rights under the Constitution, and the North has no right to decide for it, and the South undertakes to exercise rights which it thinks belongs to it, and the North resists the exercise of such rights, a conflict of some kind must ensue; and it will depend on circumstances whether it be one of litigation or of blood. If both sections followed our advice, the question at issue would be submitted to the adjudication of the supreme judicial tribunal of the country; but if the North act upon the principles enunciated by the Republican party, that there is an irrepressible conflict between the sentiment of the North, and the domestic institutions of the South, the contest which is about to ensue will be one of blood; and not upon us who counsel that the just rights of the South be conceded to them, be the responsbility, but upon those who refuse to recognize these rights, and who, after admitting their existence, refuse to permit them to be exercised."

Such are some of the sentiments which the ruling powers at Washington regard as so treasonable as to influence them to assume and exercise arbitrary power for the arrest and incarceration in one of the Lincoln Bastiles of him who uttered them.

I might quote whole columns from the Dubuque Herald to prove that I had, from the beginning of the unfortunate contest between the North and the South, besought both parties to forbearance; implored the North to concede the Constitutional rights of the South, and the South to maintain its political relations inviolate with the North. And after it became inevitable, from the refusal of the Senators and Representatives in Congress of the dominant party to meet the South in a spirit of Constitutional compromise, that war would be resorted to as the means to settle the question at issue, I repeatedly enunciated the principle that though my judgment condemned the course of the dominant party and its representatives at the head of the government, yet that in the contest as it stood, it was the duty of citizens in allegiance with the government to give it their aid and services. Such was, I believe, the position of the Democratic party, both as an organization and in the individuality of its members, with rare exception.

But were it even otherwise, and that I or any one else had violated any law, did not the law which we may have violated prescribe the mode and manner of arrest, trial, and if any one were found guilty, of punishment. And did not the Constitution of the United States, under whose authority alone the President has any right whatever to be what he is, declare most positively and emphatically that " the right of the people to be secure in their persons, houses, papers and effects, shall not be violated "? and it is a remarkable fact, worthy of special notice, that this provision of the Constitution was added to it as an amendment after the Constitution, as originally drafted, was adopted. This fact is proof demonstrative that our ancestors who laid the foundation of the government were not satisfied with leaving it to the inference of courts, founded upon the provisions of the Constitution as it was originally framed, what their personal rights were. They went so far as to have the Constitution amended in several particulars, and of the twelve amendments to the Conttitution, it is significant of the jealousy with which our patriot fathers regarded their personal rights, and of their vigilance in protecting and securing them by Constitutional restraints upon arbitrary power, that ten of these twelve amendments are restraints upon the power of the Federal Government, and reservation of rights to the people. It is far more significant of the design and object of those who have gone before us that they amended the Constitution for the greater security of their personal rights, than if this security had been incorporated into the Constitution originally. One would suppose that the Constitution as it came from the hands of Washington, Hamilton, Madison, Franklin, Livingston and Pinckney, and the other patriots, statesmen and sages who participated in its formation, needed no immediate modification or amendment to secure the freemen of America their rights of person and property, and the means, unrestrained by arbitrary power, of enjoying those rights, but our fathers had just experienced to what an extent the prerogatives of power could be used for purposes of State, and they therefore were not satisfied with even the Constitution given them by George Washington and his compatriots. They insisted upon further guarantees of their rights, upon more definite restrictions on the power of the Federal government, and on a Constitutional declaration which leaves no room for doubt as to where that power belonged which was not given by the Constitution to the Federal government.

But say some casuists, the law, the Constitution, is silent in war; and to sustain this absurd assumption they quote and pervert what was used as an indignant exclamation by a Roman orator, *Silent legis inter arma.* This expression, it is well known, was not laid down as a maxim of law, but, on the contrary, as a lament for the absence of law. We too in our day may well utter the same exclamation. The law is indeed silent and powerless. Were it not so, its flagrant violation by those who are its sworn guardians would not, as it has, go unpunished.

Admitting however for argument sake the soundness of the maxim, that the law is silent in war, whence, it might be enquired with propriety, comes the right in a constitutional government to commence and prosecute a war? If there be no law in time of war, by what authority, if not of law, does the President, aided by Congress, raise armies, appropriate money for their support, and hurl them upon the batteries and bayonets of the so-called rebels? If there be no law for this, may not every one take his own way in relation to the rebellion; nay, may not a citizen, if there be no law in time of war, resist any attempt to force him into being a combatant?

The assumption is an absurdity, that the law in time of war is silent. It is then, more than in time of peace, that the authority and power of the law should be manifested and exercised, because it is only in times of trouble that personal rights are likely to be subjected to those arbitrary restraints provided against by the Constitution of the United States, and by the Constitution of every State of the Union.

Why was it that the very first Amendment to the Federal Constitution declared that "Congress shall make no law respecting an establishment of religion, or prohibiting the free exercise thereof; or abridging the freedom of speech, or of the press; or the right of the people to freely assemble, and to petition the Government for a redress of their grievances." Was it for times of peace alone that this inhibition was placed upon Congress by a special amendment to the Constitution; and if Congress may not make a law abridging the freedom of speech or of the press, may the President nevertheless without any law, but merely by the use of his own will, set aside this restraint upon power, and do the very thing which Congress is positively inhibited in doing? Such an inference is simply absurd, yet the Executive has arrogated to itself the power to do what Congress is expressly forbidden not to do.

The Constitution, as originally drafted and as adopted, did not seem to provide for the right of the people to bear arms. No sooner was this defect observed by the vigilant perceptions of the patriots of the Revolution than another amendment was made to the Constitution providing that "the right of the people to keep and bear arms shall not be infringed," and this right was founded on the assumption that a well-regulated militia was necessary to the security of a free State. Notwithstanding this assumption of our Patriot Fathers, and of their constitutional declaration founded on it, that the right to bear arms shall not be infringed, the people of several States have, by mere executive fiat, been deprived of that means of security in which a free State is assumed to exist.

The third amendment to the Constitution, it will be seen, has reference to times of war, and subjects the quartering of soldiers upon the people to the restraints and conditions of law; thus not only recognizing the presence of law in time of war, but giving it a supremacy over the military in their relations to the people. This amendment says, "No soldier shall, in time of peace, be quartered in any house without the consent of the owner, nor in time of war, but in a manner prescribed by law." Was it to provide for a time of peace alone that this amendment was added to the Constitution; and how has this amendment been observed in the relations of the military to the inhabitants of that part of the country in which the armies have been quartered, and through which they passed? Were they quartered "in a manner prescribed by law," or were they left to commit such outrages and ravages as characterize barbarians, and as have done more to excite hostility to the Federal Government than any of its own flagitious acts?

The fifth amendment to the Constitution declares that "No person shall be deprived of life, liberty, or property, without due process of law." The provision makes no exception of persons. It is unqualified in its negation of power to any branch of the Government to deprive not only a citizen of his life, liberty and property, but to deprive any person of these rights. Is it only for times of peace that this amendment to the Constitution was made by our fathers? "But," as some of the followers of Lincoln, the "Lincoln-poops," as they are properly called, have been heard to say, "if this provision is meant to apply in times of war, how could the Government preserve its existence from the assaults of its enemies? If no person can be deprived of life without due process of law, is it not unconstitutional to kill the enemies of the Government arrayed in arms against it?" It is both unconstitutional and murderous to kill even the enemies of Government except by authority of law, and in the manner which the law prescribes. If a man who is not an enlisted soldier or sailor in the service of the United States, should kill even a rebel, that man would commit by the act, a murder, just as much as he would do who would kill a felon under sentence of death, if the person performing the act had not the authority and command of the proper Court to do it. Hence to kill even an enemy legitimately, it must be done by authority of law; and hence too the making of war in this country by mere Executive edict, instead of by the authority of Congress, is one of the most flagitious acts of usurpation of power, and in its exercise, one of the greatest crimes against the Nation and mankind, which was even committed by mortal man.

Amendment sixth to the Constitution, it will be seen, threw a shield of protection over and was interposed as a security to every person against the encroachments of arbitrary power, and even of power irregularly exercised. It reads, "In all criminal prosecution, the accused shall enjoy the right to a speedy and public trial, by an impartial jury of the State and district wherein the crime shall have been committed, which district shall have been previously ascertained by law, and to be informed of the nature and cause of the accusation; to be confronted with the witnesses against him; to have compulsory process for obtaining his witnesses in his favor; and to have the assistance of counsel in his defense." It must be borne in mind that this was not a part of the Constitution as originally drafted and adopted, but an amendment added to it by a people jealous of their rights, and who knew but too well how ready unrestrained Governments always were to assume the longest stretch of prerogative, and to exercise the greatest possible extent of power, regardless but too often of the rights or interests ef the people.

Was it only for times of peace that this precaution was taken to restrain the power of the Government, to secure even alleged criminals in their right of person, and to protect them while under the ban of a prosecution for crime. If so, why use the unqualified expression, "In ALL criminal prosecutions"? Why not have said, in prosecutions occurring in times of peace, or in all prosecutions except such as the President might deem to be of such a nature as that it may be best to have the trial private; or some other phraseology which would manifest a willingness on the part of those who adopted the amendment that exceptions may be made in certain cases, as in times of war. The reason is obvious. It was not designed that there should be any exception to this constitutional restrain upon power, and to the security and protection gven even to a criminal by this provision of the Constitution. Yet how has the Executive conformed himself and the subordinates under his command to this provision of the Constitution, which he swore, or pretended to swear, that he would "preserve, protect and defend."

How many of the hundreds, if not of the thousands, of the victims of partisan malignity and of the arbitrary despotism of our day, who were arrested without knowing for what, and in violation of other provisions of the Constitution, who were transported both out of the District and State in which they were resident, and incarcerated for long periods of time in what have become the Bastiles of America—how many of these victims were permitted to enjoy the rights suposed to be secured to the vilest wretch by this Sixth Amendment to the Constitution? NOT A SINGLE ONE. It is notorious that not only was the assistance of Counsel denied to these victims, and positively prohibited, but that Counsel who under the influence of personal friendship for some of the victims as was the case in relation to myself, or of other affecting motives, as occurred in other cases, were threatened with arrest and incarceration themselves if they did not desist their efforts in behalf of their friends and clients. Nay more, it is notorious that some Counsel who persisted in doing what they thought to be their duty, and knew to be their right, were arrested in the same arbitrary and illegal manner as were their clients, and thrust into Fort Lafayette to keep company with the other victims of partisan malignity and of arbitrary power.

And this tyranny, this despotism, this flagrant violation of their Constitution and trampling down of their personal rights under the heel of their mere fellow-citizens who happen to be invested with the constitutional authority of the government to be exercised for constitutional objects only, the American people have borne, submitted to, become almost servile to its behests, and acquiesced in its usurpations. O! God, how often did the thought attempt to burst my lips for utterance while subjected to this tyranny: have we no man among us like these who wrested our rights and liberties from the subjection of a foreign tyrant to preserve them from the despotism of our domestic rulers. Have the people of the United States ceased to be Americans with the generation of patriots who give us a continent for our inheritance and provided us with such a guide for our relations to each other while enjoying it, as would, if observed, preserve us as a people forever in peace and security, and promote our prosperity and happiness. This is a question which the people must answer to themselves, if they would preserve even the semblance of their constitutional rights. A perusal of the following pages of this work might aid in arriving at such conclusions as will have a tendency to restore our violated Constitution to its former purity, and our subverted government to its original integrity, harmony and glory.

THE AUTHOR.

THE

PRISONER OF STATE.

ASSUMPTION OF ARBITRARY POWER—INCREASE OF THE REGULAR ARMY BY PROCLAMATION—EXTENDING THE PERIOD OF VOLUNTEER ENLISTMENT BEYOND THE TIME PRESCRIBED BY LAW.

ONE of the most flagrant acts of Executive violation of the Constitution of the United States, was the proclamation of the third of May, 1861, providing for the increase in number of the regular army and navy, and prescribing that the volunteers called into the service of the United States under that proclamation should serve for a period of three years if the war might continue during that period. As a part of the history of the subversion of the government, this proclamation is referred to as evidence of fact. The Constitution, in the most positive, express, and unequivocal terms, delegates to Congress the sole authority both to raise armies and to make rules for their government, as well as of the naval force. This Constitutional provision was disregarded by the President in his proclamation of the third of May. He assumed the power in that proclamation which the Constitution had vested in Congress alone, and which no one ever supposed that the President had any right to exercise. The proclamation of the fifteenth of April of the same year, calling out seventy-five thousand volunteers, was in one aspect at least, also violative of the Constitution; but this infraction was treated lightly by most persons. Not so, however, by the writer of these papers. It was the first more than the subsequent infractions of the Constitution that alarmed me for the safety of the Republic. The President might have called out a million of men according to law, but he had no right whatever to call out a single man without authority of law, much less in direct violation of law. It is pleaded not only in extenuation of his offence, but as a justification of his acts, that the State was in danger and that there was no time to lose. To this it needs but to be replied, that dangers of this kind had been foreseen by the framers of the Constitution, and provided against by acts of Congress. Under the act of Congress of 1795, by whose authority the President acted in his proclamation of the fifteenth of April, 1861, he might have called out the whole militia of the United States, but not for a longer period than that act prescribed. But while acting under the authority of that law in calling out the seventy-five thousand volunteers, he wantonly disregarded the conditions and restraints prescribed upon such exercise of power by the same act. Thus by almost the first public act of the President, did he violate the Constitution, which a little more than a month previously he had taken an oath to "preserve, protect and defend," which oath, it seems, he has since construed so that it does not require him to obey the Constitution, as if he could both preserve, protect and defend it by the same act which disobeys it.

Whatever doubt some casuists may have had of the violative spirit of the proclamation of the fifteenth of April, there is no room for cavil on that point—the proclamation of the third of May. It was to all intents and purposes, a legislative act. It increased the regular by express terms, which I quote:

"I also direct that the regular army of the United States be increased by the addition of eight regiments of infantry, one regiment of cavalry, and one regiment of artillery, making altogether a maximum aggregate increase of twenty-two thousand seven hundred and fourteen officers and enlisted men, the details of which increase will also be made known by the War Department; and I further direct the enlistment for not less than one nor more than three years, of eighteen thousand seamen, in addition to the present force, for the naval service of the United States, the details of enlistment and organization will be made known through the Department of the Navy."

It was in vain that the Constitution vested in Congress the power to raise and support armies, to provide and maintain a navy, and to make rules for the government of the land and naval forces. The President by this proclamation assumed the right and power to do all this—a right which scarcely any monarch, if a single one, would dare to assume, and a power which no one but a usurper would attempt to exercise.

That is no newly formed opinion in the writer, I quote for the reader a few short extracts from the Dubuque *Herald* of the date of May fifteenth, 1861, the first referring to this proclamation, the others introducing it as a significant fact of history:

Dubuque Herald, May 18th, 1861.

ASSUMPTION OF ARBITRARY POWER.

The late Proclamation of the President of the United States calling for volunteers to serve for a longer period than is authorized by law, and increasing the rank and file of the regular army beyond the legal number, is the first manifest and unquestionable assumption of arbitrary power by any President of the United States. The step between this and the *coup d'etat* of a despot is short and easily taken. Those who will acquiesce submissively in the violation of the Constitution in one case are far towards the condition of becoming willing subjects to the other. While it is the duty of all to acquiesce in every constitutional and legal exercise of power by the government to preserve its existence and to perform its legitimate functions, need we say to intelligent freemen that it is no less the duty of every one of them to resist and oppose the exercise of arbitrary power by any branch or member of the Government.

Dubuque Herald, May 18th, 1861.

A FACT IN HISTORY.

The Proclamation of the President of the United States calling for volunteers for a longer period of service than is authorized by law, and for augmenting the rank and file of the regular army beyond the number prescribed by law, are such flagrant and unquestioned violations of law and arbitrary acts of power that we publish it as a matter of reference for the time when the returning reason of the people will have asserted its proper influence over the public mind, and when the public judgment will hold the highest officer of the Government as well as the humblest citizen amenable to the country for violations of law, and the exercise of arbitrary power. When we assure such of our readers as are not aware of the fact already that there is not the semblance of authority in law for the exercise of the power assumed by the President in this Proclamation, we leave them to such reflection, as this fact will naturally suggest.

Those who apologize for the course of the President, and justify his arbitrary assumption of power on the ground of State or military necessity, forget it seems that it is in the power and made the duty of the President to call Congress together whenever in his judgment the necessities of State require an extraordinary session of that body to be convened. There was therefore no good reason for anticipating and forestalling the action of Congress in a matter over which the Constitution gave Congress exclusive control. If Congress was not in session in the early part of 1861, it was the fault of the President himself, who alone has the authority to call that body together. But without any reference to this point, the President had no right to call volunteers into service for a longer period than the law giving him authority to make the call prescribed as the duration of the time of such service; nor had he any right whatever by Constitution or law to increase the number of the regular army or naval forces. "Military necessity" and "the safety of the State" are convenient pretexts for the assumption and exercise of power, but they are the pretexts of usurpers, of tyrants and of despots the world over, and in every age and country. No truly patriotic ruler ever resorted to such flagrant violations of law to promote the well being of the people, and to preserve the integrity of the Nation. On the contrary, those only have seized forbidden power and exercised it according to their own will, who made National prosperity and the people's happiness a secondary consideration in their grasp of power. Our rulers, it is now experienced, form no exception to what has been so impressively taught the people of all ages, and we American freemen while being the most diligent in placing restraints upon the exercise of arbitrary power by our rulers, have become the least vigilant in protecting our rights and liberties from the actual aggressions of unauthorized and usurped power. History has no parallel, no analogy to our shameful example.

The assumptions of power by the President which is vested in other branches of the Government when invested in any branch, and of power positively withheld by the Constitution and reserved to the people, was denounced by the writer in such terms of rebuke to the Administration as its flagitious course appeared to provoke censure, and the American people were at the same time admonished that their rights as freemen were in jeopardy, and their liberties in danger of subjection to despotic power.

The following articles from the Dubuque *Herald* are but instances of many such others which the writer could cite showing what he thought and said of this assumption and exercise of arbitrary power. No doubt it was the expression of such sentiments which influenced the Administration to subject the writer to the outrage of arbitrary arrest and the indignity of imprisonment for three months in the Old Capitol at Washington. The reader's indulgence is asked for citing these articles, and his attention is invited to their perusal, especially as on them with similar others, was based the arbitrary and extraordinary course of the Administration towards the writer, and its similar course towards hundreds of other American citizens for the expression of like sentiments.

From the Dubuque Herald, June 5th, 1861.

THE JUDICIAL AND EXECUTIVE BRANCHES OF THE GOVERNMENT IN CONFLICT.

The most deplorable, because the most dangerous, result of the civil war now pending, is the conflict of power and jurisdiction which has arisen between the Executive and Judicial departments of the Federal Government. These departments are made as independent of each other by the Constitution as their functions are distinct and of different natures; and if ever it comes to pass that the Executive successfully exercises arbitrary power over the Judiciary, that moment will have become the commencement of an era in America distinguished for the subversion of Civil Liberty.

One of the principal objections to the old Confederate form of Government established by the Revolutionary Congress was the want of a Judiciary Department whose decisions and decrees would have such a moral force as to command not only the respect of the several States of the Confederation but their acquiescence and obedience. And after a long and careful consideration of the matter, in the Convention which formed the Federal Constitution, it was agreed upon not only that there should be a Judicial Department of the Government, but that in its proper sphere it should be independent, and to a great extent be invested with attributes of such an order as to give it pre-eminence and power over the two other Departments, the Executive, and Legislative. If it were otherwise, there would be no security either from arbitrary acts of Legislation nor from the assumption of arbitrary power by the Executive. It is needless to say that it was given to the Judicial Department of the government not only to try all offenses against the Constitution and laws, except impeachments of officers, but also to issue all necessary processes of arraignment for such offences. It is not given to either of the other Departments of the Government to arraign or try offenses, except such as may be committed against the privileges of Congress. It is not a prerogative of the Executive to issue process of arraignment for any offense, much less to try any offense committed against the Constitution and laws of the Union.

The assumption of such prerogatives of power was successfully resisted by the freemen of Great Britain, and it was to provide a security against such assumptions of power by the Federal Executive that Congress alone was invested with the power to suspend the privilege of the writ of *habeas corpus*, and the Judiciary alone were invested with the authority to arraign and try offenses against the State, as well as against individuals.

There is not a more interesting lesson to freemen in the constitutional history of Great Britain than the struggle between the assumed prerogative of the Crown to deprive, at will, subjects of their personal liberty for alleged offenses, and freemen contending for their personal rights against powerful monarchs. And not only is this contest for liberty interesting, but it is equally gratifying as it resulted in the triumph of right over pretensions of Crown Sovereignty, which could not be conceded without subjecting the liberties of the people to continual constraints and violation.

It was in full view of the great struggle in England ending with the Statute in relation to the writ of *habeas corpus* passed in the reign of Charles the Second, that the Constitution of the United States separated the powers and functions of Government and put restraints upon the exercise of power by one Department of the Government which were invested in another to be exercised. The assumption of power by the Federal Executive to arrest at will, and to withhold an accused person from the effect and privilege of the writ of *habeas corpus*, is just such an assumption of power as was exercised by the British Crown, until several successive Statutes were passed to resist every encroachment upon the liberties of the people.

There is no offense known to the laws, which a citizen of the United States can commit, which is not cognizable by one or the other of the courts instituted by virtue of, or under the authority of the Constitution, and hence there is no excuse whatever for the Executive branch of the Government to arrest and hold arbitrarily, any person suspected or accused of the commission of an offense. And in the late cases occurring at St. Louis and at Baltimore, where the execution of the writ of *habeas corpus* has been resisted by military power, under, it is presumed, the direction of the President, there is presented as violent a conflict between the Judicial and Executive branches of the Government, as was foreseen might occur by the framers of the Constitution, and which they provided against so far as human forethought inspired by Patriotism, could prevent such a conflict, and protect and preserve the liberties of the people by a written law.

But now the Executive commands the services of three hundred thousand men in arms and resists and defies the authority of the courts. Of what avail is the writ of a court, served by an unarmed officer, when its execution is thus resisted by the very power by which the Constitution prescribes it should be enforced, if its execution should be resisted? What security is there for liberty or for constitutional rights in this state of things?—All depends upon the will of the Executive, nothing upon the guaranties of the Constitution.

From the Dubuque Herald, June 19th, 1861.

USURPATIONS OF POWER BY THE PRESIDENT OF THE U. S.

The Constitution of the United States, which every officer of the Government is sworn to support, from the President, who is at the head of the Administration down to the boy page in Congress whose duty it is to bring a glass of water to a Legislator, defines the duties of each branch of the Federal Government, prescribing to each branch its separate functions and putting restraints upon power which might be used to the prejudice of the people for whose benefit the Government was instituted.

For some time past, in the performance of the duties which we assumed as editor of a public journal, which professes to speak in behalf of a political party whose fundamental principles and rule of action is embraced in the Constitution, we have found it necessary to point out and animadvert upon assumptions of power by the President of the United States, which assumptions are not only unwarranted by the Constitution from which he derives any authority at all, but which are given expressly to another branch of the Government. Some persons we find do not believe that the President has usurped any power, and contend that he has acted in strict accordance with the Constitution in every act of his performed.

There is another class who admit that he has acted unconstitutionally, but justify it by the extraordinary circumstances under which he has been called upon to administer the Government.

We propose to show in this article that the President has usurped the prerogatives of the Legislative Branch of the Government and that he has in other respects set the Presidential power far above what it was created by the Constitution of the United States.

In defining and prescribing the powers and the duties of the Congress of the United States, the Constitution, Art. 1, Sec. 8, commences by saying, "Congress shall have power," and then it goes on to enumerate and prescribe definitely and in detail what Congress shall have the power to do.

Among these powers given and duties prescribed to Congress, is "To regulate commerce with foreign nations and among the several States." Yet the President has assumed to himself the prerogatives of suspending commerce between the Northern and Southern States, and of blockading the ports of certain States, a prerogative which, if it exists at all in the Government, belongs to Congress and not to the President, to exercise.

Another power vested in Congress is "To establish post offices and post roads." Now, although nothing is said in this provision of the Constitution as to the abolishment of post roads or of post offices, it is fair to presume that it is to that branch of the Government to which the power to establish post offices and post roads has been given, the power to abolish them belongs also. Yet the Executive branch of the Government has practically abolished the post offices and post roads in several of the States, thus virtually acknowledging their separate existence and putting them beyond the pale of the Constitution.

Another power given to Congress by the Constitution is "To define and punish piracies, felonies committed on the high seas, and offenses against the law of Nations."

This power has been usurped by the Executive, if common report be true, of his having given instructions to United States cruisers to treat as pirates all persons sailing under the flag of States in rebellion against the United States, and of his assuming, not only to punish offenses against the laws of Nations, but of defining what these laws are, modifying and changing these laws as they have been recognized to exist since the formation of the Government.

The next power conferred on Congress is "To declare war, grant letters of marque and reprisal, and make rules concerning captures on land and water." A war is now raging without its being declared by Congress. Captures are made on land and water without Congress having authorized it to be done; and prizes are disposed of under the authority and directions, not of Congress, but of the Executive. And it is even intimated, but we do not assert its being true, that letters of marque have been issued by direction of the President, all, to whatever extent the President has acted in the matter, in usurpation of the power of Congress.

The Constitution further says that Congress shall have power "To raise and support armies; but no appropriation of money, to that use, shall be for a longer period than two years."

See with what jealous care the power to raise and support armies is vested in Congress even. It is not in the Constitutional power of Congress, to provide for the subsistence of an army for a longer period than two years, such was the apprehensions of the patriots who gave us a Constitutional Government, of standing armies; yet the President of the United States does not hesitate to raise armies and in the face of an Act of Congress, providing that he shall not call an army into the field not even to suppress insurrection, for a longer period than till thirty days after the meeting of Congress, he raises armies to serve for three years or during a war which has not been declared by Congress and of which Congress has no official knowledge, for which it has made no appropriation, and which it has not yet recognized in any manner whatever.

The Constitution invests Congress with the power "To provide and maintain a Navy."

Never before since the formation of the Government, till recently, did the President of the United States arrogate to himself the power to build ships of war. Congress performed this duty in conformity with the Constitution, and the Presidents heretofore confined themselves to the discharge of duties in relation to the Navy prescribed by Acts of Congress.

The Constitution invests Congress also, and not the President, with the following powers:

"To make rules for the government of the Land and Naval forces:

"To provide for calling forth the Militia to execute the laws of the Union, suppress insurrection and repel invasion:

"To provide for organizing, arming and disciplining the Militia, and for governing such part of them as may be employed in the service of the United States, reserving to the States respectively the appointment of the officers and the authority of training the Militia according to the discipline prescribed by Congress."

All these powers have been usurped by the President.

He has through his subordinates, made "rules for the government of the Land and Naval forces," without authority of Congress.

He has called out the Militia for a longer period of service than is authorized by Congress, although Congress refused at its last session to give him the power to do so, even when his party friends in Congress disclaimed that it was his intention to do anything else with the forces asked for, than to reclaim the property of the United States seized by the Rebels.

He has not in a single instance attempted to execute the laws of the Union with the forces he called into service, but on the contrary has used them to violate the laws and Constitutions of States and of the United States. He has not only arrogated the power vested in Congress of organizing, arming and disciplining the Militia, but he has usurped the rights reserved by the Constitution to the States respectively of appointing the field and general officers of Militia even in cases where the Constitutions of States reserved this right to the volunteer soldiery.

He has usurped the power of Congress to suspend that great writ of *habeas corpus*, a prerogative which the Constitution of Great Britian whence it was derived, denies to the British Crown.

He has drawn money from the Treasury in violation of the Constitution which says,

"No money shall be drawn from the treasury but in consequence of appropriations made by law." See Article I. Sec. 9, of Constitution. He has created offices in the Army without the authority of Congress and appointed persons to fill these offices, which if created by Congress should be filled in accordance with the Constitutional provision, " reserving to the States respectively," the right to appoint officers of the Militia.

He has violated the provision of the Constitution, which says, Art. 2 of Amendments: "A well regulated militia being necessary to the security of a free State, the right of the people to keep and bear arms shall not be infringed." In Missouri, a body of State Militia were made prisoners and deprived of their arms under a pretext, which, if true, should have been proved, and these militia tried for treason.

He has violated the rights of the people reserved by Article 4th of the Amendments to the Constitution, which says; "The right of the people to be secure in their persons, papers, and effects against unreasonable searches and seizures shall not be violated; and no warrants shall issue except upon probable cause supported by oath or affirmation, and particularly describing the place to be searched and the persons or things to be seized."

He has violated the personal rights of the people

reserved by the 5th Article of the Amendments to the Constitution, which says : " No person shall be held to answer for a capital or otherwise infamous crime unless on a presentment or indictment by a grand jury, except in cases arising in the land and naval forces, or in the militia, when in actual service in time of war or public danger." A clause of the Constitution which gives him no power over citizens not in the actual service of the United States in war.

He has, in violation of the same article of the Constitution, deprived persons over whom he had no authority, of their liberty, " without due process of law."

He has involved the Government in debt, without the authority of Congress, the Constitution giving to Congress alone the authority to borrow money, and consequently the authority to give occasion or make it necessary to borrow it.

He has, in violation of the Constitution, which requires that no preference shall be given to any regulation of commerce or revenue in the ports of one State over those of another, blockaded the ports of States which are still constitutionally in the Union, and which he himself regards as still a part of the United States.

He took the following oath at his inauguration:

" I, Abraham Lincoln, do solemnly swear that I will faithfully execute the office of President of the United States, and will, to the best of my ability, preserve, protect and defend the Constitution of the United States."

Within three months after the taking of this solemn oath, he has totally disregarded the Constitution, and instead of preserving, protecting and defending it, he has in every instance above cited, destroyed, violated and suffered it to be outraged.

We charge it upon the President that in every

case above cited he has usurped powers denied to him by the Constitution, every one of which that it was necessary to exercise should have been done by Congress, or in pursuance of acts of Congress, as prescribed by the Constitution.

The necessity of circumstances placed in extenuation of the President's guilt, is precisely the same plea put in by tyrants, despots and usurpers, in every age of the world and under every form of government which has ever existed.

The Cæsars in Rome, the Bourbons and Napoleons in France, the Stuarts and other despots in England, all pleaded the "necessity of circumstances" for their arbitrary acts of power and their infringement on the rights and liberties of the people. Louis of France, to go back into historic times no farther, said "I am the State." James of England said to the Duke of Somerset, who told the king that he could not obey him without violating the law, " I will make you fear me as well as the law. Do you not know that I am above the law?" And the same monarch said to his Parliament:

"For matters of privileges, liberties, and customs, be not over curious. We do what is for the best, and as necessity prompts. Let not any one stir you up to law questions, debates, or that sort of thing, for of these cometh evil; but continue yourself in that honest modesty, whereby you may have my prayers to God for you, and procure the love of me, and a happy end to this Parliament."

How doth this language and the sentiment it expresses accord with what we hear at the present day. On the other hand we might cite the reasons in those days for obeying the King. "I have," said a Custom House officer who was reproached for his subserviency, "fourteen reasons for obeying the King's commands; a wife and thirteen children." Does not this reason influence the course of many in our days to acquiesce in and sustain the usurpation of power?

The same argument of necessity of changing the Constitution of France and for usurping Imperial Power and depriving the people of their rights was made use of by the Elder and the Third Napoleon, and with just as much foundation in right as it is now used.

We have done our duty. We have stated facts as they exist. We have stated analogous circumstances in the history of other peoples to those which exist among us, and we draw the conclusion that as they submitted, they became enslaved; and as they shook off the yoke of tyranny and broke the shackles of despotism, they became free and regenerated.

Let us as a people profit by the example of our ancestors, and of their kindred and neighbors of other Nations. Submission to despotism will make us slaves; resistance to the assumption of arbitrary power will preserve our rights and secure our liberties. Let the rule of our actions be, the Constitution is our rule of Government.

ASSUMPTION OF ARBITRARY POWER — CASE OF JOHN MERRYMAN—CONFLICT BETWEEN CHIEF JUSTICE TANEY AND THE PRESIDENT AND MILITARY AUTHORITIES.

Before proceeding in the relation of my personal experience, and of that of others of my fellow-victims of despotism, propriety seems to require that some reference be made both to the first aggressions on personal liberty by the Executive branch of the Government, and to the efforts as they were made at the time to resist these aggressions.

The case, so far as it is known to the writer, which brought the Executive into the first flagrant conflict with the Constitution, and with a co-ordinate branch of the Government while attempting to apply the protection of the Constitution to a citizen arbitrarily deprived of his liberty, was that of John Merryman, of Baltimore. It need not be made a part of this reference to facts what the alleged cause was for the arbitrary arrest of Mr. Merryman, and his illegal detention in Fort McHenry. It is necessary to deal with the arbitrary act only, as it is of that alone the victim or the American people have reason to complain. In the case of Mr. Merryman the facts show that he was arrested in his own house, where he was peaceably domiciled, on the 25th of May, 1861, by an armed force professing to act under military orders; that he was compelled to rise from his bed, and taken to Fort McHenry; that a writ of *habeas corpus* issued by the Chief Justice of the Supreme Court of the United States to bring the person of the prisoner before him, was disregarded by the Commander of the Fort, General George Cadwalader, who made answer to the writ that he was authorized by the President to suspend the writ of *habeas corpus*. Here was an issue between two co-ordinate branches of the government, the Executive represented by General Cadwalader, and the Judicial by Chief Justice Taney. The Executive attempting to exercise arbitrary power in relation to a citizen; the Judicial branch, as was its duty, attempting to interpose the protection of the Constitution between the tyrant and his victim. Power stood on one side regardless of its legitimate authority, and conscious of its physical ability to have its own way, while on the other on the bench of Justice, sat the Chief Justice of the United States, deciding, as was his right and duty, what were the rights of the people of the United States but powerless to protect even one citizen in the enjoyment of those rights. In that conflict as it resulted the American people lost for the time being, their liberties; and it will be only when the supremacy of the Judicial tribunals in defining the rights of the people under the Constitution, and when they will be invested with authority to carry their decrees into effect, that those lost liberties will be recovered. For let it be conceded that in a conflict of opinion or authority between the Supreme Judicial tribunal and the Executive branch of the Government on a question embracing the Constitutional rights of a citizen, that the Executive will shall have a supremacy over Judicial authority, and of what avail are those mere verbal restraints of the Constitution upon arbitrary power. They will be no more potent to effect their object than if they had never been written or expressed as the will of the people.

No government could exist any length of time in which two or more of the co-ordinate branches among which authority may be divided, would be left to determine, each for itself, the extent of its authority and power, without having some arbitor whose decision should be final. This was the opinion of the sages and statesmen who formed the Constitution, and of our patriotic ancestors who adopted, and amended it in such a manner as seemed to them remedial of its defects.

In reply to objections made to investing the Supreme Court with authority to declare legislative acts violative of the Constitution null and void, Alexander Hamilton, defending the Constitution then under discussion by the American people, said: "There is no position which depends on clearer principles, than that every act of a delegated authority, contrary to the tenor of the commission under which it is exercised, is void. No legislative act, therefore, (and he might have added with propriety no Executive act,) contrary to the Constitution, can be valid. To deny this, would be to affirm, that the deputy is greater than his principal; that the servant is above his master; that the representatives of the people are superior to the people themselves; that men acting by virtue of power may do not only what their powers do not authorize, but what they forbid." The very thing the President of the United States has been doing since he became invested with the Executive authority. He has not only done what he was not authorized to do, but arrogated to himself and exercised powers which the Constitution attempted to restrain him from assuming or exercising. But who is to be the judge of this? Let us begin with Alexander Hamilton, Federalist even as he was. In the same paper and in the same connection, Hamilton says, "The interpretation of the laws is the proper and peculiar province of courts. A Constitution is a fact, and must be regarded by the Judges as a fundamental law. It must, therefore, belong to them to ascertain its meaning, as well as the meaning of any particular act proceeding from the legislative body." Now if this be true of the law making branch of the government that it must conform its acts to the Constitution, as that instrument is interpreted by the Supreme Court, is there not a stronger reason for requiring of the mere administrator or executor of the laws that it should not assume such a superiority over the Judicial tribunal as to not only put its opinion of its Constitutional powers in opposition to that of the Supreme Court, put the Executive will in opposition to the Judicial judgment. Yet this is precisely how the case stands. The mere will of the Executive stands today, and has done since the suspension of the Constitution in the case of John Merryman, in place of the judgment of the Supreme Court not only as the interpreter of law, but the law itself in relation to the rights and liberties of the American people. It is worthy of notice that in the commentaries of the Federalist on the powers and duties of the President, there is not one word said about the power in him of suspending any portion of the provisions of the Constitution. Hence it is fair to presume that even the opponents of the Constitution, of whom there were not a few, never thought of such a thing as that the President was invested by that instrument with the authority which he assumed to exercise in relation to John Merryman, and subsequently in relation to every citizen who became the object of the malignity of the partisan party of which the President acted more as the head than he has done as Chief Magistrate of a free people.

The eminent jurist, Judge Story, in his commentaries on the Constitution, lays down the principle that—

"§ 1574. Where there is no judicial department to interpret, pronounce, and execute the law, to decide controversies and to enforce rights, the government must either perish by its own imbecility, or the other departments of government must usurp powers, for the purpose of commanding obedience, to the destruction of liberty. The will of those who govern will become, under such circumstances absolute and despotic, and it is wholly immaterial whether power is invested in a single tyrant or in an assembly of tyrants." Read this quotation again, American citizens, and compare it with the course of the Federal Executive and of Congress since the authority of the Supreme Court has been set aside and the Constitution abrogated and the government subverted, and how strikingly, aye, prophetically true are these expressions of Justice Story. A government without a supreme judicial tribunal is no better off than a ship without a compass, for no matter how skillful the pilot or master may be, they have no standard of judgment to sail by. But, alas! in what condition must be that government which throws away not only as useless but injurious the only standard of judgment by which its course can be safely guided. It will be seen by reference to the quotation from Justice Story that he claims for the judiciary not only the right to interpret and pronounce the law, but to execute it also. Well would it have been for the liberties of the American people, and for their unity as a nation, if the Supreme Court had been invested with the power to carry its decisions into effect. Had this been the case when the President of the United States commanded General Cadwalader to resist the execution of the writ of *habeas corpus* in the case of John

Merryman, that conflict of authority which has resulted in the triumph, for the time being, if not forever in the United States, of arbitrary power over the judiciary, the Constitution and the people, would have ended in restoring the Supreme Court to its legitimate supremacy, the Constitution as the fundamental law, and the government to be a means of promoting the prosperity and happines of the people instead of being made the means in the control of fanatical tyrants of destroying the peace of the people, of sacrificing their lives and of burdening them with onerous pecuniary exactions to perpetuate the power of the tyrants and to compensate the pimps and satellites of power for the base services they render.

Justice Story goes farther in maintaining the principle of the supremacy of the Judiciary than I have yet quoted him. Referring to Montesquieu he says in the same paragraph above quoted, "No remark is better founded in human experience than that of Montesquieu, that 'there is no liberty if the judiciary power be not separated from the legislative and executive powers.' And it is no less true," continues Justice Story, "that personal security and private property rest entirely upon the wisdom, the stability, and the integrity of the courts of Justice. ... When power becomes right it is of little consequence whether decisions rest upon corruption or weakness, the accidents of chance or upon deliberate wrong. In every well organized Government, therefore, with reference to the security both of public rights and private rights, it is indispensable that there should be a Judicial department to ascertain and decide rights, to punish crimes, to administer justice, and to protect the innocent from injury and usurpation."

And in a succeeding paragraph of the same work, Justice Story says "the power of interpreting the laws involves necessarily the functions to ascertain whether they are conformable to the Constitution or not, and if not so conformable, to declare them void and inoperative. As the Constitution is the supreme law of the land, in a conflict between that and the laws, either of Congress or of the States, it becomes the duty of the judiciary to follow that only which is of paramount obligation. This results from the very theory of a republican constitution of government; for otherwise the acts of the legislative and executive would, in effect, become supreme and uncontrollable notwithstanding any prohibitions or limitations contained in the Constitution; and usurpations of the most unequivocal character might be assumed without any remedy within the reach of the citizens.— The people would thus be at the mercy of their rulers." Just the condition to which the people have become subjected, and for the cause so sagely predicated for consideration. The supremacy of the Judiciary being virtually ignored, the acts of the legislature and executive have in effect become supreme and uncontrollable by any constitutional power, notwithstanding the inhibitions and restraints of the Constitution, " and usurpations of the most unequivocal and dangerous character" have been "assumed, without any remedy within the reach of the citizen," because that branch of the Government in which the Constitution invested the authority to secure the citizen in his rights, and redress his injuries, was not, unfortunately, invested with the power to carry into practical effect its decrees.

One of the most fatal errors of the Constitution was that of leaving it to the mere will of the Executive to enforce the decrees of the supreme Judicial tribunal. It ought to have been foreseen that the will of a tyrant might and probably would be

put in conflict with the judgment of the Supreme
Court, and that in such a contingency, the tyrant's
will, backed by the military power, would treat the
judgment of the Court as a nullity. But who of
the patriots of the revolutionary period could have
thought that the American people would in the
next generation imitate the degenerate Romans in
their choice of a buffoon to be their chief magistrate, and that a party would soon spring into existence whose animating principle would be hostility to the Constitution which cost so dearly of patriot
blood to establish in it a recognition of the rights
and liberties of Americans. Could they have con-
jectured that their immediate posterity would become so degenerate as to sink below the level of the
most abject serfs of despotism, the patriots of the
revolution would more likely have established a
monarchical government than that system which
only an enlightened, virtuous and patriotic people
can appreciate and maintain.

Notwithstanding the obvious intent and plain
meaning of the Constitution, Mr. Lincoln, as President of the United States, not only disregarded
those provisions of the Constitution which were added as amendments to that instrument to make it
more conformable to the views of the then people
of the United States, and to what they believed it
to be necessary it should stipulate in their behalf,
as a security and protection to their rights of person, but he went farther, commencing in the case
of John Merryman, to assume to himself the right
to perform an act made legislative not only by the
custom of Great Britain, where the *habeas corpus*,
as we understand it in our day, had its origin, by
the Constitution of the United States, in which
Congress is inhibited from suspending its privileges
except in certain prescribed cases, but also by the
very nature and object of the writ itself. For it

should be borne in mind that if there were no apprehensions of the assumption and exercise of arbitrary power, there would be no necessity of the writ of *habeas corpus* as a remedial measure of security or protection. Hence, what can be more absurd than to assume or presume that it should be left in the control of the power which was designed to be restrained by the constitutional provision of the *habeas corpus* to set aside that restraint at its own will and pleasure. What would be thought of the man who, to guard and secure his valuable treasure from the incursions of burglars, would first put on his doors and windows such fastenings as should defy the most expert thief in gaining an entrance, and then leave the key in the door, by which there was nothing more left for the thief to do than turn the key, walk in, and secure the treasure. Not less absurd than the conduct of such a man would have been that of those who formed the Federal Constitution, if they designed that after securing to themselves and to their posterity the privileges and rights of person which came down to them from their British ancestors, they should place it in the power of their rulers to deprive them of these privileges and rights.

Is it forgotten, or has it not been learned by the American people, that the writ of *habeas corpus* originated in the attempt of arbitrary power to subject British subjects to the tyranny of a despot's will; how then, without becoming both absurd and idiotic, or tyrannical, can any one assume or acquiesce in the assumption that it shall be left to the will of the power on which the writ is designed as a restraint, whether or not the victim who applies for its protection shall have the privilege of its enjoyment. The people must have become as craven and subservient to their rulers as these rulers have become tyrannic and despotic, to submit for an instant to such an assumption of power over their rights, and to acquiesce in a single instance in its exercise.

It is a fact of history significant and admonitory, that Charles the First of Great Britain lost both his crown and head for having arrogated to himself the power of suspending the writ of *habeas corpus* in relation to a few of his subjects; and is it to be presumed that American freemen will tolerate the exercise of arbitrary power in an elective functionary, for the doing of which an English king lost his head? If one may judge, as indeed must be done for want of any other standard of judgment, by the acquiescence of the people in the acts of tyranny and despotism which have so far characterized the administration of Mr. Lincoln, and which have no parallel but under the most despotic rulers and forms of government, one cannot come to any other conclusion than that the American people have degenerated from spirited freemen to the veriest slaves; so servile have we become to the despotism of our rulers, so subservient to the behests of power, and so acquiescent in the violation of every constitutional provision which recognized the personal rights of the people, and attempted to secure their enjoyment.

DECISION OF CHIEF JUSTICE TANEY IN THE CASE OF JOHN MERRYMAN.

The question of the right of the President to suspend the privilege of the writ of *habeas corpus* being elaborately discussed by Ch. Justice Taney in his written decision in the Merryman case, and it being, was universally admitted up to the presidency of as it Abraham Lincoln the right of the Supreme Justices of the United States to decide questions of constitutional law, no better service can be done the reader of this work than to give him the decision of Judge Taney in full on the assumption of the President to suspend that portion of the constitutional privileges of the people which relate to the writ of *habeas corpus*. This decision is not quoted as merely applicable to the case of Merryman, but because it applies to all the cases of arbitrary arrest and treats of the principles of constitutional law, of private rights and of Executive assumption of power. Emanating from the most eminent judge in the United States, both as regards his official position and his acknowledged ability, this decision put in contrast with the mere act of the will of an ignorant pettifogger, of a fanatical partisan and despotic ruler, would, if brought to the knowledge of the American people, restore them to a sense of their rights and prompt them to the performance of the duty by which means alone a people can preserve their liberties. Eternal vigilance is not only the price of liberty but it is one of the conditions on which political liberty can be enjoyed. The vigilance of the American people has slept upon the watch, and the penalty of this reprehensible conduct is the present condition of the country. Let us read from Judge Taney and be instructed in our rights as American freemen and in the duties we should perform to preserve our liberties:

DECISION.

Ex parte } *Before the Chief Justice of the Supreme Court of the United*
JOHN MERRYMAN. } *States at Chambers.*

The application in this case for a writ of *habeas corpus* is made to me under the 14th Section of the Judiciary Act of 1789, which renders effectual for the citizen the constitutional privilege of the *habeas corpus.* That Act gives to the Courts of the United States, as well as to each Justice of the Supreme Court, and to every District Judge, power to grant writs of *habeas corpus* for the purpose of an inquiry into the cause of commitment. The petition was presented to me in Washington, under the impression that I would order the prisoner to be brought before me there, but as he was confined in Fort McHenry, in the City of Baltimore, which is in my circuit I resolved to hear it at the latter City, as obedience to the writ, under such circumstances, would not withdraw Gen. Cadwalader, who had him in charge, from the limits of his military command.

The petition presents the following case: The petitioner resides in Maryland, in Baltimore County. While peaceably in his own house, with his family, he was, at 2 o'clock on the morning of the 25th of

May, 1861, arrested by an armed force, professing to act under military orders. He was then compelled to rise from his bed, taken into custody and conveyed to Fort McHenry, where he is imprisoned by the commanding officer, without warrant from any lawful authority.

The commander of the Fort, Gen. George Cadwalader, by whom he is detained in confinement, in his return to the writ, does not deny any of the facts alleged in the petition. He states that the prisoner was arrested by order of Gen. Keim, of Pennsylvania, and conducted as a prisoner to Fort McHenry by his order, and placed in his (Gen. Cadwalader's) custody, to be there detained by him as a prisoner.

A copy of the warrant, or order, under which the prisoner was arrested, was demanded by his counsel and refused. And it is not alleged in the return that any specific act, constituting an offense against the laws of the United States, has been charged against him, upon oath; but he appears to have been arrested upon general charges of treason and rebellion, without proof, and without giving the names of the witnesses, or specifying the acts which, in the judgment of the military officer, constituted these crimes. And having the prisoner thus in custody, upon these vague and unsupported accusations, he refuses to obey the writ of *habeas corpus* upon the ground that he is duly authorized by the President to suspend it.

The case, then, is simply this: A military officer, residing in Pennsylvania, issues an order to arrest a citizen of Maryland, upon vague and indefinite charges, without any proof, so far as appears. Under this order his house is entered in the night, he is seized as a prisoner, conveyed to Fort McHenry, and there kept in close confinement. And when a *habeas corpus* is served on the commanding officer, requiring him to produce the prisoner before a Justice of the Supreme Court, in order that he may examine into the legality of the imprisonment, the answer of the officer is, that he is authorized by the President to suspend the writ of *habeas corpus* at his discretion, and, in the exercise of that discretion suspends it in this case, and on that ground refuses obedience to the writ.

As the case comes before me, therefore, I understand that the President not only claims the right to suspend the writ of *habeas corpus* himself, at his discretion, but to delegate that discretionary power to a military officer, and to leave it to him to determine whether he will or will not obey judicial process that may be served upon him.

No official notice has been given to the Courts of Justice, or to the public, by proclamation, or otherwise, that the President claimed this power, and had exercised it in the manner stated in the return. And I certainly listened to it with some surprise, for I had supposed it to be one of those points of constitutional law upon which there is no difference of opinion, and that it was admitted on all hands that the privilege of the writ could not be suspended except by act of Congress.

When the conspiracy of which Aaron Burr was the head became so formidable, and was so extensively ramified to justify, in Mr. Jefferson's opinion, the suspension of the writ, he claimed on his part no power to suspend it, but communicated his opinion to Congress, with all the proofs in his possession, in order that Congress might exercise its discretion upon the subject, and determine whether the public safety required it. And in the debate which took place upon the subject, no one suggested that Mr. Jefferson might exercise the power himself, if, in his opinion, the public safety required it.

Having, therefore, regarded the question as too

plain and too well settled to be open to dispute, if the commanding officer had stated, that upon his own responsibility, and in the exercise of his own discretion he refused obedience to the Writ, I should have contented myself with referring to the clause in the Constitution, and to the construction it received from every jurist and statesman of that day, when the case of Burr was before them. But being thus officially notified that the privilege of the writ has been suspended under the orders and by the authority of the President, and believing, as I do, that the President has exercised a power which he does not possess under the Constitution, a proper respect for the high office he fills requires me to state plainly and fully the grounds of my opinion, in order to show that I have not ventured to question the legality of this act without a careful and deliberate examination of the whole subject.

The clause in the Constitution which authorizes the suspension of the privilege of the writ of *habeas corpus* is in the ninth section of the first article.

This article is devoted to the legislative department of the United States, and has not the slightest reference to the Executive department. It begins by providing, "that all legislative powers therein granted shall be vested in a Congress of the United States, which shall consist of a Senate and House of Representatives." And after prescribing the manner in which these two branches of the legislative department shall be chosen, it proceeds to enumerate specifically the legislative powers which it thereby grants, and legislative powers which it expressly prohibits; and, at the conclusion of this specification, a clause is inserted giving Congress, "the power to make all laws which may be necessary and proper for carrying into execution the foregoing powers, and all other powers vested by this Constitution in the Government of the United States or in any department or office thereof."

The power of legislation granted by this latter clause is by its words carefully confined to the specific objects before enumerated. But as this limitation was unavoidably somewhat indefinite, it was deemed necessary to guard more effectually certain great cardinal principles essential to the liberty of the citizen, and to the rights and equality of the States, by denying to Congress, in express terms, any power of legislating over them. It was apprehended, it seems, that such legislation might be attempted under the pretext that it was necessary and proper to carry into execution the powers granted; and it was determined that there should be no room to doubt, where rights of such vital importance were concerned, and, accordingly, this clause is immediately followed by an enumeration of certain subjects to which the powers of legislation shall not extend; the great importance which the framers of the Constitution attached to the privilege of the writ of *habeas corpus* to protect the liberty of the citizen is proved by the fact that its suspension, except in cases of invasion and rebellion, is first in the list of prohibited powers—and even in these cases the power is denied, and its exercise prohibited, unless the public safety shall require it.

It is true that in the cases mentioned, Congress is of necessity the judge of whether the public safety does or does not require it; and their judgment is conclusive. But the introduction of these words is a standing admonition to the legislative body of the danger of suspending it, and of the extreme caution they should exercise before they give the Government of the United States such power over the liberty of a citizen.

It is the second article of the Constitution that provides for the organization of the Executive Department, and enumerates the powers conferred on it and prescribes its duties. And if the high power over the liberty of the citizens now claimed was intended to be conferred on the President, it would undoubtedly be found in plain words in this article. But there is not a word in it that can furnish the slightest ground to justify the exercise of the power.

The article begins by declaring that the Executive power shall be vested in a President of the United States of America, to hold his office during the term of four years—and then proceeds to prescribe the mode of election, and to specify in precise and plain words the powers delegated to him and the duties imposed upon him. And the short term for which he is elected, and the narrow limits to which his power is confined, show the jealousy and apprehensions of future danger which the framers of the Constitution felt in relation to that department of the Government, and how carefully they withheld from it many of the powers belonging to the Executive branch of the English Government, which were considered as dangerous to the liberty of the subject—and conferred (and that in clear and specific terms,) those powers only which were deemed essential to secure the successful operation of the Government.

He is elected, as I have already said, for the brief term of four years, and is made personally responsible, by impeachment, for malfeasance in office. He is, from necessity and the nature of his duties, the Commander-in-Chief of the army and navy, and of the militia when called into actual service. But no appropriation for the support of the army can be made by Congress for a longer term than two years, so that it is in the power of the succeeding House of Representatives to withhold the appropriation for its support, and thus disband it, if, in their judgment, the President used, or designed to use it for improper purposes. Although the militia, when in actual service, are under his command, yet the appointment of the officers, is reserved to the States. as a security against the use of military power for purposes dangerous to the liberties of the people, or the rights of the States.

So, too, his powers in relation to the civil duties and authority necessarily conferred on him are carefully restricted, as well as those belonging to his military character. He cannot appoint the ordinary officers of government, nor make a treaty with a foreign nation or Indian tribe, without the advice and consent of the Senate, and cannot appoint even inferior officers, unless he is authorized by an act of Congress to do so. He is not empowered to arrest any one charged with an offense against the United States, and whom he may, from the evidence before him, believe to be guilty; nor can he authorize any officer, civil or military, to exercise this power, for the 5th article of the amendments to the Constitution expressly provides that no person " shall be deprived of life, liberty, or property, without due process of law "—that is, judicial process.

And even if the privilege of the writ of *habeas corpus* was suspended by act of Congress, and a party not subject to the rules and articles of war was afterwards arrested and imprisoned by regular judicial process, he could not be detained in prison or brought to trial before a military tribunal, for the article in the amendments to the Constitution immediately following the one above referred to, that is, the 6th article—provides that " In all criminal prosecutions the accused shall enjoy the right to a speedy and public trial by an impartial jury of the State and district wherein the crime shall have been committed, which district shall have been previously ascertained by law, and to be informed of the nature and cause of the accusation; to be confronted with the witnesses against him; to have compulsory process for obtaining witnesses in his favor, and to have the assistance of counsel for his defence."

And the only power, therefore, which the President possesses, where the "life, liberty, or property" of a private citizen is concerned, is the power and duty prescibed in the third section of the second article, which requires "that he shall take care that the laws be faithfully executed." He is not authorised to execute them himself, or through agents or officers, civil or military, appointed by himself, but he is to take care that they be faithfully carried into execution, as they are expounded and adjudged by the co-ordinate branch of the Government, to which that duty is assigned by the Constitution. It is thus made his duty, to come in aid of the judicial authority, if it shall be resisted by a force too strong to be overcome without the assistance of the Executive arm. But in exercising this power he acts in subordination to judicial authority, assisting it to execute its process and enforce its judgments.

With such provisions in the Constitution, expressed in language too clear to be misunderstood by any one, I can see no ground whatever for supposing that the President, in any emergency, or in any state of things, can authorize the suspension of the privilege of the writ of *habeas corpus*, or arrest a citizen except in aid of the judicial power. He certainly does not faithfully execute the laws if he takes upon himself legislative power by suspending the writ of *habeas corpus*, and the judicial power also, by arresting and imprisoning a person without due process of law. Nor can any argument be drawn from the nature of sovereignty, or the necessities of government, for self-defense in times of tumult and danger. The government of the United States is one of delegated and limited powers. It derives its existence and authority altogether from the Constitution, and neither of its branches,

Executive, Legislative, or Judicial, can exercise any of the powers of Government beyond those specified and granted. For the 10th article of the Amendments to the Constitution in express terms provides that "the powers not delegated to the United States by the Constitution, nor prohibited by it to the States, are reserved to the States respectively, or to the people."

Indeed the security against imprisonment by executive authority, provided for in the fifth article of the Amendments of the Constitution, which I have before quoted, is nothing more than a copy of a like provision in the English Constitution, which had been firmly established before the Declaration of Independence.

Blackstone, in his Commentaries (1st vol., 137), states it in the following words:

"To make imprisonment lawful, it must be either by process from the Courts of Judicature or by warrant from some legal officer having authority to commit to prison." And the people of the United Colonies, who had themselves lived under its protection while they were British subjects, were well aware of the necessity of this safeguard for their personal liberty. And no one can believe that in framing a government intended to guard still more efficiently the rights and the liberties of the citizens against executive encroachment and oppression, they would have conferred on the President a power which the history of England had proved to be dangerous and oppressive in the hands of the Crown, and which the people of England had compelled it to surrender after a long and obstinate struggle on the part of the English Executive to usurp and retain it.

The right of the subject to the benefit of the Writ of *habeas corpus*, it must be recollected, was one of the great points in controversy during the long struggle in England between arbitrary government and free institutions, and must therefore have strongly attracted the attention of statesmen engaged in framing a new, and, as they supposed, a freer government than the one which they had thrown off by the revolution. For from the earliest history of the common law, if a person was imprisoned, no matter by what authority, he had a right to the Writ of *habeas corpus* to bring his case before the King's Bench; and if no specific offense was charged against him in the warrant of commitment, he was entitled to be forthwith discharged; and if any offense was charged which was bailable in its character, the Court was bound to set him at liberty on bail. And the most exciting contests between the Crown and the people of England from the time of Magna Charta were in relation to the privilege of this Writ, and they continued until the passage of the statute of 31st Charles II., commonly known as the great *habeas corpus* Act.

This statute put an end to the struggle, and finally and firmly secured the liberty of the subject from the usurpation and oppression of the executive branch of the Government. It nevertheless conferred no new right upon the subject, but only secured a right already existing. For although the right could not be justly denied, there was often no effectual remedy against this violation. Until the statute of the 13th of William III. the Judges held their offices at the pleasure of the King, and the influences which he exercised over timid, time-serving, and partisan judges often induced them, upon some pretext or another, to refuse to discharge the party, although he was entitled to it by law, or delayed their decisions from time to time, so as to prolong the imprisonment of persons who were obnoxious to the King for their political opinions, or had incurred his resentment in any other way.

The great and inestimable value of the *habeas corpus* Act of the 31st Charles II. is that it contains provisions which compel courts and judges, and all parties concerned, to perform their duties promptly, in the manner specified in the statute.

A passage in Blackstone's Commentaries, showing the ancient state of the law upon this subject, and the abuses which were practiced through the power and influence of the Crown, and a short extract from Hallam's Constitutional History, stating the circumstances which gave rise to the passage of this statute, explains briefly, but fully, all that is material to this subject.

Blackstone, in his Commentaries on the Laws of England, (3d vol., 133, 134,) says:

"To assert an absolute exemption from imprisonment in all cases, is inconsistent with every idea of law and political society, and in the end would destroy all civil liberty by rendering its protection impossible.

"But the glory of the English law consists in clearly defining the times, the causes and the extent, when, wherefore, and to what degree the imprisonment of the subject may be lawful. This it is which induces the absolute necessity of expressing, upon every commitment, the reason for which it is made, that the court upon a *habeas corpus* may examine into its validity, and, according to the circumstances of the case, may discharge, admit to bail, or remand the prisoner.

"And yet, early in the reign of Charles I., the Court of King's Bench, relying on some arbitrary precedents, (and those, perhaps, misunderstood,) determined that they would not, upon a *habeas corpus*, either bail or deliver a prisoner, though committed without any cause assigned, in case he was committed by the special command of the King, or by the Lords of the Privy Council. This drew on a Parliamentary inquiry, and produced the *Petition of Right*—3 Charles L.—which recites this illegal judgment, and enacts that no freeman hereafter shall be imprisoned or detained. But when, in the following year, Mr. Seldon and others were committed by the Lords of the Council in pursuance of his Majesty's special command, under a general charge of 'notable contempts, and stirring up sedition against the King and the Government,' the judges delayed for two terms (including, also, the long vacation,) to deliver an opinion how far such a charge was bailable. And when, at length, they agreed that it was, they, however, annexed a condition of finding sureties for their good behavior, which still protracted their imprisonment; the Chief Justice, Sir Nicholas Hyde, at the same time declaring ' if they were again remanded for that cause, perhaps the Court would not afterward grant a *habeas corpus*, being already made acquainted with the cause of the imprisonment.' But this was heard with indignation and astonishment by every lawyer present, according to Mr. Seldon's own account of the matter, whose resentment was not cooled at the distance of four-and-twenty years."

It is worthy of remark that the offences charged against the prisoner in this case, and relied on as a justification for his arrest and imprisonment, in their nature and character, and in the loose and vague manner in which they are stated, bear a striking resemblance to those assigned in the warrant for the arrest of Mr. Seldon. And yet, even at that day, the warrant was regarded as such a flagrant violation of the rights of the subject that the delay of the time-serving judges to set him at liberty upon the *habeas corpus* issued in his behalf, excited universal indignation at the bar. The extract from Hallam's Constitutional History is equally impressive and equally in point. It is in vol. 4, p. 14:

"It is a very common mistake, and not only among foreigners, but in many from whom some knowledge of our Constitutional laws might be expected, to suppose this statute of Charles II. enlarged in a great degree our liberties, and forms a sort of epoch in their history. But though a very beneficial enactment, and eminently remedial in many cases of illegal imprisonment, it introduced no new principle, nor conferred any right upon the subject. From the earliest records of the English law, no freeman could be detained in prison except upon a criminal charge or conviction, or for a civil debt. In the former case it was always in his power to demand of the Court of King's Bench a writ of *habeas corpus ab subjiciendum* directed to the person detaining him in custody, by which he was enjoined to bring up the body of the prisoner with the warrant of commitment, that the Court might judge of its sufficiency and remand the party, admit him to bail, or discharge him, according to the nature of the charge. This writ issued of right, and could not be refused by the Court. It was not to bestow an immunity from arbitrary imprisonment, which is abundantly provided for in Magna Charta, (if, indeed, it were not more ancient,) that the statute of Charles II. was enacted, but to cut off the abuses by which the Government's lust of power, and the servile subtlety of Crown lawyers, had impaired so fundamental a privilege."

While the value set upon this writ in England has been so great that removal of the abuses which embarrassed its enjoyments have been looked upon as almost a new grant of liberty to the subject, it is not to be wondered at that the continuance of the writ thus made effective should have been the object of the most jealous care. Accordingly no power in England short of that of Parliament can suspend or authorize the suspension of the writ of *habeas cor-*

pus. I quote again from Blackstone (1 Comm., 136): "But the happiness of our Constitution is that it is not left to the Executive power to determine when the danger of the State is so great as to render this measure expedient. It is the Parliament only, or legislative power, that, whenever it sees proper, can authorize the Crown, by suspending the *habeas corpus* for a short and limited time, to imprison suspected persons without giving any reason for so doing." And if the President of the United States may suspend the writ, then the Constitution of the United States has conferred upon him more regal and absolute power over the liberty of the citizen than the people of England have thought it safe to entrust to the Crown—a power which the Queen of England cannot exercise at this day, and which could not have been lawfully exercised by the sovereign even in the reign of Charles I.

But I am not left to form my judgment upon this great question from analogies between the English Government and our own, or the commentaries of English jurists, or the decisions of English courts, although upon this subject they are entitled to the highest respect, and are justly regarded and received as authoritative by our courts of justice. To guide me to a right conclusion, I have the Commentaries on the Constitution of the United States of the late Mr. Justice Story, not only one of the most eminent jurists of the age, but for a long time one of the brightest ornaments of the Supreme Court of the United States, and also the clear and authoritative decisions of that Court itself, given more than half a century since, and conclusively establishing the principles I have above stated. Mr. Justice Story, speaking in his Commentaries of the *habeas corpus* clause in the Constitution, says:

"It is obvious that cases of a peculiar emergency may arise, which may justly, nay, even require, the temporary suspension of any right to the writ. But as it has frequently happened in foreign countries, and even in England, that the writ has, upon various pretexts and occasions, been suspended, whereby persons apprehended upon suspicion have suffered a long imprisonment, sometimes from design, and sometimes because they were forgotten, the right to suspend it is expressly confined to cases of rebellion or invasion, where the public safety may require it. A very just and wholesome restraint, which cuts down at a blow a fruitful means of oppression, capable of being abused in bad times to the worst of purposes. Hitherto no suspension of the writ has ever been authorized by Congress since the establishment of the Constitution. It would seem, as the power is given to Congress to suspend the writ of *habeas corpus* in cases of rebellion or invasion, that the right to judge whether the exigency had arisen must exclusively belong to that body." —3 Story's Com. on the Constitution, section 1336.

And Chief Justice Marshall, in delivering the opinion of the Supreme Court in the case of *exparte* Bollman and Swartwout, uses this decisive language, in 4 Cranch, 95. It may be worthy of remark that this "act (speaking of the one under which I am proceeding,) was passed by the first Congress of the United States, sitting under a Constitution which had declared 'that the privilege of the writ of *habeas corpus* should not be suspended, unless when, in case of rebellion and invasion, the public safety might require it.' Acting under the immediate influence of this injunction, they must have felt, with peculiar force, the obligation of providing efficient means by which this great Constitutional privilege should receive life and activity; for if the means be not in existence, the privilege itself would be lost although no law for its suspension should be enacted. Under the impression of this obligation, they gave to all the Courts the power of awarding writs of *habeas corpus*."

And again, in page 101:

"If at any time the public safety should require the suspension of the powers vested by this act in the Courts of the United States, it is for the Legislature to say so. That question depends on political considerations, on which the Legislature is to decide. Until the Legislative will be expressed, this Court can only see its duty, and must obey the law."

I can add nothing to these clear and emphatic words of my great predecessor.

But the documents before me show that the military authority in this case has gone far beyond the mere suspension of the privilege of the Writ of *habeas corpus*. It has, by force of arms, thrust aside the judicial authorities and officers to whom the Constitution has confided the power and duty of interpreting and administering the laws, and substituted a military government in its place, to be administered and executed by military officers, for at the time these proceedings were had against John Merryman, the District Judge of Maryland, the Commissioner appointed under the act of Congress, the District Attorney, and the Marshal, all resided in the city of Baltimore, a few miles only from the home of the prisoner. Up to that time there had never been the slightest resistance or obstruction to the process of any Court or judicial officer of the United States in Maryland, except by the military authority.

And if a military officer, or any other person, had reason to believe that the prisoner had committed any offense against the laws of the United States, it was his duty to give information of the fact and the evidence to support it, to the District Attorney; and it would then have become the duty of that officer to bring the matter before the District Judge or Commissioner, and if there was sufficient legal evidence to justify his arrest, the Judge or Commissioner would have issued his warrant to the Marshal to arrest him ; and upon the hearing of the party would have held him to bail, or committed him for trial, according to the character of the offense as it appeared in the testimony, or would have discharged him immediately, if there was not sufficient evidence to support the accusation. There was no danger of any obstruction or resistance to the action of the civil authorities, and therefore, no reason whatever for the interposition of the military.

And yet, under these circumstances, a military officer stationed in Pennsylvania, without giving any information to the District Attorney ; and without any application to the judicial authorities, assumes to himself the judicial power in the District of Maryland ; undertakes to decide what constitutes the crime of treason or rebellion ; what evidence (if indeed, he required any) is sufficient to support the accusation and justify the commitment ; and commits the party, without having a hearing, even before himself, to close custody in a strongly garrisoned fort, to be there held, it would seem, during the pleasure of those who committed him.

The Constitution provides, as I have before said, that "no person shall be deprived of life, liberty or property, without due process of law." It declares that " the right of the people to be secure in their persons, houses, papers and effects, against unreasonable searches and seizures, shall not be violated, and no warrant shall issue, but upon probable cause, supported by oath or affirmation, and particularly describing the place to be searched, and the persons or things to be seized." It provides that the party accused shall be entitled to speedy trial in a Court of justice.

And these great and fundamental laws, which Congress, itself, could not suspend, have been disregarded and suspended, like the Writ of *habeas corpus*, by a military order, supported by force of arms. Such is the case now before me, and I can only say that if the authority which the Constitution has confided to the judiciary department and judicial officers may thus, upon any pretext or under any circumstances, be usurped by the military power at its discretion, the people of the United States are no longer living under a government of laws, but every citizen holds life, liberty and property at the will and pleasure of the army officer in whose military district he may happen to be found.

In such a case my duty was too plain to be mistaken. I have exercised all the power which the Constitution and laws confer on me, but that power had been resisted by a force too strong for me to overcome. It is possible that the officer who has incurred this grave responsibility may have misunderstood his instructions, and exceeded the authority intended to be given him. I shall, therefore, order all the proceedings in this case, with my opinion, to be filed and recorded in the Circuit Court of the United States for the district of Maryland, and direct the Clerk to transmit a copy, under seal, to the President of the United States. It will then remain for that high officer in fulfilment of his constitutional obligation to "take care that the laws be faithfully executed," to determine what measures he will take to cause the civil process of the United States to be respected and enforced.

R. B. TANEY,
Chief Justice of the Supreme Court, U. S.

OTHER AUTHORITIES AND PROOFS TO SHOW THAT THE RIGHTFUL POWER IS NOT IN THE PRESIDENT TO SUSPEND THE PRIVILEGES OF THE WRIT OF HABEAS CORPUS, OR TO ARREST A CITIZEN OTHERWISE THAN AS THE LAWS PRESCRIBE.

UNDER ordinary circumstances it would not be necessary to add any weight to the decision of the Chief Justice of the United States in a question between him and Abraham Lincoln involving a principle of constitutional law, but as unfortunately the American public mind is as much if not more affected in these times by the mere acts of will of the President as it is by the judgment of a learned, enlightened and illustrious jurist, I have thought it becoming the object in view to add the weight of historical facts, and the opinions of other eminent jurists, to the decision of Judge Taney.

English authorities, legal and historical, Blackstone and Hallam have been quoted by the Chief Justice in support of his decision. Other British authorities might be cited confirming the same views and doctrines, but I will content myself with stating a fact which is in itself proof incontrovertible that even in Great Britain where the prerogatives of the crown are certainly more extensive in relation to the liberties of the subject than the Constitutional authority of the President is over citizens of the United States, it is not conceded to be the right of the crown to suspend the privilege of the writ of *habeas corpus*, and during the long period of time intervening between the dethronement and execution of Charles the First and the present day, no British monarch has dared to assume the prerogative of power which has been arrogantly and defiantly seized and exercised by Abraham Lincoln and subordinates under his command. During the period referred to England and Ireland were convulsed on several occasions with insurrections and rebellion; yet it was only when Parliament thought it proper to be done that the privilege of the writ of *habeas corpus* was suspended. This fact is both significant of the sacred regard entertained both in the public mind of Great Britain for the sanctity of private rights, and of the respect which the British crown is obliged to pay to these constitutionally recognized rights of British subjects.

The history of the Writ of *habeas corpus* in our own country dates properly for its origin in the Convention which formed the Constitution of the United States.

This Convention met in May, 1787, in Philadelphia. On the 29th of May, Mr. Charles Pinckney, of South Carolina, laid before the House a draft of a plan of a Federal Constitution, the VIth Article of which provided, "The Legislature of the United States shall pass no law on the subject of religion, nor touching or abridging the liberty of the press; nor shall the privilege of the writ of *habeas corpus* ever be suspended, except in the case of rebellion or invasion."

On the 6th of August the Committee of Detail, consisting of Rutledge, Randolph, Gorham, Ellsworth, and Wilson, reported a draft of a Constitution, but it contained no provision on the subject of the writ of *habeas corpus*.

On the 20th of August Mr. Pinckney submitted to the House, in order to be referred to the Committee of Detail, the following proposition, among others: " The privileges and benefits of the writ of *habeas corpus* shall be enjoyed in this Government in the most expeditious and ample manner, and shall not be suspended by the Legislature, except upon the most urgent and pressing occasions, and for a limited time, not exceeding —— months."

On the 28th of the same month, " Mr. Pinckney, urging the propriety of securing the benefit of the *habeas corpus* in the most ample manner, moved that it should not be suspended but on the most urgent occasions, and then only for a limited time, not exceeding twelve months."

" Mr. Rutledge was for declaring the *habeas corpus* inviolate. He did not conceive that a suspension could ever be necessary at the same time through all the States."

" Mr. Gouverneur Morris moved that the privilege of the writ of *habeas corpus* should not be suspended, unless when, in cases of rebellion or invasion, the public safety may require it."

" Mr. Wilson doubted whether in any case a suspension could be necessary, as the discretion now exists with judges in most important cases to keep in gaol, or admit to bail."

" The first part of Mr. Gouverneur Morris's motion, to the word ' unless,' was agreed to *nem. con.* On the remaining part the vote stood: *Aye*—New Hampshire, Massachusetts, Connecticut, Pennsylvania, Delaware, Maryland and Virginia—7. *Nay*—North Carolina, South Carolina, Georgia—3." (Elliott's Debates, Vol. V., pp. 131, 376, 445, 484.)

It will be seen from this original draft of the proposition to incorporate the *habeas corpus* clause in the Constitution that it was manifestly the design to restrain the Federal Legislature from suspending the privileges of the writ except in the prescribed contingency. There was no thought that the Executive would either possess that right by virtue of office or by any implication whatever, and therefore no reference was thought to be necessary to the executive in this connection. Without this qualified restraint proposed by Mr. Pinckney upon the power of the Legislature, it would perhaps be inferred that as Congress would hold nearly the same relation as the law-making power in the United States that Parliament held to Great Britain, Congress, unless restricted by constitutional inhibition, might assume to exercise the same power in the suspension of the writ of *habeas corpus*, and in passing laws in relation to the religious worship.— And as there is no restraint upon the British Parliament nor contingency prescribed to it when it may or may not suspend the privilege of the writ of *habeas corpus*, it was obviously Mr. Pinckney's object to restrain Congress from suspending the privilege of this great writ of right at its own discretion. Hence the restriction on its power to the contingency of rebellion or invasion.

But some sophist might say just as Mr. Lincoln has assumed the right to do, this restriction upon the power of the Legislature only proves the greater power in the President, for the power must be lodged somewhere. According to this theory, which is not merely a theory now-a-days, any power of government withheld from Congress is by implication vested in the President, so, it should be concluded, according to this, that whenever the Constitution says Congress shall not do a thing the President has a right to do the act inhibited ; and where Congress is permitted to do an act under certain prescribed contingencies, the President may act in such cases, his own discretion only being the rule and limit of his power.

Absurd as this theory is to common sense, it is nevertheless made the rule of action by Mr. Lincoln in his administration of the Federal Government. Legislative powers denied by the Constitution to the Legislative Department are assumed by him as if it were a matter of course that what the Constitution withheld from Congress it vested in the President. Still more absurd is Mr. Lincoln's assumption that the power not vested in him as President belongs to him by virtue of his being Commander-in-Chief of the Army and Navy, a position which he holds only by virtue of his being the President, an ex-officio position which derives no power or authority from any other source than the Constitution of the United States and through no other means than that of the Presidency. But as Mr. Lincoln is more used to illustrations than he is to arguments to guide or influence his actions, he might better appreciate the force of an attempt to hold himself up by the seat of his breeches, an experiment it is suggested to him to make, than of any argument, however conclusive in reason or law which might be made for him from common sense, historical facts and judicial authority to prove to him the absurdity of the pretensions he makes to a right of setting aside the Constitution, and existing nevertheless as President of the United States. He forgets that the act of his which destroys the Constitution puts him out of existence as Chief Magistrate of this Republic, and that if he continues in power after his destruction of the Constitution and his subversion of the government, he does so only as an usurper. But let us continue our historical proofs. I quote from Bullitt's compilation of such facts.

In the Massachusetts Convention, called to determine whether the Constitution should be ratified or not, the *habeas corpus* clause being under consideration on the 26th of January, 1788, "Dr. Taylor asked why this darling privilege was not expressed in the same manner as in the Constitution of Massachusetts? . . . He remarked on the difference of expression, and asked why the time was not limited?

"Judge Dana said: The answer in part to the honorable gentleman must be that the same men did not make both Constitutions; that he did not see the necessity or great benefit of limiting the *time*, supposing it had been as in our Constitution, 'not exceeding twelve months;' yet, as our Legislature can, so might *Congress* continue the suspension of the writ from year to year. The safest and best restriction, therefore, arises from the nature of the cases in which *Congress* are authorized to exercise that power at all, namely, in those of rebellion or invasion. These are clear and certain terms, facts of public notoriety; and whenever these shall cease to exist, the suspension of the writ must necessarily cease also. He thought the citizen had a better security for his privilege of the writ of *habeas corpus* under the Federal than under the State Constitution for our Legislature may suspend the writ as often as they judge, 'the most urgent and pressing occasions' call for it.

"Judge Sumner said, that this was a *restriction on Congress*, that the writ of *habeas corpus* should not be suspended, except in cases of rebellion or invasion. The learned Judge then explained the nature of the writ. . . . . The privilege, he said, is essential to freedom, and, therefore, the power to suspend it is restricted. On the other hand the State, he said, might be involved in danger; the worst enemy may lay plans to destroy us, and so artfully as to prevent any evidence against him, and might ruin the country, without the power to suspend the writ was thus given. 'Congress have only power to suspend the privilege to persons committed by their authority. A person committed under the authority of the States will still have a right to the writ.'" (2d Elliott's Debates, 108.)

In the act of ratification by the Convention of New York is this remarkable clause, among others, explanatory of their understanding of the Constitution: "That every person restrained of his liberty is entitled to an inquiry into the lawfulness of such restraint, and to a removal thereof, if unlawful; and that such inquiry and removal ought not to be denied or delayed, except when, on account of public danger, *the Congress* shall suspend the privilege of the writ of *habeas corpus*.*

" Under these impressions, and declaring that the rights aforesaid cannot be abridged or violated, and *that the explanations aforesaid are consistent with the said Constitution,* . . . . we, the said delegates, in the name and on behalf of the people of the State of New York, do by these presents assent to and ratify the said Constitution." (Supplement to the Journal of the Federal Convention, published in Boston in 1819, pp. 428 and 431.)

The Convention of Rhode Island also ratified the Constitution with certain explanatory declarations; among them is the following:

" VII. That all power of suspending laws, or the execution of laws, by any authority, without the consent of the representatives of the people in the Legislature, is injurious to their rights, and ought not to be exercised." (Idem, p. 455.)

In the debate in the Virginia Convention, Mr.

---

* No proof can be more conclusive than this is as to the understanding and intention of the framers of the Constitution. This action of the Convention is in itself a complete corroboration of the argument under consideration. No ingenuity can mystify it. No controversal skill can weaken or destroy its force.

Patrick Henry, in speaking of the 9th section, used this language:

"The design of the negative expressions in this section is to prescribe limits beyond which the powers of *Congress* shall not go............The first prohibition is, that the privilege of the writ of *habeas corpus* shall not be suspended, but when, in case of rebellion or invasion, the public safety may require it. It results clearly that, if it had not said so, *they* could suspend it in all cases whatsoever.... (Elliot's Deb., Vol. III, p. 461.) See also remarks of Gov. Randolph, quoted *ante*, p. 9.

These were the declarations in four Conventions called for the ratification of the Constitution; and in that of New York, it will be observed, that it is expressly set forth, in their act of ratification, that the power of suspension is in Congress.

The first occasion for the consideration of the question of the suspension of the writ of *habeas corpus* after the Federal Government went into operation, arose in consequence of Burr's conspiracy.— Mr. Jefferson was then President, and it is well known was not a personal friend of Burr. It ought to be presumed that Mr. Jefferson knew as much as Mr. Lincoln does of the intention, objects and designs of the framers of the Constitution, and whether he, as President, was invested by the Constitution or otherwise with the power assumed by Mr. Lincoln. Mr. Jefferson not only recognized Congress as the depositary of this power, but requested that body to exercise it so that he might be better able to suppress the impending insurrection. The Senate passed the bill, " An act to suspend the privilege of the writ of *habeas corpus* for a limited time in certain cases." The vote on the passage of this bill in the Senate appears to have been unanimous. In the House the bill was rejected, so jealous was this body of the rights of the American people.—

The following extracts from the debates on the question, as collated by Mr. Bullitt in his Review of Binney's pamphlet on the suspension of the writ of *habeas corpus*, will show that there was no question then as to where the power was vested to suspend the privilege of this act.

Mr. Burwell said, "If that be the case, upon what ground shall we suspend the writ of *habeas corpus?* . . . . . Nothing but the most imperious necessity would excuse *us* (i. e. Congress,) in confiding to the Executive, or any person under him, the power of seizing and confining a citizen, upon bare suspicion, for three months, without responsibility for the abuse of such unlimited discretion.". . .

Mr. Elliott said, "We can suspend the writ of *habeas corpus* only in a case of extreme emergency. . . . . But we shall be told that the Constitution has contemplated cases of this kind, and, in reference to them, invested us with unlimited discretion. When any gentleman shall advance such a position, we shall meet him upon that ground, and put the point at issue." . . . .

Mr. Eppes said, "By this bill we are called on to exercise one of the most important powers vested in Congress by the Constitution of the United States. . . . . . . The words of the Constitution are, 'The privilege of the writ of *habeas corpus* shall not be suspended, unless when, in cases of rebellion or invasion, the public safety may require it.' The wording of this clause of the Constitution deserves peculiar attention. It is not in every case of invasion, nor in every case of rebellion, that the exercise of this power by Congress can be justified under the words of the Constitution. . . . . . . The Constitution, however, *having vested this power in Congress*, and a branch of the Legislature having thought its exercise necessary, it remains for us to inquire, whether the present situation of our country authorizes, on our part, a resort to this extraordinary measure." . . . .

Mr. Varnum said, "I consider the country, in a degree, in a state of insecurity; and if so, *the power is vested in Congress, under the Constitution,* to suspend the writ of *habeas corpus.* . . . .

Mr. Smilie said, "A suspension of the privilege of the writ of *habeas corpus* is, in all respects, equivalent to repealing that essential part of the Constitution which secures that principle which has been called the palladium of 'personal liberty.' If we recur to England, we shall find that the writ of *habeas corpus* in that country has been frequently suspended. But under what circumstances? . . . . . . We have taken from the statute of this country (England) this most valuable part of our Constitution. The Convention who framed that instrument, believing that there might be cases when it would be necessary to vest a discretionary power in the Executive, *have constituted the Legislature* the judges of this necessity; and the only question to be determined now is, does this necessity exist?" (3d vol. Benton's Deb., 504–514.) On the 17th of February, 1807, the House of Representatives proceeded to consider the motion of Mr. Broom, to wit: "Resolved, that it is expedient to make further provision by law for securing the privilege of the writ of *habeas corpus* to persons in custody, under or by color of the authority of the United States."

Mr. Broom said, "This privilege of the writ of *habeas corpus* has been deemed so important that by the ninth section of the first Article of the Constitution it is declared that it 'shall not be suspended, unless when, in cases of rebellion or invasion, the public safety may require it.' Such is the value of this privilege that even the highest legislative body of the Union—the legitimate representatives of the na-

tion—are not intrusted with the guardianship of it, or suffered to lay their hands upon it, unless when, in cases of extreme danger, the public safety shall make it necessary. . . . .
This constitutional provision was intended only as a check upon the power of Congress in abridging the privilege, but was never intended to prevent them from intrenching it around with sound and wholesome laws; on the contrary, it was expected that Congress were prohibited from impairing at their pleasure this privilege,—that they would regard it as of high importance, and, by coercive laws, insure its operation." . . . .

Mr. Bidwell said, "The Constitution, by restricting the Legislature from suspending it, except when, in cases of rebellion or invasion, the public safety may require a suspension, had recognized it as a writ of right, and our statutes had authorized certain courts and magistrates to grant it."

Mr. G. W. Campbell said, "*This provision evidently relates to Congress*, and was intended to prevent that body from suspending by law the Writ of *habeas corpus*, except in the cases stated, and has no relation whatever to the act of an individual in refusing to obey the writ,—such refusal or disobedience would not certainly suspend the privilege of that Writ, and must be considered in the same point of view as the violation of any other public law made to protect the liberty of the citizen."

Mr. Holland said, "But, sir, so far as respects the *habeas corpus, the suspension of it applies to the Legislature*, and not to persons. The Constitution says, it shall not be suspended but in case of rebellion, or when the public safety requires it. *This prohibition manifestly applies to the Legislature*, and not to persons in their individual capacity."

Mr. J. Randolph said, "The Writ of *habeas corpus* is the only Writ sanctioned by the Constitution.

It is guarded from every approach, except by the two Houses of Congress." (3d vol. Benton's Debates, pp. 520—540.)

In 1842, in the debate on the bill to idemnify Gen. Jackson for the fine imposed on him by Judge Hall, at New Orleans, Mr. Bayard said, " Congress may indeed suspend the privilege of the Writ of *habeas corpus*, but cannot declare martial law to be the law of the United States, or any part of them...... The Constitution says, Congress shall have power to declare war, to raise armies, to provide a navy, to provide arms and munitions of war, and to make rules for the government of the land and naval forces. On these limited and specific powers it has been inferred that Congress may declare martial law. To avoid this very conclusion there is an express provision in the very next section, among the restrictions on the powers of Congress, declaring that the remedy of the Writ of *habeas corpus* shall not be suspended, unless in cases of rebellion or invasion. . . . . All Congress can do, even in cases of rebellion or invasion, is to suspend the privilege of the Writ of *habeas corpus*; and that can be done by *Congress only*—not by an officer of the Government—without its authority." (Vol. XIV Benton's Debates, pp. 627.)

On January 14, 1843, the same subject was discussed in the House of Representatives.

Mr. Hunt said (after quoting the ninth section of the first Article of the Constitution, which provides that the privilege of the writ of *habeas corpus* shall not be suspended, unless when, in cases of rebellion or invasion, the public safety may require it), " Who was to be the judge of that necessity? Was it the President of the United States, or any subordinate officer in command? No; it was the Legislature of the country that was the judge, and the only judge of that necessity. He supported the position by citing the practice of Mr. Jefferson, who, in 1807, as President of the United States, applied to Congress for a temporary suspension of the writ of *habeas corpus* for three months; which, however, was refused by the House of Representatives, where the bill was defeated, which had passed the Senate for that purpose."

In the House of Representatives, in the debate on the bill to indemnify General Jackson, January 2, 1844, Mr. Barnard said, " The Constitution gave Congress authority to pass laws for the regulation of the army and navy of the United States, and under that, Congress have passed laws for the government of the army and navy and the militia. That code was applicable to the officers and soldiers, and to the militia, when in service; but it was not applicable to any other human being. Congress itself could not proclaim martial law. *It might suspend the habeas corpus act,* but it could not suspend the Constitution. A proclamation of martial law by the Congress of the United States would, of itself, be a violation of the Constitution." (Vol. XIV. Benton's Debates, p. 657.)

In an opinion delivered by Mr. Attorney-General Cushing, upon the subject of martial law, and the suspension of the *habeas corpus,* in February, 1857, growing out of a proclamation of martial law by the Governor of Washington Territory, in order to suspend the *habeas corpus,* this language is used : " The opinion is expressed by commentators on the Constitution, that the right to suspend the writ of *habeas corpus,* and also that of judging when the exigency has arisen, belongs *exclusively to Congress.* ....It may be assumed, as a general doctrine of constitutional jurisprudence in all the United States, that the power to suspend laws, whether those granting the writ of *habeas corpus,* or any other, is vested exclusively in the Legislature of the particular State." (Opinions of Attorneys-General, Vol. VIII, p. 365.)

So much for historical proofs embracing also the opinions of the statesmen, patriots and jurists of the better days of the Republic.

Judge Taney having already quoted the opinion of his illustrious predecessor, Chief Justice Marshal, I shall not repeat the opinion of that eminent jurist as given in the case, ex-parte Bollman and Swartwout, but refer the reader to it as quoted by Judge Taney. I will only add one quotation from Judge Story, who in his commentaries on the Constitution, says: Sec. 1336, " Hitherto, no suspension of the writ has been authorized by Congress since the establishment of the Constitution. It would seem, as the power is given to Congress to suspend the writ of *habeas corpus* in case of rebellion or invasion, that the right to judge whether the exigency had arisen, must exclusively belong to that body."

To the understanding and judgment of the reader, these facts, historical proofs, decisions of illustrious judges, and opinions of eminent jurists are committed in contrast with the act of will of Abraham Lincoln; and unless the interested motive of the partisan has usurped the place in the American mind which was once occupied by patriotism, it will not be in vain for our country's well being that history, common sense and the judgment of our most illustrious ancestors have been cited to prove how utterly absurb are the pretensions to power of Abraham Lincoln, how unwarrantable has been his assumptions of right to set aside the Constitution, to subvert the government, and to deprive individual citizens of their rights of person; and how dangerous to liberty it is to permit these assumptions of power to pass unrebuked, and to be exercised unrestrained.

CONFLICT WITH MISSOURI — CAPTURE OF CAMP JACKSON — MASSACRE IN ST. LOUIS — MISSOURI DRIVEN TO REBELLION.

As a part of the history of the arbitrary course of the Administration at Washington, and of its determination to press the irrepressible conflict by driving every slaveholding State into rebellion, its relations to Missouri are referred to here as evidence of its reckless disregard for State rights. The impartial world as well as the Patriotic American will be amazed at the arrogance of the Executive in assuming power and at the boldness with which this assumed power was exercised.

A law of the State of Missouri, enacted in accordance with constitutional requirements, made it the duty of the organized Militia to meet in May of each year for drill and camp instruction.

In accordance with this law a brigade of State Militia were in camp near St. Louis early in May, 1861, under the command of Gen. Frost, a Militia officer. While thus conforming to a law of Missouri which these Militia could not disregard under penalties of fine at least, they were surrounded by United States troops, part regulars and part volunteers, under the chief command of Captain Lyon, and the whole brigade made prisoners. Very naturally a flagrant outrage such as this, accompanied as it was with the massacre of a number of citizens, created a profound sensation, and excited hostility in thousands of Missourians against the Federal Government. Many who till then thought of holding no other relation to the Government than that of fealty, wavered in their allegiance, and thousands, who up to that time, were wavering in their course between preserving their relations to the Federal Government and joining their fortunes to the seceded States, were driven by this high-handed outrage of the Administration, to become Rebels, in defence of State Rights. It would seem from all the circumstances which were then known and which have since come to light, that it was systematically arranged between partisans of the Lincoln Administration and the leaders of that party at Washington, that Missouri should be driven into revolt for the purpose, and by that means, of placing the State in the control of such partisans as Frank Blair and his fellow spoilsmen. The assemblage of the State Militia at Camp Jackson afforded the first opportunity to the conspirators against the dignity and peace of Missouri to commence operations. Gen. Harney, who was in command of the Western Department, was disposed of temporarily, so as that the more ready tool of the designs of the Administration and its partisan friends, Captain Lyon could be placed in command of the Federal forces at St. Louis; this done, the capture of the State Militia at Camp Jackson was effected. This occurred on the tenth of May, 1861. The State of Missouri had till then made no demonstrations of hostility to the Federal Government, nor had the State Militia, even those under the command of Gen. Frost, manifested any design to array itself against the constituted authorities; on the contrary the Legislature of Missouri had taken means to preserve the peace of that State, and Gen. Frost had made a tender of his own services and of those of his command to the Federal authorities.

These are not mere assertions without foundation in fact. The Acts of the Missouri Legislature previous to this occurrence, the published correspondence between Gen. Frost, and the Federal authorities and the testimony of Camp Jackson prisoners, all go to prove that the State of Missouri and for aught that appeared to the contrary, all its people were truly loyal: but this condition of things did not suit the Administration and its Missouri partisans; the State was under the control of others than creatures and parasites of the Administration. Something must be done to afford Frank Blair and company a pretext for seizing on the State Government, not to preserve the State from seceding, but to use it for partisan and personal purposes, to strengthen the hands of the Administration in the abuse of power which it had already commenced to exercise, and to fill the pockets of its needy and greedy followers. Such was the "Military necessity" which the diabolical machinations of Blair & Co. in Missouri, and the leaders of the Administration at Washington contrived to bring about and apply to Missouri; and behold the result in the devastations of the homes of Missourians, in the massacre of thousands who, were it not for the partisan policy of the Administration and for the satanic selfishness and ambition of the Blairs, would be living evidences of their devotion to the Union.

But no, Missouri must be scourged into servility to the Administration and to Blair & Co., and as Gen. Harney would not be used for that purpose, he was called to Washington on the pretense of important business and Blair found the scourge in the person of Captain Lyon, who had orders from Washington how to proceed in laying the lash on the Missourians.

The first blow, as we have seen, was to be inflicted on the State militia and on the people of St. Louis, who were to be massacred if they manifested any hostility. If their capture in a camp organized under the requirements of a State law, would not subject the militia to the behests of Blair, or, what would do just as well to serve the same purpose, excite them to defend their person from outrage and their State from the indignity of such a proceeding, other means to effect the object were not unprovided. But nothing more was necessary than this, to rouse the spirited freemen of Missouri to a sense of the design of the partisans in power. The capture of the militia at Camp Jackson was a flagrant violation of State rights and of the sovereignty of Missouri; and no wonder that such an act, done at the instigation of Missouri abolitionists and by command of the Administration, drove many of the people of that State into rebellion. It has been attempted to justify the capture of Camp Jackson, by the allegation that the troops there were to be used against the Government. The proofs, however, are all the other way. The camp was established not only in compliance with law, but under the requirements of law; and the militia officers would have subjected themselves to fine and made themselves amenable to other penalties of military law, had they neglected or failed to perform the duty of organized troops in camp. This is but one proof that the State militia were not assembled for any other intent than to comply with the law which gave them existence as a military body. Another is that already cited, of their offering their services to the Government. These facts disprove all and every allegation made by partisans of the administration, who are notoriously given to lying when their objects can be accomplished, their interests promoted, and their real designs concealed, by that means. The subsequent course of some of the Camp Jackson prisoners is adduced as a proof of their disloyalty at the time of their capture. As well in propriety might it be asserted that the whole South was in favor of secession when South Carolina seceded. It was only by such flagrant acts of folly, of rashness, of violations of constitutional rights as the outrage on Camp Jackson, the assumption and exercise of legislative and judicial power by the administration, and its manifestly partisan course, that drove the greater portion of the South into revolt; and it was this course which had its influence on the Camp Jackson prisoners.

Even Gen. Price, who has since then become one of the most influential as he is one of the ablest confederates, was so manifestly solicitous to preserve the peace in Missouri, and to secure that State in the Union, made an arrangement to effect that object with Gen. Harney, who returned to his command at St. Louis after Capt. Lyon had been used to inflict the indignity on Camp Jackson. Gen. Price succeeded Gen. Frost in the command of the State militia at St. Louis, and when Gen. Harney returned after the capture of Camp Jackson, these two Generals, Harney and Price, both having the well-being of their country at heart, entered into an agreement, one on behalf of the United States, the other for Missouri, that the respective forces under their command should be used to keep the peace. This arrangement, however, instead of being gratifying to the administration, gave it such offense that Gen. Harney was immediately removed from his command, and the scourge of Missouri, Lyon, was substituted. Is any other evidence, than what has been adduced, needed to convince the reader that it is not peace the administration desired or wanted in Missouri but civil war, that the administration seemed determined to provoke, at all hazards, and no matter in what consequences it might end. Step by step, blow by blow, civil war was provoked, and the end is not yet; desolated as Missouri has been, plundered, burned, ravished and subjected to every outrage and horror of war as it has been in the person of its people and in their property, History will not rehearse the thousandth part of the outrages on person and property committed under the authority of the Federal Government on Missouri, but it will tell enough to convict the administration of Abraham Lincoln of the crime of driving that State into rebellion for the purpose of subjecting it to the domination of a few partisans whose services the administration found it necessary or useful to requite, even at the sacrifice of the peace, constitutional rights, liberties, lives and property of more than a million of the American people.

Referring to the condition of Missouri at the time of these occurrences, and subsequently to the course of Governor Jackson, of that State, the writer of this work expressed the following sentiments, which were submitted then to the reason of the people and to their judgment when the passion of the hour had ceased to have its influence. Has not the time nearly come when this judgment can be appealed to with confidence of its decision being on the side of right, justice and truth. The following allegations and sentiments expressed in the Dubuque Herald of August 19, 1861, are submitted to the judgment of the reader as a part of the defense of the writer against the imputations of disloyalty implied in his arbitrary arrest and imprisonment by the Administration, and as a part of his arraignment of the Administration before the bar of American public opinion for its manifold and flagrant crimes.

From the Dubuque Herald.

CONDITION OF MISSOURI.

The most unfortunate, the most deplorable and the least inexcusable act of the Administration in the unfortunate conflict which has been precipitated upon the country was the removal of Gen. Harney from the command of the Western Department of the Army, and his supercedence by Gen. Lyon in the administration of Federal affairs in Missouri.

Gen. Harney, even after the affair of Camp Jackson, had restored a calm to the public mind and had secured the confidence and regard of the people to such an extent that any suggestion coming from him would have been respected and coincided in without hesitation.

But it seemed as if the demon of discord had taken possession of the President and his advisers, and that it was determined on that Missouri should have no peace. It was not enough that a Convention of her people, elected by univeral suffrage, resolved most solemnly that Missouri would remain a faithful member of the Union. It was not enough that even the volunteers at Camp Jackson had offered their services, their arms and their lives to sustain the Federal cause in St. Louis. No; nothing would satisfy the suspicions of the Administration—nothing would gratify the Abolition fanatics who controlled the President but to plunge Missouri into the same fratricidal strife in which the other Southern States had become involved with their sister States of the North. If ever an effect could be traced to its legitimate cause, the condition of Missouri to-day is owing to the course of the Administration towards that State. Every life lost in the conflicts within her borders, every home made desolate, every affliction to which both her people and those who have been sent into the conflict with them have been subjected, are the effects of the policy, the cruel, unrelenting, fanatical policy of the Administration towards the unfortunate State of Missouri; and the judgment of posterity will pass a sentence of condemnation, aye and of retribution upon the guilty men who plunged the people of that State into the barbarities and inflicted upon them the horrible cruelties of civil war.

From the Dubuque Herald.

MISSOURI DECLARATION OF INDEPENDENCE.

Governor Jackson has issued a Provisional Declaration of Independence for the State of Missouri dated at New Madrid on the 5th of August. The Lieutenant Governor of the State, Reynolds, has issued a Proclamation from the same place on the 31st of July against the new Government, instituted by the Convention, under the executive lead of Judge Gamble.

Thus is Missouri distracted, torn, ruined by conflicting and hostile Governments, to which the Federal Government, without solicitation by the lawful authority of that State, has become a party. The Federal Government, if it did anything, should have recognised the constitutional Government of Missouri, no matter what became of Governor Jackson nor in what manner he may have acted.

Suppose that Governor Kirkwood of Iowa should become recreant to his trust and his position as Governor of this State, would that be a sufficient cause, or would it have justification or apology for overthrowing our whole State Government, changing our Constitution, subverting the State Authority and making it a subservient instrument of despotism to the People. Surely not in Iowa, why then is it so in Missouri.

With regard to Governor Jackson's Declaration of Independence, that is no less revolutionary, unauthorized, and unwarranted than is the act of the

Convention which superceded him as Governor, by the substitution in his stead of Judge Gamble. Governor Jackson should have contented himself with endeavoring to restore his legitimate authority in Missouri, as Governor of that State, as a member of the Union, and not assumed the prerogative nor attempted to exercise the power of separating Missouri from the Union. Missouri has voted to stay in the old Union; and until her people express themselves differently in some official manner, it is nothing short of treason in any one to attempt to wrest the State from the Union.

While expressing this as our opinion, we are not the less convinced that the course and policy of the Federal Government towards Missouri is unconstitutional, unwise, and better calculated to produce the worst disasters than to remedy any evils it might have perceived or averted those it may have apprehended in that State.

The best thing all parties in Missouri could do now, if they could be brought to it, is to restore the Government of that state, and to subject Governor Jackson and his accomplices to impeachment, or to such other trial as his alleged dereliction and crimes may warrant. To effect this, all parties should lay down their arms, the Federal forces should be withdrawn, and the civil authorities and civil tribunals should be restored to power and respected according to law. There is no other remedy, that we can pe rceive, to restore peace to Missouri. Unless this be applied, that State will be hopelessly, irretrievably ruined.

SUPPRESSION OF THE MARYLAND LEGISLATURE—ARREST OF THE MEMBERS.

ONE of the most arbitrary and despotic acts of the President was the suppression of the Legislature of Maryland, or the prevention of its holding a session, by the kidnapping of certain members of that body. This was done in September, 1861.

The pretext for this high handed measure was the alleged design of a majority of the members of the Legislature to pass an Ordinance of Secession; but the real design was, as it was avowed by Mr. Seward in an official interview with Lord Lyons, to affect the elections, soon to take place, in Maryland.

That there was no well-founded ground to apprehend that the Legislature of Maryland would pass an Ordinance of Secession, it will be sufficient to refer to the action of that body at the convened session in April previous. That action is given here as related by Hon. S. Teackle Wallis, a member of that body, one of the victims of arbitrary power, in a letter addressed by him to Senator Sherman, from Ohio. Mr. Wallis says:

"The special session of the Legislature of Maryland, called by Governor Hicks in 1861, was opened in Frederick on the 26th of April in that year On the next day, April 27, a select committee of the Senate reported to that body an address to the people of Maryland, which on the same day was unanimously adopted, and was shortly afterwards published, with the individual signatures of the Senators, in all the newspapers of the State.

"The principal feature of that address, in fact almost the only purpose of its promulgation, is developed in the following extract—

"'We cannot but know that a large portion of the citizens of Maryland have been induced to believe that there is a probability that our deliberations may result in the passage of some measure committing this State to secession. It is, therefore, our duty to declare that all such fears are without just foundation. *We know that we have no constitutional authority to take such action. You need not fear that there is a possibility that we will do so.*

"'If believed by us to be desired by you, we may, by legislation to that effect, give you the opportunity of deciding for yourselves your own future destiny. We may go thus far, but certainly will go no further.'

"You will find the whole address on pages 8 and 9 of the printed journal of the Senate, which is no doubt accessible to you in the library of Congress. It could not be more clear than it is upon the point in dispute. On the 29th of April, the day after the address was communicated to the House of Delegates by the Senate, an opportunity was afforded for the House to announce its own conclusions, in the most direct and unequivocal manner, upon the constitutional authority of the Legislature to alter the Federal relations of the State. On page 19 of the printed journal of the House of Delegates you will find that, on the day last named, a memorial was presented 'from 216 voters of Prince George's county, praying the Legislature (if in its judgment it possesses the power) to pass an ordinance of secession without delay.'

"This memorial was at once referred to the Committee on Federal Relations. Desirous of putting the question at rest, as it was then greatly agitating the public mind, the committee determined to report upon it before the adjournment. There was no difference of opinion among the members of the committee as to reporting unfavorably to the prayer of the memorialists, nor, with five out of seven, was there any doubt as to the propriety of stating, explicitly, as the ground of our recommendation, that the measure proposed was unconstitutional. Two reports were accordingly made. You will find them both on page 21 of the House journal. That of the majority, which I myself signed and presented, as chairman of the committee, contains the declaration, in words, '*that in their judgment the Legislature does not possess the power to pass such an ordinance as is prayed, and that the prayer of the memorialists cannot, therefore, be granted.*' The minority report asks leave simply 'to report unfavorably to the prayer of the memorialists.'

"With the concurrence of the whole committee, I stated to the House the difference of opinion which had caused two reports to be made, and the importance of having the deliberate sense of the House, on the question, announced to the people at once. The grounds upon which it was believed to be beyond the constitutional authority of the Legislature to pass an ordinance of secession were then briefly stated, and a test vote thereupon was taken, by common understanding, on the minority report, which received only thirteen votes to fifty-three. The majority report was then adopted without a division. From that time, down to the forcible suppression of the Legislature by Mr. Lincoln's orders, the subject was never again mooted, but was considered, on all hands, as absolutely and permanently disposed of. Without pretending to know what was in the breast of every member, I know enough to assert, in the most unhesitating manner, my belief that at the time of our arrest, no individual, of either House, had a thought of again recurring to it. I positively know that if such recurrence had been attempted, it would not have been, for a moment, entertained in the House of which I was a member. From all that I knew then, and know now, of the purposes of the members of the Legislature and their opinions—and I think I was not and am not ill-formed—I have no doubt that if they had been permitted to hold the session which was prevented by the arrests of September, 1861, they would have adjourned, in three days, for lack of business to occupy them.

"Not only have I given you the facts truly in regard to the supposed intention of the members of the Legislature to pass a secession ordinance themselves, and their actual determination to the contrary, but if you will take the trouble to examine the journals (Senate journal, 133, 134, and House journal, 108, 121,) you will further see that as early as May 14, 1861, the House of Delegates, by a vote of forty-five to twelve, and the Senate unanimously, had adopted a resolution against the expediency of even calling a sovereign convention of the people of the State. The reasons assigned for that action, in the report which accompanied it, you will find to have been even more conclusive, when the Legislature was suppressed, than when the resolution was adopted.

"All these facts are well known to be true by every member of the Legislature, no matter what may be his political sentiments. They were equally well known, at the time of our arrest, to every man in Maryland who had troubled himself to follow the course of our legislative proceedings. They were perfectly accessible to Mr. Lincoln at the time when, if Mr. Hickman truly represents him, 'he thought it better to arrest the members of the Legislature and put them in jail,' merely because he thought it 'not unlikely' the facts were otherwise. If what I have stated is not true, its untruth can be shown. If, as Mr. Fessenden suggests, the President has 'evidence' upon which his alleged belief to the contrary can be justified, such 'evidence' can be easily produced. *I assert to you that there is no such evidence, and that there can be none, because the fact which it is supposed to establish it did not exist.* I am willing to stake my veracity and integrity upon the issue, and I challenge the public production of any proof to the contrary of what I have asserted. Doing so, I leave it to your candor and sense of right, to give to gentlemen whom you have been instrumental in injuring, an opportunity of being heard in their own vindication, through you, in the same public way in which the injury has been done."

But admitting that it was the design of the Legislature of Maryland to pass an ordinance of secession, or any other unconstitutional act, did that justify the President in preventing the meeting of the State Legislature? Such an act would be either unconstitutional or valid constitutionally. If unconstitutional, it would be void *ab initio* without any intervention. If constitutional, what right had the President of the United States to prevent its enactment? Void or not, what right in law, or by authority had he to interfere with the acts of a Sovereign State?

In relation to States, he is a mere individual as other citizens are; no more. The fact of Mr. Abraham Lincoln being President of the United States does not change his relation as an individual to other individuals, much less to the States of the Union. As President he is invested with certain authority in law, but beyond this investment of authority, he has no more rightful power to interfere with the acts of individuals, much less of States, than has any of the victims whom he subjected by arbitrary power to the constraints of his will. He is President by the Constitution, and as such has authority conferred on him by the Constitution, no more, and when he disregards the Constitution, he disregards the only source of his authority and power, and subjects himself not only to impeachment in his official character, but to such personal consequences as both the laws contemplate and as those who may be outraged and injured in person and property by his despotic assumptions and arbitrary exercise of power choose to inflict; for surely those who have been made the victims of Lincoln's despotism without a shadow of a warrrant on his part in law, have some right to be avenged on him for the wrongs, and outrages, and injuries to which they have been subjected.

MARYLAND, it was necessary for the designs of the Administration, should be placed under the heel of the dominant power. To effect this object, the first step was to seize and imprison the prominent and influential members of the State Legislature, under the assumed pretext, (assumed, for there was no foundation in fact for it,) that the Legislature, if allowed to assemble, would take the State out of the Union. Mr. Wallis shows conclusively that the Legislature not only favored no such design but were decidedly opposed to it, and did not believe they had the right to pass an ordinance of secession. The first step being taken, and most of the prominent public men of the State being kidnapped and immured in the loathsome Bastiles provided by the Administration for the punishment of freemen who dared to love their country more than they did the despots, and tyrants, and officers who had obtained control of the government, the next step was to prevent a free election by the people of Maryland. To this end Federal troops were quartered in all the principal cities and towns of the State, and, in fact, at almost every election precinct, and those only were permitted to vote at the fall election who gave good evidence of what the Administration calls "loyalty," which is synonymous for a servile acquiescence, base submission to and hearty approval of the despotic and tyrannical course of the Administration, and an approval of the villainous conduct of the leading members of the party in power, from Members of the Cabinet, aye, from the President's household down to the meanest pimp of the Administration. Whoever in Maryland could not measure his conduct as a citizen by this standard of loyalty, would be thrust from the polls by Federal bayonets, and may consider himself fortunate if he escaped being kidnapped and sent to one of the Bastiles.— Yet, it is claimed that the American people are not only living under the constitutional government which they adopted, but are enjoying and exercising their rights as the Constitution professed to guarantee them and protect the people in their enjoyment.

Maryland, since September, 1861, is as much under the subjection of arbitrary power, exercised over it by the Executive Department of the Federal Government, as any subjugated portion of Russia is under the despotism of the Czar; much more so than Hungary is subjected to Austria, and infinitely more so than any dependency or colony of Great Britain is subject to the British Crown. There has been no free election in Maryland since the spring of 1861, and the freedom enjoyed by the citizens of that State is simply to live and act as it is desired they should by the Lincoln Administration. That the people of Maryland submit to such subjection is neither creditable to their courage, their honor, or their patriotism. They should either cast away the forms of constitutional government entirely, or live, aye, and if need be, die, freemen in accordance with the form and system of government established for them by their ancestors when they shook off the yoke and burden of a foreign tyrant. Domestic tyranny, it would seem, is more tolerable or less odious than that of Great Britain was to the sturdy patriots of old Maryland; although, as a matter of fact, the despotism of British tyranny was mild in its form and light in its burden, compared to the relentless grasp, the remorseless rigor, and the callous heartlessness of the despotism to which Maryland is subjected by Abraham Lincoln and his minions and satellites.

USURPATION OF LEGISLATIVE POWERS BY THE PRESIDENT—CREATION OF A JUDICIAL TRIBUNAL WITH CIVIL JURISDICTION IN NEW ORLEANS.

ANOTHER of the flagrant acts of the President violative of the Constitution of the United States and usurpative of the authority and powers of Congress, was his creation, by an order dated at the Executive Mansion, of a provisional court invested by him with civil jurisdiction, at New Orleans. It would be difficult to believe that so flagrant and daring an act of usurpation, as this is unquestionably, had been committed were not the evidence of it existing, both in the order itself and in the fact that the court created by it is exercising the functions with which it was invested by the Executive decree.

It is needless to say that the Constitution of the United States invests Congress alone with the power to constitute judicial tribunals other than that of the Supreme Court, which is created by the Constitution itself, but both to prevent cavil and to enlighten the uninformed the provision of the Constitution is referred to. The ninth clause of Sec. VIII. of the Constitution says the Congress shall have power "To constitute tribunals inferior to the Supreme Court." It does not anywhere say that the President shall have this power, but that Congress only shall have it. Yet the President assumed

USURPATION OF LEGISLATIVE POWER. 107

and exercised this power, unconstitutionally and arbitrarily there can be no question, as will be seen by the decree itself, which is as follows:

EXECUTIVE MANSION,
Washington, October 20, 1862.

The insurrection which has for some time prevailed in several of the States of this Union, including Louisiana, having temporarily subverted and swept away the civil institutions of that State, including the judiciary and the judicial authorities of the Union, so that it has become necessary to hold the State in military occupation; and it being indispensably necessary that there shall be some judicial tribunal existing there capable of administering justice, I have, therefore, thought it proper to appoint and I do hereby constitute a Provisional Court, which shall be a court of record for the State of Louisiana; and I do hereby appoint Charles A. Peabody, of New York, to be a Provisional Judge to hold said court, with authority to hear, try, and determine all causes, civil and criminal, including causes in law, equity, revenue, and admiralty, and particularly all such powers and jurisdiction as belong to the District and Circuit Courts of the United States, conforming his proceeding, as far as possible, to the course of proceedings and practice which has been customary in the Courts of the United States and Louisiana—his judgment to be final and conclusive. And I do hereby authorize and empower the said Judge to make and establish such rules and regulations as may be necessary for the exercise of his jurisdiction, and to appoint a Prosecuting Attorney, Marshal, and Clerk of the said Court, who shall perform the functions of Attorney, Marshal, and Clerk according to such proceedings and practices as before mentioned, and such rules and regulations as may be made and established by said Judge. These appointments are to continue during the pleasure of the President, not extending beyond the military occupation of the city of New Orleans, or the restoration of the civil authority in that city and in the State of Louisiana. These officers shall be paid out of the contingent fund of the War Department, compensation as follows: * * Such compensation to be certified by the Secretary of War. A copy of this order, certified by the Secretary of War, and delivered to such Judge, shall be deemed and held to be a sufficient commission:

Let the seal of the United States be hereunto affixed.

[L. S.] ABRAHAM LINCOLN.

By the President:

WILLIAM H. SEWARD,
Secretary of State.

How a partisan, partial as he may be to the President, and prejudiced against the President's political opponents, can palliate the guilt of this offense, much less justify the commission of so palpable an outrage on the Constitution, it is impossible to conceive. And not only does the President create a court and appoint a Judge independent of any action of Congress, but he delegates, as it will be seen, the authority and power to the Judge so constituted to appoint not only a Marshal and Clerk of the court, but a Prosecuting Attorney.— Now the acts of Congres, which have become the laws of the United States, prescribe that the Marshals and Attorneys of United States Courts, or of courts created by acts of Congress, shall be appointed by the President, by and with the consent of the Senate, and not by the Judge ot such courts, as this order of the President gives the Judge not only the authority to do, but requires him to exercise that authority as part of the functions of his office. But it is useless to argue the question involved. The act of the President is fairly a usurpation of power, a wilful disregard of the prescriptions and restraints of the Constitution.

Nor is this all. The Presidential decree creating this court makes the decisions of its Judge final. From him there was to be no appeal, the Constitution of the United States to the contrary notwithstanding. "His judgment to be final and conclusive," decrees the President. In vain does the Constitution prescribe and stipulate that the Supreme Court shall have appellate jurisdiction, both as to law and fact. Abraham Lincoln's fiat is above the Constitution—the Executive decree is the Higher Law.

ORDERS OF THE WAR DEPARTMENT ON WHICH AMERICAN FREEMEN (?) WERE KIDNAPPED AND IMPRISONED—SUSPENSION OF THE *HABEAS CORPUS*.

The first public order which emanated from the War Department directing the kidnapping of American citizens, and indeed of every one else who might fall under the ban of the displeasure of the Administration, was dated the 8th of August, 1862.

A number of cases of arbitrary arrests had occurred before this, some of them as early as May of the previous year, but there was no general order it seems to warrant or direct such proceedings. A telegraphic dispatch or a private order from the State or War Department was the usual warrant previous to the 8th of August, 1862, for depriving American freemen of their liberty.

To preserve a record in connection with the recital of the outrages to which so many freemen have been subjected without just cause, without a judgment of any court and without any warrant whatever in law, the orders by whose authority alone these outrages were committed are here published. The first was as follows:

WAR DEPARTMENT, Aug. 8th, 1862.
ORDERED—
First. That all United States Marshals, and Superintendents and Chiefs of Police of any town, city or district, be and they are hereby authorized and directed to arrest and imprison any person or persons who may be engaged by act, speech or writing, in discouraging volunteer enlistments, or in any way giving aid and comfort to the enemy, or for any other disloyal practice against the United States.

Second. That immediate report be made to Major L. C. Turner, Judge Advocate, in order that such persons may be tried before a military commission.

Third. The expense of such arrest and imprisonment will be certified to the Chief Clerk of the War Department for settlement and payment.

EDWIN M. STANTON,
Secretary of War.

On the same day another order was issued, which among other things, suspended the writ of *habeas corpus*, not by authority of Congress as required by the Constitution, nor even by the President, granting that he had the authority to do so, which the writer does not, but by Edwin M. Stanton, who was holding a mere statutory office, and who at most had the right to exercise only such powers as the Statute creating the office gave him authority to do. But here nevertheless is his order suspending the writ of *habeas corpus*:

"WAR DEPARTMENT,
Washington, August 8th, 1862.

Order to prevent evasion of military duty and for suppression of disloyal practices, and for the suspension of the writ of *habeas corpus.*

First—By direction of the President of the United States, it is hereby ordered that until further order, no citizen liable to be drafted into the militia shall be allowed to go to a foreign country, and all Marshals, Deputy Marshals and military officers of the United States, are directed, and all police authorities, especially at the ports of the United States on the seaboard and on the frontier are requested to see that this order is faithfully carried into effect. And they are hereby authorized and directed to arrest and detain any person or persons about to depart from the United States, in violation of this order, and report to L. C. Turner, Judge Advocate, at Washington City, for further instruction respecting the person or persons so arrested or detained.

Second—Any person liable to draft, who shall absent himself from his county or State, before such draft is made, will be arrested by any Provost Marshal or other United States or State officer, wherever he may be found within the jurisdiction of the United States, and conveyed to the nearest military post or depot, and placed on military duty for the term of the draft; and the expenses of his own arrest and conveyance to such post or depot, and also the sum of five dollars as a reward to the officer who shall make such arrest, shall be deducted from his pay

Third—The writ of *habeas corpus* is hereby suspended in respect to all prisoners so arrested and detained, and in respect to all persons arrested for disloyal practices.

[Signed] EDWIN M. STANTON,
Secretary of War."

It was by virtue of the first of these two orders, and before an attempt had been made to assume the arbitrary power to suspend the writ of *habeas corpus*, that most of those who had been kidnapped during the months of August and September, 1862, were deprived of their liberty.

It will be noticed—and the reader's attention is specially called to the fact—that it was designed to try those who may be arrested under the order of the 8th of August by a military commission. Why this was not done is simply because the elections in October admonished the Administration that it could not go much farther in subjecting American freemen to the despotism of arbitrary power, with impunity. The Military Commission was named, and ready to try the victims, and of course to convict them of any crime of which the tyrants chose to accuse them; but after the result of the elections became known, the Commission was diverted to another purpose.

It was not till the 24th of September, 1862, that the President ventured to assume to himself arbitrary power, and avow the act publicly. This he did by an order of that date, which is as follows—

PROCLAMATION OF SEPTEMBER 24, 1862.

" Whereas, It has become necessary to call into service not only volunteers, but also a portion of the militia of the States by draft, in order to suppress the insurrection existing in the United States, and disloyal persons are not adequately restrained by the ordinary processes of law from hindering this measure, and from giving aid and comfort in various ways to the insurrection.

"'Now, therefore, be it ordered—

" 1. That during the existing insurrection, and as a necessary measure for suppressing the same, all rebels and insurgents, their aiders and abettors, within the United States, and all persons discouraging volunteer enlistments, resisting militia drafts, or guilty of any disloyal practice, affording aid and comfort to the rebels against the authority of the United States, shall be subject to martial law, and liable to trial and punishment by court martial or military commission.

"2. That the writ of *habeas corpus* is suspended in respect to all persons arrested, or who are now, or hereafter during the rebellion shall be, imprisoned in any fort, camp, arsenal, military prison, or other place of confinement, by any military authority, or by the sentence of any court martial or military commission.

"In witness whereof, I have hereunto set my hand, and caused the seal of the United States to be affixed.

"Done at the city of Washington, this twenty-fourth day of September, in the year of [L. S.] our Lord one thousand eight hundred and sixty-two, and of the Independence of the United States the eighty-seventh.

"ABRAHAM LINCOLN.

"By the President:
"WILLIAM H. SEWARD,
Secretary of State."

It looks significant that this order is countersigned by Wm. H. Seward and not by Edwin M. Stanton.

Following this order for the suspension of the *habeas corpus*, the following extraordinary announcement was made from the War Department.

ORDERS OF THE SECRETARY OF WAR, PROMULGATED SEPTEMBER 26, 1862.

First. There shall be a Provost Marshal General of the War Department, whose head quarters will be at Washington, and who will have the immediate supervision, control and management of the corps.

Second. There will be appointed in each State one or more special Provost Marshals, as necessity may require, who will report and receive instructions and orders from the Provost Marshal General of the War Department.

Third. It will be the duty of the special Provost Marshal to arrest all deserters, whether Regulars, Volunteers or militia, and send them to the nearest military commander or military post, where they can be cared for and sent to their respective regiments; to arrest upon the warrant of the Judge Advocate, all disloyal persons subject to arrest under the orders of the War Department; to inquire into and report treasonable practices, seize stolen or embezzled property of the Government, detect spies of the enemy, and perform such other duties as may be enjoined upon them by the War Department, and report all their proceedings promptly to the Provost Marshal General.

Fourth. To enable special Provost Marshals to discharge their duties efficiently, they are authorized to call on any available military force within their respective districts, constables, sheriffs, or police officers, so far as may be necessary under such regulations as may be prescribed by the Provost Marshal General of the War Department, with the approval of the Secretary of War.

Fifth. Necessary expense incurred in this service will be paid in duplicate bills, certified by the special Provost Marshal, stating time and nature of service, after examination and approval by the Provost Marshal General.

Sixth. The compensation of special Provost Marshals shall be — dollars per month, and actual travelling expenses, and postage will be refunded on bills certified under oath and approved by the Provost Marshal General.

Seventh. All appointments in this service will be subject to be revoked at the pleasure of the Secretary of War.

Eighth. All orders heretofore issued by the War Department, conferring authority upon other officers to act as Provost Marshals, except those who receive special commissions from the War Department, are hereby revoked.

By order of the Secretary of War.

L. THOMAS, Adjutant General.

This completed the assumption of arbitrary power, nothing more was needed to exercise it universally throughout the whole country, in that portion of it where the people were pursuing their usual peaceful avocations in life as well as in that portion of it occupied by hostile armies.

These orders, one and all not only usurped the Legislative powers of Congress, but the judicial authority of Courts; nay powers of Government are assumed in these orders which the Constitution does not invest in any department of the Federal Government but on the contrary, reserves them specially to the people. But of what avail is it that such is the fact, The people aquiesce in these assumptions of power, and many of them approve of and commend the act. Who could have believed this of the American People.

KIDNAPPING OF D. A. MAHONY—INCIDENTS CONNECTED WITH IT, AND ON THE WAY TO WASHINGTON—MEETING WITH MR. SHEWARD, A FELLOW-PRISONER—INTRODUCTION TO THE OLD CAPITOL.

On the morning of the 14th of August, 1862, a loud rapping was heard by my wife at the front door of our residence on Bluff street, in Dubuque, Iowa. It was still early morning, between three and four o'clock. I was in a sound sleep, having been up most of the night before with a number of other Democrats who had been in attendance at a Democratic Convention at Delhi, some forty miles from Dubuque. My wife—hearing the rapping, rose from her bed and looked out one of the front windows, when she discerned the figure of a man at the door. She enquired of him what he wanted, and who he was. He informed her that his name was Gregory, and that he desired to see Mr. Mahony at his office on business. She told him that I was asleep; that I had been up the night before, and that I was tired and fatigued, and that she did not like to wake me, unless his business was of such emergency as to make it necessary. By this time the loud talking had awaked me, and I went to the window. I made the same or similar enquiries to those my wife had done, and receiving similar replies, I observed to Mr. Gregory that I could do nothing for him at that hour of the morning at my office; that I had not the keys of the place, and could not get in, and that even if I had, the business he professed to have with me should be transacted with the clerk, and that at all events there would be time enough for him to attend to it before the cars left for the West, he professing to be destined for Cedar Falls that morning, and at the time the cars did not leave Dubuque till about 11 o'clock. He persisted so in his manner that I should come to the office, that I began to suspect that some foul play was intended; and as I had received several anonymous letters threatening my life for the course I had taken towards the Administration, it occurred to me that Mr. Gregory, as he called himself, might be one of a number to put the threat in execution. So I told him that I would not go to the office with him at that time. He then gave a signal by whistling, which confirmed me in my suspicions, especially as I observed several other persons peeping around the corners above my residence. Presuming that my suspicions were well founded and confirmed, and that the object of Mr. Gregory and his confederates was to deal foully with me, I attempted to raise an alarm by crying out murder. This brought out Marshal Hoxie, of Iowa, his Deputy at Dubuque, P. H. Conger, and several soldiers who had remained out of sight with them. They threatened to shoot me if I did not cease making a noise, and as soon as I recognized the Marshal and his Deputy, with both of whom I was personally acquainted, I felt relieved of my apprehensions entertained of Mr. Gregory's object, and reproached the Marshal for having taken such a means to arrest me, as I saw it was his object to do. He replied to my reproaches that he feared a rescue of me would be attempted if he had waited till the citizens should be awake. I enquired of him by whose direction or authority he came to make the arrest. He replied, the authority of the Secretary of War. By this time my wife had become almost frantic with fear and apprehension. The array of soldiers around the house, and their threatening menaces and violent language wrought so violently upon her feelings that she became almost insensible to any other thought or feeling than that I was to be taken away from her and murdered. She implored the soldiers not to injure me, when one or two of them brutishly told her to hush up, or they would blow her brains out. The Marshal and myself engaged in a brief conversation, the substance of which was that on his pledging to me his word of honor, I was credulous to think for the moment that Mr. Hoxie had some honor, that he would take me to see Governor Kirkwood before doing anything further towards carrying into effect his order, whatever it may have been, I would surrender myself to him as a prisoner, and give him no trouble whatever. On these conditions I prepared myself as hastily as possible to accompany the Marshal and his escort to the Key City House, where he proposed to have breakfast. Mr. Hoxie professed to be in such a hurry to reach the steamboat which was to convey us to Davenport, that he did not give me time to prepare a change of clothes, intimating that it was not necessary, as in all probability when I had seen the Governor, the matter of my arrest could be satisfactorily arranged, so that I could come back home.

My object I should state, in desiring to see the Governor was, that regarding him as a personal friend though a political adversary, and having known that he had declared on a former occasion that no one should be taken out of the State of Iowa without having a trial to ascertain whether or not the accused may have been guilty of any crime, I thought I would have such a hearing before him as would impress him with the true position in which I stood towards the Administration, and that my discharge would follow as a matter of course.

Having delivered myself to the Marshal, I asked him his authority for arresting me. He refused to let me see it, and surrounding me with his Deputy and the soldiers under command of Captain Pierce, of the Regular Army, marched me off. After proceeding a short distance, I observed other soldiers in such positions as was evidently designed to resist any attempt at my rescue; and fearing that a collision might take place between the people, if they should hear of my arrest, and the military, I suggested to Marshal Hoxie, that he send the soldiers to their quarters, and that he and I go alone and unattended by any other force to the hotel. The Marshal stepped aside and consulted Captain Pierce on the matter, when it appearing that they approved of my suggestion, the soldiers took another course, and the Marshal and I went alone, followed by Deputy Marshal Conger to the Key City House.

After placing me there in the safe keeping of Mr. Conger, Mr. Hoxie went out to, as I learned afterwards, make his report of the exploit he had performed to his political friends, who chuckled and rejoiced over what had occurred with fanatical zest. After remaining for about half an hour in this state I suggested to both Mr. Hoxie as soon as he returned and to Mr. Conger the propriety of taking me on board the steamboat at once, as it was not unlikely that some trouble might be experienced. At all events, to prevent anything of the kind, I thought it would be best remove me at once from the city. The Marshal thought well of the suggestion, and we started as soon as possible for the steamboat, the Bill Henderson. Notwithstanding my evident and manifest design and desire to avoid anything that might lead to a conflict between the people and the Marshal in the execution of his illegal and arbitrary warrant, if he had one, which is somewhat doubtful, I was informed afterwards that he circulated the repor' that I tried to resist the execution of his writ, when had I remained in the house till he could have entered it by force, in all probability both himself and his posse would have been massacred, as soon as it should become known that there was no legality in his proceedings. And I would take this opportunity to say, that never did the American people make a greater mistake or sacrifice their rights so cheaply as to have submitted to these arbitrary and illegal arrests. I blame myself as well as others for having submitted as I did to be taken from my home by Marshal Hoxie without making some effort, even though it should have been unsuccessful to preserve my personal rights as an American citizen. Had I shot him down, or any one of the party who accompanied him, I would have only performed my duty and exercised my inalienable and constitutional rights as an American.

ON THE STEAMBOAT.

Having arrived at the steamboat, a company of soldiers were drawn up on the levee; two guards with loaded muskets and fixed bayonets were placed by me, and my friends were not allowed to come on board to see me, except in twos, and even under this restraint, but very few, including half a dozen of my office boys, printer's devils, as they are called, were suffered to approach me. One would have thought, from Mr. Hoxie's precautions, that I was a desperado of herculean strength and terrific appearance, else that my friends were numerous, indignant, and determined to see me have fair play. As soon as I could find an opportunity, I wrote the following brief note of my arrest, and desired its publication.

On board the Steamer Bill Henderson,
May 14th, 1862.

Fellow-citizens of Iowa,—I have been arrested by an arbitrary and illegal order from the War Department for my fidelity to the Constitution of our common country. As I am at the disposal of tyrants who care for no law but that of their own will, I know not what might befall me. To your care and protection I commend my wife and children.

D. A. MAHONY.

It so happened that a committee of citizens of Dubuque were on board the boat on their way to Savanna to invite some excursionists who were expected at the latter place to Dubuque. Among them I recollect D. S. Wilson, who had his wife with him, the late Surveyor-General Townsend, and I think one of the Langworthys of Dubuque. All but Mr. Wilson looked askant at me, and even he was more formal than a personal friend should have been, under such trying circumstances.

During our stay at the levee, among the few persons who were allowed on board to approach me was Hugh Treanor, one of my warmest personal friends. An objurgation of some kind having escaped his lips, the effect of the indignation with which he was convulsed, the guards deliberated whether it would not be well to arrest him. They debated in an angry tone; but on consulting some one in authority, my friend Treanor was suffered to remain at liberty, and to soliloquize upon the nature of American Liberty under Lincoln's Administration of the Government.

After the steamboat had got fairly under way, and the passengers became settled in their respective positions for the voyage, I went up on the hurricane deck, where my two guards accompanied me with their loaded muskets and fixed bayonets. These guards were two sergeants—one an orderly, and the other a duty sergeant. They were evidently selected, from their manner and bearing towards me at first, for their antipathy to a Democrat. They guarded me for a while as if I were a wild beast whom it was as dangerous to approach as it was to let me roam at large. But it was not long before they and I engaged in conversation on the hurricane deck, and they soon became so much at ease, and their apprehensions of me became so far removed as to invite me to take a " slug " with them from a flask of whiskey which either one of them or a fellow-soldier on board had provided—a condescension and familiarity which I appreciated by thanking them, but declined to participate in the familiarity. The sergeants consulted aside for a few moments, when, as the probable result of the conference, they took their muskets down stairs, and I did not see those formidable and menacing weapons again in their hands till we reached Davenport.

I inquired of one of the guards why was it that two sergeants were selected to be my guards instead of privates. He replied that the Marshal was instructed to treat me with proper consideration and respect, and that he and his companion were a guard of honor. " A guard of honor," thought I. This is a strange mode of honoring a man. But the fellow's reply put me more at ease as to the ultimate designs of the Administration than my first apprehensions after being kidnapped had forebode.

On the way down the river the steamer took aboard some recruits who had scarcely reached the boat before they were informed by the Marshal of the conquest he had made. These recruits dogged me around so that I was obliged, to avoid their impertinent stares, to confine myself to a state room, and even in this seclusion I was intruded on by the unmannerly fellows who would open the door and place their faces against the glass panels to have a stare at me. All this the Marshal not only tolerated but evidently encouraged.

In due time towards evening we arrived at Davenport, and were driven to the Burtin House, partly I believe on account of my preference over any other hotel, for that hospitable and well regulated establishment. The Marshal directed that a suite of rooms be placed at his disposal, mine to be in the center of the suite and the one on either side to be occupied by himself and my guards, an open communication being secured between my apartment and that of my custodians. We were disappointed at not finding the Governor at Davenport where we had expected to meet him, but the Marshal assured me that he would be in the city the next day, especially as Adjutant General Baker, who joined us at Clinton, on our way down the river, wanted to meet him on important business which required the Governor's special and immediate attention. This satisfied me for the time and reconciled me to the disappointment of not meeting the Governor, as Hoxie assured me I would do at Davenport. During the evening however, one of my guards who had become a little communicative hinted to me that the Governor would not come to Davenport next day, and that Hoxie did not mean to take me to see him. I sought the Marshal immediately and enquired of him if it was his intention or not to comply with the promise, or word of honor such as Hoxie understands such an obligation, which he had given me at Dubuque, on the condition of my voluntary surrender of myself to him as a prisoner. All that I could elicit from Hoxie in reply to my enquiries and in compliance with my demand that he kept his word was, that the Governor would come to-morrow. I felt assured at the time that Hoxie wrote to the Governor not to come from the manner in which he acted, and from a reply I received from the Governor to a letter which I had written soliciting an interview, which he declined to give me, impliedly, either at Iowa city or Davenport.

This settled the conviction in my mind that I was the object of partisan malignity and the victim of the tyranny which had then begun to manifest itself in the most arbitrary and despotic manner at Washington. I felt all the premonitions that I was to be sacrificed in every way that the malignant partisans in Iowa and the tyrants in Washington needed to use me for the accomplishment of some sinister purpose of their own. What it was time would develop. I took the first opportunity afforded me to write some letters, to my wife first, then to some friends, as I thought, at home, and to others in Iowa, informing those who could not yet have heard of it, of my arrest, and suggesting to some of them the interposition of their known personal influence with the Secretry of War to obtain for me an early hearing. It will be as well for me to observe here as any where else that the only effect of the requests to those whom I presumed to be my personal friends, was a letter in my behalf written by Senator Grimes, a political adversary of mine, but since our first acquaintance in 1854, a personal friend, a friendship which I reciprocate and appreciate the more as it exists in a political opponent. There were others, Democrats too and professed friends of mine who had sufficient personal influence I was satisfied with the Secretary of War, to have drawn his attention to my case immediately on my reaching Washington and to have caused an early investigation into the accusations against me, but political and personal friends never wrote a line in my behalf. On the contrary they, or at least some of them, took a mean advantage of my confidence in them, exhibiting my letters as an evidence, as they assumed, of my backing down. When I learned these facts as I soon did, I felt for the first time in my life the baseness of ingratitude, the vileness of hypocrisy, the deception of pretended friends.

MY FIRST NIGHT UNDER GUARD.

After spending the evening at the Burtis House as best I could under the surveillance of my custodians and in communion with my thoughts, for I had but few visitors, when it came to bed-time, my guards held a counsel in their room, the result of which was that one of them was to sleep with me, and the other was to keep watch and ward over me during the night. To this proposition I flatly and unqualifiedly demurred, notwithstanding the apparent cordiality and familiarity which had grown up between them and me. The room in which I was to sleep was, I think, on the third story of the building; their room was contiguous to it, and there was a communicating door between the two rooms. Besides this they could, I told them, lock the door of my room, and fasten the windows, if they were afraid that I was silly enough, or as they might have thought, bold enough to attempt an escape. They argued the matter for some time with me, but I had made up my mind to sleep alone, so far as they were concerned, and would listen to no modification of my determination.

So after examining door locks and window-fastenings, they concluded that I could not escape provided that both of them sat up to watch me. I told them they were a pair of fools to imagine for a moment that I would attempt to escape. I told them both to go to bed, and they would find me in the morning where I was, even if they should leave the doors unlocked and the windows unbolted; but the Lincoln Angel who had me under his guardianship impressed the poor guards so strongly with some peculiarity he imagined me to possess, that my suggestions to them to go to bed were only regarded as an evidence of what Hoxie had said of me. So they remained up all night for all that I know to the contrary, and I slept soundly till morning after I had once got to sleep.

A DAY IN DAVENPORT.

I awoke on Friday morning out of a dream. I looked about me, and could not realize at once what had become of me—but the nodding figure of one of the guards who occupied a recumbent position on a chair, soon brought me to a consciousness of my situation. I was a prisoner, and beginning to feel the fact, but I was not yet under much restraint. After breakfasting, I requested Mr. Hoxie to give me permission to see some friends in the city, in company with the guards. He refused at first, but one of the guards volunteering to see that I was returned to safe keeping, Hoxie reluctantly assented, remarking that there was a great deal of feeling in the city on account of my arrest, and that he did not like to excite it any further by my appearance in the streets. I assured him there would be no trouble on my account—so, with his permission, the guard and I sauntered out.

The first person I met to know was Judge Grant, who having heard of what had taken place, inquired if any thing could be done for me. I replied, nothing—that I would submit to what disposition might be made of me, presuming that when I reached Washington, if I could not in the meantime see Gov. Kirkwood, that I should have a hearing—and as I knew myself to be guiltless of any crime, expected my discharge immediately. I was not aware then, credulous man that I was, that our Government had fallen into the hands of tyrants, who subverted it from its beneficent designs to be the means of bringing destruction upon the country by inciting one portion of the people to do violence to the rights of the others, and these others to rise in revolt against their persecutors. I was under the impression that, for all that had been done to prove the contrary, the heads of the Government had not set wholly at naught every provision of the Constitution which recognized and aimed to protect personal rights, and that it had not become, as I found it to be subsequently, subservient to so small a design as to become used for the purpose of preventing the election of my humble self to Congress, and of securing in my stead, by means of its patronage, my imprisonment, and the terror it attempted to inspire in the Congressional District of which I was resident, the election of one of its tried satellites. So I told Judge Grant that it was needless and useless to do any thing looking to my release.

I met a few other warm personal friends at Davenport, some of whom ventured to call upon me. Among those who did so was Mr. Richardson, of the Democrat and News, who though no hearty friend of mine, still risked himself to come and see me. Counsellor Parker was one of the very few whose friendship towards me influenced them so far as to make me a visit. An old and tried friend who was my neighbor in Dubuque, H. V. Gildea, spent a few hours with me—and Mrs. D. V. Wilson, of Dubuque, who was on a visit to friends in Davenport, not only called to see me, but, woman-like, aided in procuring me some necessary changes of clothing.

There were other ladies whom I would delight to mention as having more than all others whom I met subsequent to my arrest, contributed to my comfort and alleviated my apparently forlorn and destitute situation. These, finding I was denied the poor privilege of taking with me a change of clothing, went of their own accord and purchased for me such changes of underclothing, stockings, handkerchiefs, &c., as they knew I might need, both on my journey and during my prospective and probable incarceration. But these angels of compassion do their deeds for a higher motive and nobler reward than earthly fame and human applause. I can only allude to them as I do, lest I might violate the sanctity of emotions which no other than a friend in distress could have prompted into being.

I soon found that the sergeant's intimation to me that Hoxie would not take me to see the Governor, was about to be confirmed, by seeing the Iowa City train start from the depot without the Marshal or I on board. So I sent a letter which I had prepared for such an anticipated emergency, to Gov. Kirkwood, informing him of what had taken place, and requesting an interview. He wrote me back by the evening train, a cold, formal, and in some respects insulting letter, assuming that I was disloyal to the government. This, from a person who had heretofore taken occasion, in public and private, to manifest his personal regard for me, and to speak of me as one of the best of men, and whom I had treated with more than reciprocal consideration, and whose well-being, even as a politician, I had endeavored to promote among his party friends, was the first of those daggers of faithlessness, ingratitude and hypocrisy of presumed friendship, which I felt to pierce my soul. I never felt more disappointed and deceived in one whom I regarded as a friend, than I was in Governor Kirkwood. His treatment of me called to my mind all that I had ever read of friendly confidence misplaced in a deceitful heart, and made me regret that he had ever called me friend, or done me a kindly act. Had I been Governor of Iowa, and he been one of my fellow citizens, to say nothing of any other personal relations between us, before he should be taken from my gubernatorial jurisdiction by any power on earth, illegally and arbitrarily, it should be over the prostrate power of the commonwealth of Iowa, and of its executive.

And here, by the way, lies the danger that Federal power might overawe and subject the State sovereignties to its domination. This it can do easily, when the Executives of the respective States become the subservient instruments, the supple and willing implements by which the rights of States and people are ruthlessly torn from them and they subjected to arbitrary power. What security is there in State governments from the encroachments of Federal power, if the Governors of States become, whether through dread of power or influenced by its favor, recreant to their duty and treacherous to the trust reposed in them by the people. Governor Kirkwood of Iowa has given an illustration of how the sovereignty of a State may be subjected in a moment to the domination of arbitrary power; and how with equal impropriety a citizen may be dragged forth by a power foreign to the State in the respect in which the arrest and imprisonment of myself and others under similar circumstances was effected. For, it should be borne in mind that neither the President of the United States, nor *a fortiori* of any of his subordinates, had any more rightful authority to arrest a citizen in Iowa and have him taken to Washington and imprisoned, than Queen Victoria or any other European monarch had or has, to arrest and take him to London or any other European capital a prisoner. The President or any one else would have a right to complain of me before a magistrate in Iowa, and if there appeared to be probable cause for binding me over to stand a trial for the offense alleged against me, to have me so held, or if need be kept in custody till the day of trial; and if innocent, acquitted, or if guilty, that I might expiate the offense or crime by suffering the imposed penalty. But beyond that, the President of the United States has no more rightful power over a citizen than a citizen has over him. Any one of the so-called prisoners of State have just as much right in law to seize Abraham Lincoln and imprison him in the Old Capitol, as he or any of his minions had to arrest and imprison any of us. But I digress.— My outraged feelings as an American citizen will vent themselves even to the prejudice of the continuity and harmony of my narrative.

Friday the 15th of August was passed in Davenport. I spent most of the day in visiting friends and acquaintances in company more than in charge of the guard, who had become on very intimate and friendly terms with me, so much so indeed that rather than keep the two poor fellows up all Friday night, as was the case on the night before, I proposed that one of them should sleep in the same bed with me.

The Abolition paper of Davenport, the Gazette, which had no little effect, I doubt not, in procuring my arrest by its libellous attacks and calumnious misrepresentations of me, gloated over my arrest.— I replied to its attacks briefly, repelling its infamous allegations of disloyalty.

OFF FOR BURLINGTON.

On Friday night it was intimated to me that instead of proceeding direct to Washington I was to be taken down the river to Burlington, Iowa. I could not understand the object of this excursion at first, but after we had got on board the steamer, the

Marshal intimated to me that he had other arrests to make, and he informed me subsequently that Mr. Sheward, editor of the Constitution and Union, at Fairfield, Iowa, was one of the persons who was to be seized. The guards who had been placed over me as custodians at Dubuque were here dismissed by the Marshal, I thought because they had become too friendly with me, although at first, when placed over me at Dubuque, they acted as if they were purposely selected for qualities best suited to the infamous purpose of those who had procured my arrest. A single guard was placed in charge of me down the river to Burlington, who scarcely noticed me during the trip. We arrived at Burlington on Saturday night late, and walked to the Barrett House, the Marshal selecting rooms at this house for the party, securing one for himself in the best part of the establishment, and two others in another part of the building for myself and the guard. My custodian very unconcernedly left me to occupy the room next the door, while he stowed himself away in the inner room, leaving me in the most unrestrained manner to do as I pleased. This was not, of course, the design of the Marshal, and was more the result of thoughtlessness or indifference on the part of the guard than it was intended as a favor or leniency to me. The Marshal designed the inner room for me, of course, because he seemed to be full of the notion that somehow or other I might escape from his clutches, although I assured him and would have kept my word, that if he would only direct me where to go and report myself, he and his guards might stay at home. But this would not carry out one of the objects of my arrest, which was to give Marshal Hoxie a job that secured him pay and mileage to Washington.

A DAY IN BURLINGTON.

During Saturday night it became noised about Burlington that I had arrived there a prisoner. My personal and political friends, of whom I have the pleasure to count many in that city, manifested more feeling and sympathy than had been done in my observance at Davenport. They crowded the hotel on Sunday morning, and became so demonstrative, in Mr. Hoxie's estimation, of their disapprobation of my treatment, that he directed me to confine myself as much as possible to my room, and when my friends sought access to me there, they were obliged to obtain a pass from Hoxie, which was granted grudgingly and to only two at a time. I requested the Marshal's permission to go to church, it being Sunday. After some hesitation, he consented, placing me in charge of an orderly sergeant of the regular army, who accompanied me and sat with me in the pew, a most singular and significant sight in these United States. A political prisoner at church under guard in free America, where the liberty of speech and of the press is a constitutional guarantee to the people and a part of the compact between them and their government. I could not help reflecting during the church service on this anomalous state of things.

The Abolition paper of Burlington, the *Hawk-Eye*, being duly informed of my arrest on Saturday night, it took the opportunity to take advantage of my position—a prisoner—to both defame and insult me. In the edition of the paper which was to appear on Monday morning, and a copy of which was left with me by a friend, I perceived this attack of the *Hawk-Eye* and replied to it in the Burlington *Argus* of Monday morning. This reply will show both the nature and object of the attack and my position and sentiments. I give it as part of the record embracing my relations to the people of Iowa and to the questions of the day:

LETTER FROM MR. MAHONY

BURLINGTON, IOWA, }
August 18th, 1862. }

Editors of the Argus:—Permit me, a prisoner of State, gentlemen, to repel the insults offerred me in the *Hawk-Eye* of this morning. That paper, not satisfied with having poisoned the sentiments and feelings of its readers against me to such an extent as to influence the Government to cause my arrest, continues still to follow my track to the military prison to which its false accusations have had a large influence in consigning me. In the *Hawk-Eye* of this morning I find such allusions to me as follows:
"Dennis Mahony has openly opposed the war for the Union almost ever since the rebels opened the ball at Sumter."

"Dennis Mahony managed the recent State Convention and drew up its platform."

"With Dennis Mahony they (alluding to others, whom the *Hawk-Eye* designs to have served as I have been), believe that Rebellion can only be put down, Constitutionally, through the State Governments."

Now for the satisfaction of my personal and political friends in Iowa, more than for my own, I want to assure them that it is not true as alleged by the *Hawk-Eye*, that I have been, either openly or secretly, opposed to the prosecution of the war in the sense it evidently means to imply. I was not in favor of producing such a state of things as would lead to war, and in that sense I was opposed to it. But once war became inevitable, by, as I firmly believe, the determination of the dominant party that there should be war, cost what it might, and be the result destruction of the Union, the subversion of the Government, and the utter ruin of the country, I bowed my will to that of the ruling powers, reserving to myself the poor privilege of mourning over the loss of the heritage bequeathed to posterity by the Fathers of the Republic. This has been my offense. I have bewailed, sometimes in language stimulated by the poignancy of feeling for my country, the sad condition to which partisanship has driven our once glorious Republic, our once powerful Union, our long happy country, and I have in my judgment come to the conclusion that our present condition is owing to a disregard and violation of the fundamental agreement on which we exist as a Nation.

But nevertheless to the full extent and degree that the Administration has a right to control the Government, to make and prosecute war, as well as to preserve peace, I have never questioned its right, never interfered with the exercise of its authority, and only admonished it not to transcend its legitimate authority in assuming and exercising arbitrary power.

It is not, be it ever borne in mind by my fellow citizens of Iowa, that I have violated any law, but that I have given offence to its violators, that I am accused of being opposed to the war, and of discouraging enlistments, pretexts, which are used as causes for my arrest. Had I encouraged the Executive Branch of the Government to usurp the functions of the Judicial Branch or approved of the usurpation; had I encouraged the Administration to violate the Constitution of my country, which every member of the Administration is sworn to maintain and uphold, had I proclaimed with others that the Union was a league with hell, and the Constitution a covenant with death, had I in a word encouraged, countenanced or approved the subversion of the Government by its Constitutional guardians, is there a fellow citizen of mine in Iowa who believes that I would be a prisoner of State to day? Not one, I can safely answer. My fault is, too much loyalty to the Constitution, not the want of it. I would not bend, therefore I must be broken.

As to my relation to the late State Convention, the truth is not as the *Hawk-Eye* alleges, and as it states no doubt for mere effect, and not with any regard for truth. I had as little to do with the "management," of the State Convention as any member in it, and was only one ninth part of its committee on resolutions. But suppose it were true that I did all that the *Hawk-Eye* alleges, what is there in the proceedings of that Convention or in its Platform to subject me or any one else to the pains of disloyalty. Is there a sentiment in that Platform repugnant to the principles on which the Government was supposed, till of late, to have been founded; or is there a suggestion in it objective in spirit to the best interests of our country. I see none.

It does state as matter of fact a thing I do not believe, that the civil war in which we are engaged was caused by secession. I believe it was caused by abolitionism, without whose existence there would have been no such heresy as secession. And speaking of secession let me say for the thousandth time to the People of Iowa, that I never have been, am not now, nor do I expect, or intend to be a secessionist. To put this matter beyond question and dispute so far as I am concerned, I would not be in favor, even now, of reconstructing the Federal Union on the principle that any State might secede from the others at will, for no federation could be held united on such a hypothesis, unless by the mere dread which would deter the Federal Govern ment from giving offense to any of the individual States.

As to the other charge of the *Hawk-Eye* that I with others believe, "that the rebellion can only be put down constitutionally through the State Governments," it is a pure invention of that paper, if anything but abolitionism in its rankest form can be pure coming from such a corrupt and infamous source.

The *Hawk-Eye* is not satisfied with trying to make me out a disloyalist, but a fool also; and having done everything to its malignant satisfaction, it swoops vulture-like upon what it presumes to be a powerless victim. But, prisoner of State as I am, no vile mouth-piece of Abolitionism shall insult me with impunity, till I be deprived of the right of self-defense, as the *Hawk-Eye* supposed, no doubt, had been the case already.

People of Iowa, believe nothing that you may hear discreditable or derogatory to me as your fellow-citizen, both of the United States and of the State of Iowa, till my revilers and accusers prove something involving guilt. That, I assure you, it is not in their power to do, other than by bearing false testimony against me, a resort to which they probably will not hesitate to have recourse, judging some of them by their newspaper organs.

As I said at the outset, I write these remarks to remove from the minds of my friends any apprehensions, if any there be, of my having by word or act committed any offense warranting or justifying the arrest to which I have been subjected, other than to be loyal to the Constitution as it is, to be in favor of restoring the Union as it was, and to having the Government administered as it should be.

I remain, Messrs. Editors, and people of Iowa,
   Yours truly,   D. A. MAHONY.

ARREST OF DANA SHEWARD.

During the day, the object of our visit to Burlington was revealed by the arrival in the city from Fairfield of Mr. Sheward, Editor of the Constitution and Union. To secure his arrest Marshal Hoxie engaged a powerful locomotive in the morning from the Superintendent of the Burlington and Missouri Railroad. The Marshal and Superintendent started early for Fairfield, which place they reached at dinner time. Mr. Sheward was dining at the house of a friend when the Marshal informed him that he was his prisoner.

As a separate account is designed to be given of the arrest of each of the political prisoners as such an account can be procured from, I shall pass over Mr. Sheward's case, except as it is connected with my own; and connected with me, not only as a prisoner but as more than friend, as Mr. Sheward was to me from the moment we met as fellow prisoners, for the first time, that eventful Sunday, the 17th of August, 1862, in the Barrett House, Burlington.

The locomotive made good time back to Burlington from Fairfield. Indeed owing to the influence of whiskey on the special engineer as well as of steam on the engine machinery, the locomotive which bore Mr. Sheward a prisoner from Fairfield made the best time ever before run on the Burlington and Missouri Railroad. Mr. Sheward arrived early in the afternoon, was brought to the room occupied by me, introduced, and thenceforward we became for three months fellow prisoners of State, fellow martyrs in the cause of constitutional liberty, fellow objects of partisan malignity, fellow victims of the arbitrary tyranny which has usurped despotic power at Washington, but in pleasing contrast to this aspect of our condition, fellow-men in mutual friendship and affection for each other, and in devotion to those principles of human and political rights which God bestowed upon his creatures, which the Constitution of our country recognized and guaranteed, but which tyrants have dared to attempt to take away.

The excitement at Burlington increased ten fold when it was heard that Mr. Sheward was arrested. Under the pre'ext of removing us to more comfortable quarters, Hoxie had us placed in a part of the hotel more remote from access to our friends. Our guards were quadrupled, and armed with both muskets and revolvers, with orders from Hoxie to shoot down either of us who would manifest the least attempt to elude their vigilance. I came very near becoming a victim to this order, by an attempt to speak a suggestion to the guard respecting an over familiar friend of ours who having imbibed a little more stimulant than his judgment could control, became disagreeable to our other visitors, Sstepping to the door and whispering to the guard in the most friendly manner to suggest that our noisy visitor be removed, the fellow rushed at me with a loaded revolver with the imprecation from his lips, "Damn you, stand back or I'll shoot you," thrusting me inside the door as if I were a wild beast. My indignation was naturally aroused. I felt for a moment a conflict of emotions struggling within me; indignation of being a victim of despotism and the humiliation of being in the power of my partisan enemies and obliged to suffer with impunity their taunts, jeers and insults.

The evening of Sunday and part of Monday, was spent in receiving and by me in making visits to friends, Mr. Sheward having for some time previously to his removal to Fairfield, been a resident of Burlington, was regarded by his many friends and acquaintances of that place as their fellow-citizen. A large number of persons called to see him, but only a few of them were permitted to enjoy that gratification. Hoxie made his head quarters at the office of the Abolition paper, and there any one who desired to see Mr. Sheward or myself was obliged to seek him to obtain a pass to reach us. Of course many of our democratic friends rather than subject themselves to the designed humiliation forewent the pleasure of making us a visit.

During my absence from the Hotel making calls on friends, one curious visitor presented himself at our rooms. He inquired of Mr. Sheward if I was in. Mr. S. replied, No—I was out visiting some friends, but would be in soon, probably. Visitor remained for a couple of hours. At length Mr. Sheward inquired of him if he were an acquaintance or friend of mine. The fellow replied, no, he was not, but that he had a curiosity to see me. O! said Mr. Sheward, if that be all you want to see him for, I can assure you that he has neither hoofs, horns, nor tail—and, putting on an expression of countenance significant of contempt, scorn, derision, and indignation, which few men can do better than Mr. Sheward when a proper object presents itself for the purpose, he looked my curious visitor out of the room, and I never heard of him after, except as Mr. Sheward told me of his visit.

Although I have alluded, in another part of this narrative, to the friendly interposition of Senator Grimes of Burlington in my behalf, I will take this occasion to give that gentleman the credit which belongs to him of having made me a friendly visit at Burlington, and of having, as he promised he would, written a letter to the Secretary of War, demanding for me an early trial. This promise he fulfilled in a delicate, dignified and friendly manner, of which I have the evidence in my possession.

I would also speak gratefully of Mr. Postlewaite of Burlington, who forced upon the acceptance of Mr. Sheward and myself the contents of his purse, observing to us, prophetically as it turned out, that we might need it while under the subjection of our tyrant keepers.

OFF FOR WASHINGTON.

Burlington was considerably agitated during Monday, as rumors had been circulated that other victims designated for sacrifice, Gen. Dodge, Mr. Carpenter, Mr. Postlewaite, and some other prominent and esteemed citizens of that place, were on the tongue of rumor as the proscribed victims, and I have little doubt but that it was the design of the Marshal to make more arrests, as he had told me going down the river to Burlington, that he had orders to arrest some four others besides Sheward. But the day passed on to the time for the starting of the eastern train and no arrests were made. Messrs. Dodge, Carpenter, Corse, Postlewaite, Judge Hall, Browning and several other friends, made us visits during the day, regardless of the rumors which designated nearly all these gentlemen as our fellow-victims. Evening came, and with it the order for us to prepare for Washington.

We had but little to get ready. I was taken away from home without a charge of clothing, and with but little means to procure any necessaries that I might require. Mr. Sheward was taken equally short, and would have been equally destitute in that respect with myself, had not his wife arrived on Monday with a carpet sack of clothing for his use. My leavetaking, sudden and unceremonious as it was, had been made at Dubuque. It was now

Mr. Sheward's turn to undergo the agony of parting from his wife for a destination which he could only conceive the end of by knowing that he was in the hands of his enemies, from whom the infliction of death on a short shrift would be pr ferable to the hardships, outrages, and subjection of one's manhood to their despotic will, inflicted during a three months' incarceration in the Old Capitol. I leave the reader, especially if he be a husband or she a wife, to imagine if they can the agony of such a parting. Death has its terrors, but one can comprehend its horrors, and see the end of it, and know its effects. It kills only the body, but it releases the soul from captivity. But who can conceive of the tortures a spirit endures in a man subjected to the despotism and tyranny of rulers who usurp power over him by virtue of mere might, inflamed by the passions of hate, spite, revenge, and an ambition which would trample country in the dust to gratify its lust of power. All this was to be experienced in the Old Capitol; but who of us knew it? Hence that agitation of emotions produced in one's mind by doubt, apprehensions of evil, and gloomy forebodings influenced by the certainty that not only one's life is in the hands of his enemies, but that his spirit, his manhood, is the subject of their will, caprice, and enmity.

But we must off to Washington. We are soon ready. A guard is detailed to conduct us to the ferry boat, and we are off, gazed at in mute astonishment by some, in silent pity by others, with indignant scowls at our custodians by many, and with marked evidences of gratification on the countenances of the Lincolnpoops, as we learned to call the followers of Father Abraham in the Old Capitol.

In the cars at last for Chicago towards Washington. We are accompanied by Marshal Hoxie and Sergeant (I forget his name,) the latter to be used as guard, &c. An accident by the collision of two freight trains detained us some hours on the road, so that we did not reach Chicago on time next morning. Although the news of the arrest of Mr. Sheward and myself had preceded us by telegraph, and that we remained in Chicago some hours, not one, friend or foe, came to see us. We began to experience our situation in its existing reality. We felt that we were being separated indeed from friends and home, and that we were about to pass into the gripe of those who would rejoice in tormenting us.

The Marshal, after providing himself at the Quartermaster's office with transportation for us to Washington, took us to the cars of the Chicago, Fort Wayne and Pittsburg Railroad. Here we, as every one else leaving Chicago, had to pass through the inspection of an official who was stationed at that time at every railroad depot at Chicago, to see that no one attempted to leave for Canada or other foreign countries to escape or evade the draft. Traveling in the service of our good Uncle Samuel, and by direction of his high Steward Abraham, we had permission, of course, to pass.

Nothing of much moment worth reciting occurred to us on our journey to Baltimore. Most of the way instead of being under the guard of Marshal Hoxie and his Sergeant, they were the objects of our care. At one place where we stopped both Hoxie and the Sergeant were fast asleep. Mr. Sheward called the conductor's attention to the sleeping sentinels, observing that he and I had taken their places in keeping watch, with an injunction on the conductor that he should not mention the circumstance. At every place where we remained for any time, Marshal Hoxie, when awake, took special pains to inform the by-standers that he had two Democrats as Prisoners of State in his custody, bound for Washington, one of them being the notorious Mahony, whom the Administration papers had published into a traitor, and the other the not less traitorous, only younger in iniquity, Sheward. This official news, of course, had the effect to direct upon us the gaze of every one who had heard of our arrest.

When we had reached Harrisburg we found ourselves already within the influence and immediate power of Military as well as Martial law. The railroad from that place to Baltimore was under the guard of armed men. The railroad cars were filled with soldiers returning from furlough, or going for the first time to join the Army in the field. Travelling civilians were painfully the exception, military the rule. And so it was all the way to Washington, which we reached on the 21st of August.

AT WASHINGTON.

We reached the Capital of our once happy country about noon, and Mr. Hoxie enquiring the way to the office of the Military Governor, Mr. Wadsworth, we set out on foot for the office of his dread mightiness, General Wadsworth. Not only did the city appear to be under martial law, but almost every house on the streets through which we passed seemed to be under the special care of soldiers. Footmen and horsemen were patroling or galloping through the streets, very many of the cavalry presenting the ludicrous appearance for armed horsemen of holding on to their horses' mane on a gallop. In spite of my condition, tired and hungry, (for we had eaten nothing since we had left Altoona,) and the thoughts which arose on my mind when giving way to reflection, I could not help speculating upon the probable effects of a battle between such cavalry as I saw in Washington and the dashing, daring, intrepid troops of Rebeldom. It struck me at once that there was something radically wrong, or defective in the organization of our Army, that men were mounted as cavalry who neither knew how to ride a horse in a charge, and who would never, probably, learn.

I had not much time for observation, however. We were hurrying as fast as weary feet could carry us along towards the office of the Military Governor. On the way we fell in with one Hawkins Taylor, of Keokuk, Iowa, who seemed to be *au fait* with Marshal Hoxie. The two walked together apart from us, and as Sheward and myself were the topic and objects of their conversation, their chuckling over us attracted our attention and stung us to the quick. We took the street cars a part of the way to the Governor's office, Taylor accompanying us and keeping up a conversation all the time with the Marshal. From the antecedents of this Taylor, and from the fact, which we learned afterwards, that he was an applicant for some of the crumbs which were bestowed upon needy followers whose services could be had for the privilege of using them, by the dominant party, we concluded, and very properly, as events confirmed, that between Taylor and Hoxie we should be represented to the Military Governor in all the deformity of character in which a Democrat can be pictured by malignant fanaticism and partisan enmity.

When Hoxie had arrested me in Dubuque, and when I had demanded to see his warrant for so doing, he informed me that his orders were from the Secretary of War, without exhibiting to me any evidence of the fact, and that he was directed to take me before the Military Governor for an examination. Instead of doing this he merely took Mr.

Sheward and myself to the foot of the steps approaching the entrance to the office of this Military Governor, while he and the fellow Taylor, whom we met on the way, went in together. What transpired between them and the Military Governor and the other implements of despotism in the same place, it is not given to me to divulge, but this I am permitted to say, that everything these men could do to make us odious, and to bring us under the subjection of the most relentless tyranny which could be exercised towards persons in our condition was applied by both these fellows to effect that object.

After being kept waiting outdoors with our carpet sacks at our feet for more than an hour, Hoxie and Taylor made their appearance, the Marshal, Hoxie, pointing out Mr. Sheward and myself to an orderly who had a paper in his hand, our commitment, it appeared, to the Old Capitol. So without hearing, examination, investigation—without being informed of what offence, if of any, we were charged we had committed, here we were handed over to a soldier to be incarcerated, we know how long, in the Old Capitol.

The prison van was at the door, and we were ordered to get in. As I attempted to obey the order, I sickened with emotion. Never before till then did I realize or experience the feeling of being a prisoner—of being thrust into a vehicle which characterized those who may enter it as prisoners.

THE OLD CAPITOL.

We arrived in due time at the entrance door to the Old Capitol, and our arrival being announced by the sentinel who is patrolling the pavement in front of the door, who calls out, "Corporal of the Guard, No. 1," Corporal makes his appearance and takes charge of us. Now we are ushered into the prison, and within its doors several dirty looking soldiers are lounging around. One of them is stretched out on a sort of lounge, and the others, except the corporal of the guard, are sitting at ease. We are kept in this ante or waiting room for some time, there being a visitor, we were told, in the inner room, through which we must pass for inspection, examination of our baggage and person, and to be duly registered. After waiting longer than I ever afterwards knew a visitor to be allowed at an interview with a prisoner, we were ushered into the august presence of Lieutenant Holmes, whom we afterwards learned was known in the prison by the significant, if not elegant, name, "Bullhead." This officer was, no doubt, one who, like many other civilians who never before had any authority over one of their fellow men, on becoming a military man arrogated to himself all the power as well as authority which he dared to exercise with impunity over the defenseless victims entrusted to his guardian care. After receiving our commitment from the orderly who had brought us from the office of the Military Governor, Lieutenant Holmes enquired if we had any arms, liquors or other contraband goods. Sheward and I replied, no, we had none, but Holmes was not satisfied with our answer. He took hold of us roughly, felt our person, and finding nothing to gainsay our word, he directed us to open our carpet sacks. This done, he thrust his hands into them, and after a careful and diligent search, finding nothing that he could appropriate to himself, according to military law, and the prevailing custom of persons in authority in Washington, Holmes handed us over to a guard with directions to take us to Room No. 13.

Up to the third story we followed the guard, who, stopping at the head of the stairs, ushered us into this room. We took in its aspect, its occupants and its accommodations, at a glance. And first, of its occupants. There were two Virginians, one who had been an officer in the Confederate army, the other a civilian, and Dr. J. C. Stanley, of Chicago, Illinois. The three were seated at a small pine table, amusing themselves with a game of cards, as we entered. Dr. Stanley, who put us at our ease as soon as we were introduced to him, acted as the spokesman of the room. He inquired who we were, where from, what we had done, and if we were secessionists; to all of which we made the appropriate replies, giving as good an account of ourselves as we knew how, except as to being secessionists, which we observed we were charged with having been. The Doctor said we would do, and inquired if we had had anything to eat. We replied no, that we had eaten nothing since the day before. He said he was sorry, but could not help us. He then asked if we would have something to drink, to which invitation we replied, that being very fatigued and weary, we would have no objection. We ventured to ask, how did he manage to have anything of the kind to offer us in the prison? "Oh," said he, "it's all owing to the way you hould your mouth. I hould my mouth right, and I can get whatever I want." This was some comfort. "Perhaps," thought Sheward and I, "we can learn how to 'hould' our mouth." We did; but it took us a good deal of practice, and a long time to do it.

DESCRIPTION OF ROOM NO. 13, AND ITS FURNITURE.

The buildings now known as the Old Capitol were not all erected at once. The Old Capitol proper, included only the building fronting on First street, that on A street adjoining and now forming a part of the prison, was built subsequently when the whole concern was used for a boarding-house. Room No. 13, forms a part of the addition to the Old Capitol proper. This room is in the third story, at the head of the stairs passing up from the officers' quarters. It is by rough measurement eight feet wide by fourteen feet long from the door to the window facing the street opposite. The floor proper extends over only about ten feet of the length of the room, a raised sort of platform occupying the remainder of the space. This platform extends across the width of the room and is raised to a level with the bottom of the window facing North. The furniture of the room consisted of a small table and two chairs, which had been purchased, as we understood, by some of the former prisoner occupants of the place. Besides this there were two bunks for sleeping, each one having a place for two occupants, canalboat fashion. These bunks were furnished with a tick each, having in them but a scanty quantity of old straw which had done service ever since the place was used as a prison, and were probably the cast-away rubbish of some tavern. Each berth was also furnished with a dirty quilt, and there were two small dirty blankets among them all which did service for the occupants in their turn. For a pillow, a board was morticed into the head end of the berths. As we were now five occupants of this room, and only four places to sleep in, Doctor Stanley who acted as Procurator, sent word to the officials that another bed was needed for the fifth of our number. After awhile Corporal Brown who was acting as commissary and quartermaster of the prison under Superintendent Wood, brought an old, dirty straw-filled bed-tick for our fifth prisoner. This happened to fall to my lot. It was placed on the platform I have described, lengthwise of the room but across the platform, so that the end of the tick extended over the edge of the platform. For a pillow, I found a chunk of fire-wood. On this bed, which was about four feet and a half long, while I am nearly six feet in height, I was to take such repose as I might.

In due time, one of the colored servants, a fugitive contraband, brought us, including now all five who were in this room, something to eat. This consisted of bread, which was of very good quality, and a liquid which was called coffee, but which had such a nauseating smell that it was almost sickening. To this, however, we became so used in due time, that the sensation of smell became so reconciled to it, that we drank it without hesitation, and even without dislike. This was our first meal in prison; and Sheward and I having eaten nothing since leaving Altoona the day before, it was partaken of by us heartily, notwithstanding our feelings and the depression of spirits under which we labored.

Up to this time, we had seen nothing of the superintendent nor of any other official of the prison except Lieutenant Holmes, or as he was aliased by the prisoners, "Bull-head," and Corporal Brown of the commissary department. Being fatigued, weary, dispirited and given over to such emotions as would be naturally excited by the treatment to which we had been subjected and which we expected to be continued in a harsher degree of tyranny, we confined ourselves closely to our quarters, which was the general rule of the place, although we had not yet been so informed. Nor indeed were we ever informed of any rule we were obliged to keep, until we had violated one of the established orders of the place. The first intimation one had of transgressing a rule of the prison was generally a threat of one of the guards to stab or shoot him. I came near having a bayonet run in me several times, and of being shot at for violating rules I was never informed had existence, and others had similar experiences.

The Old Capitol Prison situated on the corner of A and First sts., Washington, is an old and dilapidated brick building, which was erected in 1817, to accommodate the National legislature, the Capitol building having been destroyed by fire. It was used for this purpose until the Capitol was rebuilt, when it was by means of additions and alterations, fitted for a boarding house, and as such was for many years patronised by Members of Congress and others who visited Washington during its session, and whose daily attendance on the legislative halls, made a contiguous dwelling desirable.

It was in this building that the Hon. John C. Calhoun breathed his last, and little did this revered champion of liberty or his compeers who legislated within its walls or reposed beneath its roof, think that the day would come when this building, within sight of the Capitol of the Nation, which, when complete, will be surmounted with a statue of liberty, should be turned into a Bastile and dungeon for the victims of despotism and tyranny.

The building forms two sides of a square. The entrance is on First street, under a large arched window, which lighted the former Senate chamber, but which now through its broken and filthy panes give entrance to the winters' wind and drifting snow on the unhappy inmates of the famous room, 16.

On entering the building from First street, a large hall or passage-way presents itself. This is now used as an anteroom, or lounging place for the soldiers who form a part of the military guard of the prison, and does not vary from the filth and reeking atmosphere of most guard houses. On the right there are two rooms which are used as offices in which the prisoners are taken on arrival, questioned, and searched by one or more of the officers of the guard. In the discharge of this and kindred duties, a Lieut. Miller, of the 16th New Jersey Volunteers, has made himself so unenviably notorious and tyrannically officious, as to merit and call forth the unanimous execrations of every inmate of the prison, not excepting the officers, guards, and negro attendants, but for which he was promoted to the office of Chief Jailor of the adjoining Bastile called Duff Green's Row. The innermost of these offices opens into a hall on which there is one room for prisoners, about twenty feet square, containing a number of bunks or sleeping berths, like to those used on canal-boats, but having three berths, one over the other. These berths are about three feet wide, and six feet long, and from constant use, and want of cleaning, are literally alive with bed-bugs and other vermin. Indeed, this but faintly describes the condition of every room in the building, and the weary hours of its inmates are often unpleasantly spent in the disgusting occupation of hunting and killing those vermin.

From this hall the principal stairway leads, at the end of and opposite to the first flight of which is room No. 19, for some time past used as the private office of the Superintendent. Not a few of my readers will recall to mind his visits to this inquisitorial chamber; for it is here that Detective Baker and Superintendent Wood hold their interviews with their innocent victims, and torture their harmless though often fearless expressions into evidence against them; and in hundreds of cases the only evidence they possess, and with which they hope to criminate or intimidate them into tacitly submitting to the terms of extortion proposed as a condition of their release.

Following up the stairs from this room, we arrive on the principal floor of the building, which contained the Halls of the Senate and House of Representatives, but which are now divided into five large rooms, numbered respectively from 14 to 18—room 16 being the centre and largest. Those rooms strongly resemble that described, in their being fitted with similar bunks filled with filth of every imaginable kind, and entirely destitute of any furniture or necessary accommodations indispensable in the humblest cabin. These rooms usually contained from eighteen to twenty-five prisoners in each; their average size is under thirty feet square, and the accumulated filth of them, the inevitable consequence of over-crowding and neglect of cleansing, or regard to their sanitary condition, can better be imagined than described. The hall or vestibule in front of those rooms, and from which they all open, is continually paced by a sentry, whose duty it is, not to allow more than two of the prisoners at a time to leave their rooms for the purpose of obeying nature's calls, and on their doing so to shout to the sentry on the next landing that all is right, No. 6, that being the number of the post, as each sentry has a number to his post, and one is stationed on every landing in the building, so that the new-comer to this terrible dungeon, from the continued calls of the sentries, the clanking of their arms, and the changing of the guard once in every two hours, has but little hope of finding oblivion to his sorrows, or forgetfulness of his wrongs in sleep.

Rooms No. 14, 15 and 18, were usually filled with citizens of Virginia owning farms and their stock of cattle within the Federal lines or on debatable ground; and many of these gentlemen, among whom were not a few of the highest respectability, education and patriotism, found themselves inmates of the Old Capitol, because they owned a fine horse coveted by some shoulder-strapped upstart, or because they refused to swear allegiance to a Government that was powerless to protect their persons or their property. I recall to mind with pleasure the acquaintance I made with many of those Virginia gentlemen, and hope the day is not far distant when the wrongs which they have sustained, the recital of which has often made my ears tingle with shame and indignation, shall be redressed, and the desolation caused by a brutal soldiery on the happy homes of the old dominion shall be forgotten and its outraged people indemnified for the losses and indignities they have suffered.

Room 17 was filled with officers of the Federal service, many of whom were ignorant of the cause of their arrest; others were sent here because Provost-Marshal Doster wished to coerce them into compliance with his dictates, and proposed to release them on their sending an unconditional resignation of their positions. In this room there was confined a Lieut. McClure, of the 135th Pennsylvania Volunteers, whose offense consisted in saying he disapproved of President Lincoln's Emancipation Proclamation. For this grave and heinous crime he was immured for four months without trial, and when tried, the Colonel of his regiment, who desired his position for a friend of his own, was made President of the Court-Martial in his case. The result, as might be expected, was finding him guilty and sentencing him to dismissal from the service and imprisonment *during the war.* Adjoining this is room No. 16, famous alike for being the quarters of the western prisoners, and for containing the leading spirits of the prison. Here was the project formed of submitting these pages to you, reader, and thus informing the American people how their rights in the persons of hundreds of American citizens have been outraged; and of handing down to posterity this record of the illegal and tyrannical acts of an administration blinded with fanaticism and sustained by corruption. This room, like the others, contained 21 bunks, but few of which could be used by the inmates, as they were so thickly inhabited or infested by vermin that a mattress on the floor was deemed far preferable to a night-long conflict with those gigantic and blood-thirsty chargers of the O. C. P. Here the writer and some 12 or 14 others, gentlemen from Maryland, Pennsylvania, Illinois, Iowa, Indiana and New York, all of whom he is proud to call friends, and all of them honorable representatives of the learned professions, or merchants, in the best sense of the term, formed a mess and association to meet at a future day for the purpose of obtaining redress for the wrongs sustained and interchange of sentiment and congratulation at their escape from the clutches of the venal crew who then held them in duress. The reader, to form a correct idea of the mess of room No. 16, must imagine he sees before him a large and desolate-looking room with one very large window at the end, opposite to that from which the room is entered. In the centre a large, dirty cylinder stove, around the room and against its dirty walls, the whitewash on which, discolored with age and festooned with spiders' webs, were distributed those bunks already mentioned, and in addition three or four iron bedsteads. These bunks, filled with boxes, bags, valises, pots, pans, newspapers, pipes, cigars, old playing cards, empty bottles, and one or more of every garment of mens' wear indiscriminately packed together in the most chaotic confusion with the *debris* of the last meal and materials for the next. Sitting on chairs, benches, and impromptu contrivances for seats, around two dirty pine tables, each about five feet along, are seated twelve or fourteen gentlemen, of all ages from twenty to fifty. These form the mess, and are diligently discussing a ham bone or a piece of commissary beef, which, from its quality, is by common consent called mule. When the reader reflects that these gentlemen were kidnapped from their homes where they were always surrounded with the comforts and luxuries of civilized life, for no earthly reason and without any crime, and immured in this filthy pen, destitute of every comfort, cut off from all correspondence with families or friends, denied the well-known rights of any accused person, he will cease to wonder at the wrecks of mind and body produced by their incarceration.

Scattered around the room in every imaginable attitude, or crowding to the window to see the latest arrival whom within an hour they may greet as a fellow-prisoner and sharer of their privations, is seen the other occupants of the room. Suddenly a shout of "fresh fish" is raised, when all rush eagerly to the large window to witness the arrival under an escort of one or more detectives, of the last victim of military necessity; or it may be that the call is "a sympathizer," when with equal avidity they press forward to salute or return the friendly but furtive greeting of some one of the many ladies of Washington, whose noble hearts, touched with sympathy for their sufferings, daily pass the prison to give them a cheering and kind look; which, though harmless, often involves them in difficulty; for scarcely a day passes without the sentry, under orders from Lieutenant Miller, or some other down-east aspirant for administration favors and promotion, arresting on the side-walk or from carriages, ladies or gentlemen who dare to recognize, by look or salutation, a relative or friend that has had the misfortune of incurring the displeasure of the War Department.

It will doubtless astonish the reader, but it is nevertheless true, that these arrests are of daily occurrence, nay, hourly; and I have known ladies of the highest respectability dragged from their carriages for saluting a relative in the window of this prison, taken into the office, and for hours subjected to the insulting familiarity and impudent questioning of those uniformed plebeians who are paid and pampered for the protection of those defenceless women that they thus outrage. Nor is this the only consequence of a friendly look or word, for if the prisoner receiving or returning it, could be discovered, he is at once locked up in a dark, dirty, narrow hole, alive with vermin, and unfit for a coal hole, but which is dignified with the name of the guard-house, where he is closely confined, without food or bed, until the wrath of these officials is appeased by some fellow-prisoner, or the soothing influence of a consideration; and those discoveries were not infrequent, for the War Department secured daily reports of all the movements and conversations of the prisoners, by placing a spy in each room, who, though ostensibly a prisoner, was the paid informer of the officials. I recall one marked case of this kind, which occurred in room 16. A fellow named Corbett, acting in this capacity, wrote daily reports to Detective Baker, one of which described the indignant denunciation by a prisoner of the corruption of this official, for which, this Baker had him placed in solitary confinement. During the half hour allowed for recreation to the occupants of those large rooms in the yard of the prison, those spies, assuming the air and bearing of injured victims of despotism, mingled freely with the other prisoners, obtaining their confidence with the intention of betraying it.

Ascending a short flight of rickety stairs, from the floor on which those large rooms are situated, we arrive at room 13, which, with four others of unequal size, but of equally filthy condition, opening on to a corridor, were lately devoted to prisoners kept in solitary confinement, and cut off from all conversation or privilege of recreation. It was in a room on the second floor of this part of the prison, that Belle Boyd was confined; and the list of occupants written on their walls, vie in length and respectability, with the registers of our largest and best hotels. These rooms are in the wing of the building on A Street, and from the windows of some of them a view of the Railroad Depot, Camp Sprague, now used as an hospital, and the euphonious negro village of Swamppoodle, can be had. The barred casements of these rooms are constantly lined with the pallid and anxious faces of their inmates, who gaze with envy on the contrabands enjoying that liberty of which they are so unjustly deprived. That portion of the building containing these rooms are as before stated, used for prisoners kept in close confinement, who never breathe the fresh air of heaven, but once a day, when they are allowed under escort of a corporal, to visit the sink, the revolting condition of which I will attempt a description of, in its proper place. On the lower floor of this building, which we reach by a tumble down and dangerous stairway, used by the prisoners, none of them being allowed to use the principal stairway, which is reserved for the officers, guards, and negroes, are two rooms, one of them running the entire width of the building, in which confederate prisoners of war are confined, but from which they were removed in the coldest part of December, to an out-house. This change was made to accommodate the negro washerwomen, who are by far the most important of the prison inmates.

From this floor we pass to the prison yard, about 100 feet square, one half of which is paved with brick or round stones; the remainder is, (in wet weather,) a quagmire. It was here during the summer months that five large Sibley tents were erected, in which and on the brick pavement, several hundred prisoners of war were huddled together night and day for many weeks. In a line with that portion of the prison last described there extends a two story wooden building, the upper part of which is used for a hospital, with its steward's rooms and apothecary shop. The approach to it is by a flight of steps outside of the building, at the foot of which stands a sentry to prevent intrusion by any but the favored few who have succeeded in getting a whiskey pass from the superintendent. This is obtained by first procuring from the surgeon in charge a written permit to purchase and keep in the hospital, liquor for the bearer's use, which on being countersigned by the superindendent, allows the fortunate possessor to open negotiations with Corporal Brown, the sutler or commissary of the prison, for the purchase of whiskey, and as Corporal Brown sets an exalted estimate on his time, and says, " He never buys but the best," the liquor, including the samples taken out of it in the office for examination as to its quality by the guard, who having the health and welfare of the prisoners at heart, jealously scrutinize whatever they purchase for consumption, it costs more than Lachryma Christie or Imperial Tokay by the time it reaches its owner, who or days has been watching its arrival.

The hospital accommodations are with some exceptions as good as could be expected in a place conducted without any regard for system unless it be for a system of plundering the unfortunate prisoners, which is done in a hundred different ways. Conspicuous among them is the sale to the prisoners of certain articles, such as tobacco, cigars, matches, stationery, pies, bread, cheese, and other edibles, all of them of the poorest quality, but for which a profit of 500 per cent. is charged by Corporal Brown or his partner, who holds this lucrative, if not dignified office, by virtue of his being a nephew of the superintendent. The only opportunity given to make these purchases is during recreation, when the space in front of the sutler's shop is crowded with the eager throng, cash in hand, which they are glad from necessity to exchange for the miserable rubbish peddled to them at ten times its value, and in addition submit to the impertinent and obscene familiarity of a vulgar puppy who presumes on his relationship to the superintendent to take advantage of their peculiar position. The scenes of daily occurrence in front of this swindling shop are often rich. The friendly badinage of the prisoners to each other as they call out their wants, (for an armed sentry prevents their approaching within several yards of the door,) is highly amusing, often witty, and but seldom personal, as the quality of the articles, the enormity of the charges, and the childish tyranny of the ever-changing prison rules, form fruitful topics for the exercise of their wit and repartee, while many of the prisoners are thus engaged. If the weather permits, others are vieing with each other in exhibitions of strength or agility, or seeking exercise for their limbs, weary with the confinement, by repeated marchings around the narrow limits of the yard. To these varied modes of passing the coveted half hour for recreation, sudden stop is put by a sergeant calling out, "Time is up. Repair to your rooms," when they again return to their overcrowded rooms to inhale their fetid and unwholesome atmosphere. Adjoining the sutler's shop and nearer the hospital is the mess room of the prison, for the use of those who have not the means or privilege of procuring their own food. It is a long, dimly-lighted room with a pine bench running its whole width and around its walls, on which at meal hours the prisoner's food, consisting of half-boiled beans, musty rice, and pork or beef in a state of semi-putrefaction, was thrown in heaps, from which they helped themselves without knife, fork, or plate. The accumulated filth and grease of the floor and tables sent forth such an odor, that many, nay, most of them, on snatching a piece of meat in one hand, and of bread in the other, were obliged to go in the open air to eat it.

The total disregard of cleanliness of this hog-pen, and the fetid effluvia from the half cooked and decomposing food, was a fruitful source of the diseases of the prison, and its proximity to the hospital must have caused or hastened the many deaths that occurred there. Opposite to this, and extending to the gate, a stone building, one story high, containing the cook-house, wash-rooms, and the guard-house already described, the two former of which must be a source of profit to some official, as the cooking of the food and the washing of the prisoners' clothes was charged for at an exorbitant rate, and frequently incurred their loss. Behind this building, and at the west of the wood-shed, the sinks are situated, and consist of wide trenches, covered over but open in front, with a long wooden rail on which the eighteen or twenty persons using them all the time were obliged to stand. The accumulated excrement for months of several hundred men, many of them suffering from diseases of the intestines produced by these sinks, sent forth such an offensive effluvia as poisoned the atmosphere of the whole prison and disgusted the sickened senses of its inmates. In front of the cook-house, and on the west side of the yard, a wooden fence is placed to divide it from that portion set off for the use of the guards. At the end of this fence are two other sinks, differing from those described only by being enclosed. These are reserved for the officials and a favored few who are admitted by card, which is closely scrutinized by the sentry in front of them, and any person who approaches them is ordered to halt and show his ticket, of which this is a fac simile, and without which no one can enter either of these reserved though almost equally loathesome premises:

**FURNISHED
ROOMS TO LET,**
BY
R. WEINHOLD,
No. 6 4½ Street North,
WASHINGTON, D. C.

The negroes have also for their use covered privies; as in this and every other particular their comfort is of vastly more importance than the prisoner's.

Running along the southern side of the yard a two story rough wooden building was erected to accommodate, or rather contain, a portion of the Confederate prisoners. Its interior, for want of cleanliness and light, beggars description. Adjoining it is the gate, opening into an alleyway, where are continually congregated a herd of hungry pigs waiting for the slush that oozes from the prison yard, the daily offal of several hundred men.

In December last, the President having ordered the execution of a soldier in the prison yard, the gallows was erected in front of the Confederate quarters last mentioned, and as visitors were expected, the prison generally received a long-needed cleaning and whitewashing. For several weeks after the execution the revolting instrument of death was left standing in the yard, as, it was said, to be a terror to the prisoners. Since the November elections, the number of arbitrary arrests having greatly decreased, the condition of the prison is somewhat improved; but this description is literally true in every respect, and in no other city or country would such a nuisance be tolerated or allowed to pollute the atmosphere by its existence. On the same street, in the adjoining block a row of houses, known as Duff Green's Row, is also used as a prison for the incarceration of prisoners of state. Its condition and management is so like the Old Capitol as to render unnecessary a detailed description of it.

EXPLORING THE PRISON.

We soon learned that there was no guard on the third story, which we found to be occupied besides the five in No. 13, by the following gentlemen; in room No. 10, Messrs. McDowell, Barrett, Foster and Jones, of the Harrisburg Patriot and Union, and in four other rooms, nineteen gentlemen from Fredericksburg, Virginia, who were taken and kept as hostages for some Union men alleged to have been arrested and kept in custody by the Confederate Government.

These hostages were thus described by the Christian Banner, a Fredericksburg, Va., newspaper:

"Thomas B. Barton was the oldest lawyer at the Fredericksburg bar, and Attorney for the Commonwealth. He was originally an old line whig, and a member of the congregation of the Episcopal church.

"Thomas F. Knox was a large wheat speculator and flour manufacturer, an old line whig, and a prominent member of the Episcopal church.

"Beverley T. Gill was for a number of years a large merchant tailor, but for several years past had retired into private life, was an old line whig, and a prominent member of the Presbyterian church.

"C. C. Wellford was an extensive dry goods merchant, the oldest in town, than whom none stood higher, was an old line whig, and an elder in the Presbyterian church.

"James McGuire was one of the oldest merchants in Fredericksburg, an old line whig, a prominent member of the Presbyterian church, and a most excellent man.

"James H. Bradley was a grocery merchant, an old line whig, and a deacon in the Baptist church.

"Dr. Wm. F. Broaddus was the pastor of the Baptist church in Fredericksburg, and an old line whig.

"M. Slaughter, Mayor of Fredericksburg, was a large wheat speculator and flour manufacturer. was an old line whig, and a member of the Episcopal church.

"G. H. C. Rowe was a talented jurist, a democrat and a Douglas elector during the late Presidential election, and a member of the Baptist church.

"John Coakley was for many years a merchant, but for several years past had retired from business, and at the time of his arrest, was Superintendent of the Fredericksburg Aqueduct Co.; he was an old line whig, and a very prominent member of the Episcopal church.

"Benjamin Temple was a wealthy farmer, an old line whig, and we believe a member of no church, but a most excellent man.

"Dr. James Cooke was a druggist, owning the largest establishment, perhaps south of the Potomac river, was an old line whig, and a prominent member of the Episcopal church.

"John F. Scott was proprietor of the large Fredericksburg Foundry, and carried on an extensive business up to the time the Union troops took possession of the place, was an old line whig, and a prominent member of the Episcopal church.

"John H. Roberts lived off his income, was an old line whig, and, we believe, a member of no church.

"John I. Berrey, formerly engaged in a large produce business, but at the time of his arrest connected with a hardware store, was an old line whig, and a member of no church.

"Michael Ames was a blacksmith, and old line whig, and a member of no church.

"Abraham Cox was a tailor, a Breckenridge democrat, and a Southern Methodist.

"William H. Norton was a house-carpenter, an old line whig, and a member of the Baptist church.

"Lewis Wrenn—no particular business—an old line whig, and a member of the Baptist church.

"Of the nineteen citizens of Fredericksburg arrested and sent to Washington, it will be observed, that seventeen of the number were whigs, one a Douglas democrat, and one a Breckenridge democrat, six Episcopalians, three Presbyterians, five Baptists, one southern Methodist, and four who are not members of any church.

"Mr. Knox had some 13 or 14,000 barrels of flour, which, up to the present time is lost to him; the party has lost full one hundred thousand dollars worth of negroes."

The Harrisburg prisoners and the nineteen hostages from Fredericksburg, were comparatively well off, having provided themselves or being provided by their friends, with many necessaries which the government did not afford. These gentlemen cooked most their own food, which as it had to be done in the small rooms they occupied, was anything but agreeable during the warm months of summer. As there was no apparent restriction on the prisoners in those rooms of the third story of the building from visiting each other, they took advantage of this circumstance to make each other's acquaintance. The Virginia prisoners, or hostages as they were, maintained a dignified reserve, even long after their acquaintance had been made by their fellow prisoners. While they were gentlemanly and polite in their intercourse with their neighbors, there were but few of them who descended to the familiarity one might expect under the circumstances in which they found themselves placed. They were nearly all of what is known by the term Old School in their manners, deportment and intercourse with strangers. This, some of them carried to an excess which became disagreeable to their neighbors. There is evidently a notion of what constitutes gentlemanliness prevailing among some Southern people which regards haughtiness of deportment, and austerity of manner, a stiffness of person, and a silent reserve as among the leading traits characteristic of the real gentleman. However this may appear to Southern people, it certainly was no commendation in the estimation of their fellow prisoners of such of the Fredericsburg hostages as stood too much upon this sort of dignity.

Mayor Slaughter, Messrs. Scott, Knox, Broaddus, Ames and Dr. Cook, and one or two of the others, came nearer the standard of gentlemanliness in the broad and true sense of the term than most of their companions.

These and one or two others returned the visits of their fellow prisoners, and conversed freely with Northern men on the state of the country, while some of their companions scarcely returned the civility of a "good day," to their fellow prisoners.

VISITS OF FRIENDS.

Next day after the arrival in prison of Messrs. Sheward and myself, we were visited by a friend and fellow citizen of Iowa, Judge Charles Mason, who volunteered to act as our counsel. Some idea may be formed by the reader of how a visit is made and an interview conducted between a friend and a prisoner from the following extract of a letter descriptive of an interview between Judge Mason and myself. It is needless to say who wrote it:

"I doubt whether you have a full idea of the way in which this business of visiting prisoners is managed. You go with your pass to the Capitol prison, and are stopped by the sentinel in front of that building who sings out lustily for the corporal of the guard. The corporal makes his appearance with his musket at his shoulder, and conducts you into the building to the august presence of the sergeant of the guard. The sergeant seizes his musket and enters an inner room to announce your presence to the lieutenant. If that dignitary is disengaged, he permits you to enter, and the sergeant announces that permission accordingly. As there is only one reception room for the visitors of all the prisoners, and as they allow only one person to enter that room at a time, you have to await your turn in this ante-chamber, until you can be permitted to penetrate into the real presence. The lieutenant examines your pass inside and out,—spells out some of the words and guesses at the rest, and asks you the name of the person you wish to see, for it is very doubtful whether the Military Governor is able to decipher the manuscript. Once my pass, by mistake, had the name of Mr. Lane instead of Mr. Mahony, and I did not observe the mistake until too late to have it rectified; but although the lieutenant U. S. A. looked very grave over the pass for a long time, he failed to see the error, and I did not tell him, and he ordered Mahony to be brought down.

"After all these preliminaries are gone through with, the corporal is directed to bring down Mr. Mahony from room No. 16. In due time he comes— we shake hands and seat ourselves. The military keeper seats himself right directly in our front at three feet distance—listens attentively to every word —catches every motion, and sees that nothing is done to overthrow the government. To see a perfect stranger thus intermeddling in our private conversation excites in one almost irresistible impulse to insult him in some way as an evesdropper and intermeddler. When fifteen minutes have elapsed, our conference is abruptly brought to an end, and I go home musing on the glorious privileges of an American citizen.

"Yours truly."

During the interview with Judge Mason, I enquired of the Judge what the news was out doors. The Judge had scarcely opened his mouth to tell me the current public news of the day, than he was interrupted by Lieutenant Holmes, alias "Bullhead," with the remark that it was not permitted to the prisoners to be informed of what was occurring out doors. "But," interposed Judge Mason, "what I was going to say is merely what is published in the papers." "No matter for that," said Bull-head, "no conversation can be permitted on such matters."

"What then may we speak of?" enquired the Judge, and before he had the enquiry quite out of his mouth, Bullhead looked at his watch, and declaring the fifteen minutes allowed for an interview with a prisoner to have expired, he opened the door leading to the prisoners' apartments, and motioning me to go, thus unceremoniously closed the interview. A glance at Judge Mason's countenance revealed in its indignant expression the workings of a spirit which could scarcely repress the emotions excited into fury by the despotic arrogance and tyranny of this satellite of arbitrary power.

During this interview an arrangement was made to bring the cases of myself and Sheward to the notice of the Secretary of War, with a view to have a trial or hearing as speedily as possible, the result of which will appear further on. A few days after I was visited by F. B. Wilkie, Esq., who was then acting as a Washington correspondent of the Chicago *Times*, but who had been the local editor of the Dubuque *Herald*, of which paper I was the principal editor. During the conversation which took place between us, Mr. Wilkie remarked to me, "I presume you have heard of your nomination for Congress." This allusion to a circumstance which was evidently displeasing to the Administration, was regarded by the lieutenant on duty, who was present at the interview, as contraband information, so nothing more was said of the matter. Here, however, was a key to unlock the motive of the Administration and of the Abolition partisans in Iowa, who had been the means of having me arrested.

As soon as I reached my room, a consultation was held at which it was advised that a letter be written by me, accepting of the nomination for Congress, although it was morally certain that my acceptance would protract the length of my imprisonment. It was considered likely that a letter or letters had been, or would be, written by my friends informing me of the nomination, and that in all probability these letters would not be allowed to reach me, as there was evidently a determination concluded by the Administration to defeat me for Congress at all hazards, and by any means possible to the tyrants in power. The result of the consultation was that I should accept of the nomination, and that a letter signifying this design should be written. This I did, addressing the letter to my friend, Stilson Hutchins, Esq., who was conducting my paper in my absence. This letter was returned to me from the Provost Marshal, with a note saying:

HEADQUARTERS, PROVOST MARSHAL'S OFFICE,
WASHINGTON, D. C., —— 1862.

Nothing but *family* and *business letters* are allowed to pass.

W. V. C. MURPHY.

It might gratify the reader to see a copy of the letter which was thus prevented from reaching my fellow citizens. It is, with the exception of some business matters, as follows, the original being now in my possession as evidence of what I allege:

OLD CAPITOL PRISON, WASHINGTON, D. C.,
August 25th, 1862.

DEAR HUTCHINS:—Say to my friends that I accept the nomination for Congress, and that I thank them for having conferred on me the honor of that nomination; that I am now and expect to ever remain true to the Constitution as it was made a compact between States and people; true to the Union as it was framed by the Constitution, and true to the Government as the Constitution gave it an existence; and that neither persecution, nor threats of violence, nor imprisonment, nor desertion of friends, nor opposition of enemies, will wean me from this position.

To traitors to the Constitution, North, South, East and West, I am opposed. To those who would subvert, corrupt or revolutionize the Government, as to those who would overthrow it by force of arms, I am opposed. To the plunderers of the Treasury, I am opposed. To those who defraud the Government, and to those who permit frauds to be perpetrated, I am opposed. To every person and to every act which violates the Constitution, subverts the Government, threatens ruin to the country, I am opposed.

I am to-day what I have ever been, an uncompromising Constitutionalist, and come wo or weal, I shall so remain till the people of the United States change their form of Government, which I hope they never will, or permit it to be done by others.

* * * * * *

Yours truly,
D. A. MAHONY.

Such were the sentiments which the Administration tyrants would not permit a candidate for Congress, who was a victim in their custody, to address to the people. It was perfectly consistent with their violations of the Constitution, with their subversion of the Government, with their plunderings of the Treasury, with their destruction of the country that such a letter should be suppressed. The only wonder is that it was not destroyed, and that the prisoner was not left in ignorance of what became of it. But the letter was returned, and I have it in my possession; an evidence of the tyranny of Lincoln's Administration, and of the despotism which reigned over the Old Capitol.

No sooner was this letter returned than I resolved to send out another surreptitiously, addressed to my fellow-citizens of the Third Congressional District, Iowa. This was accomplished, by what means and how it is unnecessary to say.

As copies of this address have been solicited for preservation, by the prisoners who heard it read in the Old Capitol, and by several others, it is republished here, with the hope that it contains matter worthy of consideration, and that it embodies doctrines in which the great body of the American people believe, sentiments which they approve, and contains statements of fact which they know to be true in relation to the existing rebellion:

ADDRESS OF D. A. MAHONY, TO THE CITIZENS OF THE THIRD CONGRESSIONAL DISTRICT, IOWA:

OLD CAPITOL OF THE UNITED STATES,
Now A PRISON OF DESPOTISM,
WASHINGTON, D. C., Aug. 25th, 1862.

Fellow-Citizens of the Third Congressioual District of Iowa:

I have been informed to-day of my nomination as a candidate for Representative in Congress by a convention representing such of you as believe that the Constitution of the United States is the supreme law of this Nation, a law which is designed to afford security and protection to life and property, and to be a restraint on evil doers, as well on those invested with attributes of authority in the State as those who are merely citizens of this once happy Republic. I have signified my acceptance of the nomination referred to, and promised, if an opportunity were offered, to address you more at length. This opportunity has now presented itself, not with the consent of those who have arrested and brought me here, but despite their determination that I should not be afforded the privilege which every American freeman has been taught to believe it was his right to exercise.

As I am taken from among you by an arbitrary and illegal decree of some minion of the ruling powers and thus prevented from addressing you in person, I am obliged to have recourse to such means as this prison affords, a scanty portion of ink and paper, to appeal to your manhood, to your intelligence, to your patriotism, and to your interests, to rebuke the arbitrary, illegal, and outrageous course of the Administration and its partisan supporters who have converted this building, consecrated by the patriotism of other days, into a prison in which loyal citizens are immured for our devotion and fidelity to the Constitution of our fathers. Rebuke these outrages by transferring me to the Capitol, as your representative, from this Abolition Bastile to which I, among others, have been consigned for pleading the cause of the people and a conformity to the Constitution by the Executive and Legislative Branches of the Government. Your relations to the Government, your interests in the future, your rights as citizens, your all that you value as freemen, are as much at stake as are my rights and interests. Whatever arbitrary action of the Administration or of Congress affects one portion of the people will affect us all. One portion of us cannot be outraged without affecting the other. One portion of us cannot be affected injuriously by the violation of the Constitution or by a subversion of the Government without affecting us all. The outrages inflicted upon me to-day might be the fate of some of you to-morrow, should arbitrary power be suffered or encouraged to usurp the place of law. Reflect, therefore, on your condition and act accordingly. Many of you know my sentiments already on the principles of Government and on the questions of the day. Many others of you know my sentiments only through the misrepresentations of my personal enemies and political adversaries, while there may be some who have not heard one way or another of what my political opinions are, and what course I would take if I had an opportunity to act as your Representative in Congress. It is due to all of those whom I address on this occasion that my sentiments and views in relation to Government affairs and the state of the country, be fairly, distinctly, and unequivocally set forth, and this I propose to do, reminding the reader that being debarred of all means to consult records or to make references to well known facts, I shall have to depend entirely upon my memory in referring to such matters as I introduce as testimony to the truth and as facts of history.

Let me dispose first of the misrepresentations of my political adversaries who, for nearly two years past, have diligently and perseveringly belied and maligned me.

Accused of being a Secessionist.

I am accused by these partisan malignants, and I am in this Abolition Bastile on the accusations, that I am a Secessionist, a sympathizer with Rebellion, a disloyalist, in a word a traitor. No proofs of these accusations have ever been presented or will ever be presented. The files of the Dubuque HERALD will prove the negative of these charges. They will prove that I was the first person in Iowa who declared that a State could not constitutionally secede from the Union, an opinion which I have ever held and in which I am more than ever confirmed by the longer study of the question. I not only believe that it is unconstitutional for a State to secede from the Union, as I have ever and always believed and maintained, but I am opposed to making the right of secession a constitutional right. This does not deny the right of revolution, which is held by most persons of all parties, but revolution is quite different from secession. Mr. Lincoln and his party admit and advocate the right of revolution, but deny the exercise of the right; but it is needless to argue this question. I refer to it merely for the purpose of correcting misrepresentations, and misapprehensions of my position.

Accused of Disloyalty.

I am accused by my adversaries of being disloyal to the Government. What is a disloyalist? Disloyalty consists in being unfaithful to the Government. What has been my course? I have ever and always advocated a compliance with and conformity to the Constitution, which is the Supreme law, both over the Government, Administrators of the Government, and individual citizens. Is this disloyalty? Is it disloyalty to believe and to say that the President of the United States has no more right to trample on the Constitution and to subvert the Government than any other citizen has? The President is obliged to take a special oath to support the Constitution. Is it treason in me or you, fellow-citizens, to say that that oath ought to be kept by the President inviolate? If this be treason we are all traitors.

Opposed to the War.

I am accused of being opposed to the war. To a certain extent this is true. I believe that the war in which the country is engaged should have never been commenced; that it never would have been commenced were it not for the determination of the Abolitionists and some Republicans to divide the Union, to kick the South out of the Union whether it would go or not. What else but this was the meaning of the "Irrepressible conflict?" Did not the Abolitionists and Republicans proclaim that the North and South could not live together in peace under the same Government, and believing that they could not live in peace, these Northern sentimentalists determined that there should be war. Did they not refuse to settle the questions of difficulty between the North and South by a vote in Congress? There would have been no war had the Abolitionists and Republicans so desired. But they desired war, not to save the Union, but to destroy it. To effect this object they passed Personal Liberty bills, resisted the execution of the Fugitive Slave Law, and provoked the "Irrepressible Conflict." They forced the South into war. To save the Union, think you? Not at all. Peaceful and conciliatory measures must be adopted by the North and South. The only way to preserve the Union when re-formed is to have recourse to the same means as did our fathers when the Union was first established.

Hence I am opposed to war except as it might be made a means of an early restoration of peace, Union, prosperity and happiness. A vindictive war a war of subjugation, a war of spoliation, a war of devastation, in a word, a war as the Abolitionists desire and design to have this war waged, will never end in peace, will never restore Union, prosperity, or happiness, to the American people.

My political sentiments are embraced in the following motto.

THE CONSTITUTION AS IT IS.
THE UNION AS IT WAS.
THE GOVERNMENT AS IT SHOULD BE.

The Constitution as it is.

How do you understand the constitution, Fellow Citizens? It is not only an agreement among the people at large to be governed in the manner which it provides, but an agreement also among the States by which they, as political sovereignties, delegated a portion of their state rights to a general agent of the whole, called a Federal Government.

Recollect that the original thirteen states existed before the Constitution. They were brought into existence by the declaration of the 4th of July 1776, and from that time forward they were *de facto* and *de jure* Sovereignties. When their Independence was acknowledged by Great Britain, the Independence of each of them separately and distinctly was recognized. So at the close of the Revolutionary war, there were thirteen Sovereign and Independent States. It is true they were confederated together for mutual defense, protection and interest, but neither of them was obliged to hold that relation to the others. They were free to unite themselves to each other, or to remain separate and distinct sovereignties. They chose to form a Federal, or as some call it, a National Union.

How did they do this? By selecting delegates

to represent them in a convention, which body was vested with the authority to draft a new agreement, by which the States were to be governed thenceforth, should they agree on the terms of the contract. This convention produced the Constitution of the United States, and when ratified by the requisite number of two-thirds of the thirteen States, it became the fundamental contract among the States, according to its provisions.

Now what is this agreement or constitution? It is simply a delegation of certain authority and power of sovereignty, from the states respectively, to an Institution of their own creation, called the Federal Government; and a direction to the respective branches of Government, as to what power and authority they should each exercise, and under what circumstances and conditions this delegated power and authority should be brought into requisition and manifested.

The Constitution is the contract among the States and people as to how National affairs shall be conducted, as to how laws affecting the general weal shall be enacted and come into effect, as to how the rights and liberties of the People shall be secured and protected. This agreement expressly reserves to the People their individual rights of person and property, and to the States their right of Sovereignty, as these rights existed before the Constitution was formed, except such portions thereof as the States through the Constitution delegated to the General Government.

I need not enlarge upon the provisions of the Federal Constitution, Fellow Citizens, to explain to you its provisions in detail. It is quite sufficient to remind you that it is the evidence between the States and the General Government of the creation of the latter and of its existence at present. Without the Constitution there is no Federal Government, with the Constitution there is no other legitimate Government than that which exists by virtue of the Constitution and is administered in accordance with its provisions. Should the will of the people as manifested in the Constitution, and the will of the Administration as manifested by its acts of arbitrary power conflict with each other, which should—which will the people obey? Let them answer.

I answer for myself, I abide by, and will conform to, and to the best of my ability, power and influence, will uphold and sustain the Constitution. It is to the Constitution as the Patriot Fathers agreed to it and bequeathed it to us that I owe allegiance, and not to the dogmas of the sectional party, which has forced the people of the North and South into an "irrepressible conflict," and which threatens to destroy the Union, subvert the Government and ruin our Country.

The Constitution as it is, in conformity to the Government, if preserved by the people, will save the Union unbroken and perpetuate free Government so long as the Constitution endures. Let the Administration be permitted to violate the Constitution, and there will remain to the people no other evidence of Free Government, or of political rights which it was the pride, the boast and happiness of American Citizens that they so long possessed.

Now shall we have a Constitutional Government in which the authority of the ruling powers shall be defined, prescribed and restrained as our Fathers provided in this Constitution they gave us? or shall we suffer this Constitution to be taken away from us and the will of our public servants become our Government as it is at the present time? This is as much for you, Fellow Citizens, to decide, as it is for any portion of the American people. And before you decide, take into consideration the facts of history, and the causes, which have effected the downfall of Governments in other nations, and the reasons why despotisms still exist in this enlightened age. There can be no free government but as it is established constitutionally, nor can free Governments be preserved and perpetuated, but by holding its administrators to a strict account.

The Union as it was.

The object of the Constitution was, principally, to form a Union of the Thirteen Original States, and of such other states as might be thereafter admitted into the Federation. What sort of a Union was it which the Constitution formed? Was it such a Union as the "Irrepressible conflict," as taught by Lincoln and Seward and their followers would have established? Was it a Union in which the people of the North were taught to hate their fellow citizens of the South, and to meddle with their rights of property and domestic affairs? Was it such a Union as the Abolition and Republican party have endeavored and are endeavoring to bring about, in which the equality of States will be no longer recognized, in which distinctions will be made among citizens according to their pecuniary means and political opinions?

In the Union of our Fathers, every State was equal in sovereignty with her sister States, every citizen was the equal in rights with his fellow citizen; but in the Union which Abolitionism and Republicanism propose to give us, one State, according as its institutions may conform to Abolition politics will have a higher rank in the scale of sovereignty than other States which will not conform to the Abolition standard of politics. So as between individuals, the citizen of constitutional proclivities in politics will be treated as a dangerous person in the Union of Abolitionism, while he who disregards all law, high or low, except as Abolitionism gives the law, will be recognized and respected as a patriot of the new order.

Fellow citizens, which of these Unions are you in favor of? A Union of equal States and of equal persons politically, or a Union in which some States will be deprived of sovereignty, and in which the large mass of the people will be subjected to the rule of those who, by pecuniary means and political influence, will have acquired power.

It is the ambition of human nature to dominate. They who once acquire power, will stop short of the use of no means to perpetuate their power. But in the Republic of Federal States like ours, there must be equality among the States as sovereignties and among the people politically, or there can be no lasting Union. The Union our Fathers made was a perfect, harmonious, and, as it proved to be, a prosperous and powerful Union; but the Irrepressible conflict of Abolitionism has disorganized it, broken it into fragments, brought upon it misery and woe, and reduced it to such a state of impotency as to be powerful only in committing self-destruction.

Do you, fellow citizens, favor the continuance of the destruction which is tearing the Union down to its foundation, or do you desire that the old fabric should be built up in the same form, proportions, strength and beauty in which it was the pride and boast of every American and the admiration and envy of civilized man the world over? You fellow citizens have much to say and much to do in determining this question. Elect my competitor to Congress, and you vote that the Union of the Fathers shall be destroyed. Believe me, the Union can never be restored by the partisans who now control the Federal Government. Recollect that the

Union was preserved for several years past, despite the efforts of the Abolitionists to destroy it, by the Democratic party, and I say it reproachfully to the leaders of that party, that had they remained faithful to its principles and consistent with its historic name it would not have been in the power of Abolitionism to force the country into war, and to have brought upon the people the miseries they now endure.

The sectionalism of Abolitionism, can you not perceive fellow-citizens, is in antagonism to the Union. Now can a man be for and against the Union at the same time? Abolitionism tells you it is in favor of Union, but not of the Union. They want a Union with emancipated slaves, but not with slaveholders. They affect such a horror of slavery that they will jeopard the existence of the Union to get rid of slavery in States where they have no property, no interest, no rights to be affected one way or another. Why should we lose the Union to abolish slavery? Why should we interfere between master and slave, to bring upon ourselves the burden of maintaining pauper negroes? Why should we deprive the people of the South of negro labor to bring this labor in competition with free white labor? Why should we endeavor to transfer to our own doors and to our homes the moral evils which are said to be the effect in the South of a commingling of the black and white races? Answer these questions, fellow-citizens, and as you answer them to your judgment and to your conscience, so vote at the polls.

The government as it should be.

I am in favor of the government as it should be, not as it has become by subversion and usurpation. The government as it should be is the government as it was, when the people of the United States, were a free, happy, prosperous people in the enjoyment of peace among themselves and at peace with all the world.

The government as it should be is the government as the constitution made it, one in which the Executive, Legislative and Judicial powers were invested in distinct, separate, independent, co-ordinate branches, and in which the humblest citizen of the Republic was guaranteed security and protection for his life, property, liberty and rights. Is this the character of the government as it is and has been administered by Mr. Lincoln and the party which has acquired power by his election? Let us see. The Constitution says that the government shall consist of three distinct branches, the legislative, to make the laws, the executive, to carry the laws enacted into proper effect, and in case there should be a question as to the conformity of these laws to the Constitution, the Judiciary, to judge of the question. The Executive was not to make laws but only to put the laws into execution.

The Congress was not to put laws into execution, or to judge whether the laws were in conformity to the Constitution, but only to enact, to the best of their judgment and ability such laws as they might deem best for the interests of the people; and the Judiciary were not to enact laws, but only to pass judgment upon disputed questions.

This agent, or government, received whatever power and authority it possesses through the Constitution from the people. It could not receive power or authority by any other means than through the Constitution, nor from any other source than from the people, in a Constitutional manner.

The government was not created to do as those who might be selected from time to time to administer it pleased, but to carry into effect the will of the people as they have manifested it in the Constitution and as it might become their interest to change their will from time to time, not arbitrarily, or whimsically, nor capriciously, nor violently, but Constitutionally.

As every creature is properly subordinate and subject to the power which created it, so is the government of the United States subject and subordinate to the will of the people. The government is superior, and should be obeyed only when it acts in accordance with the will of the people as they have manifested their will in the Constitution. Whenever the government undertakes to abridge the freedom of the people, or to circumscribe, or violate the rights which they reserved to themselves by the Constitution, and some of which they expressly declared should not be abridged, circumscribed or violated, the government, or any branch of it in so doing, subjects itself to reprehension, and if necessary to bring it to a sense of its duty, to opposition.

Let us have an illustration of this doctrine. Suppose that Congress should undertake to lay a more onerous tax upon some of the States and upon the people of those States, than upon others, which might have more influence in that branch of the government, and that the executive should approve of such a measure, and suppose that such an act should be declared unconstitutional by the judicial branch of the government, but nevertheless that the executive would attempt to enforce such an act upon the people, would they be obliged to submit to it? Clearly not. No man who knows the nature of the government, and the conditions on which it was instituted by the people, will say that one or more branches of the government has the right to do a wrong, not only to the people of one or more States, but to a single individual of any State. The difference, the long boasted difference, between our government, and that of most other countries, is that our government is Constitutional, while most other governments are more or less absolute, arbitrary, tyrannical, or despotic. Even in our school geographies we are told that there are different forms of government, and what these forms of government are, and in what they differ from each other. We are told that in absolute Monarchies the will of the ruler is the supreme law, while in Constitutional governments, the will of the people, as expressed in their compact of government, is the supreme law. Now, fellow-citizens, in what material respect does our government as administered by Mr. Lincoln, differ from the government of Russia, which we have been taught to regard as an absolute monarchy. Nominally, it is true, we have a Constitutional government and we had one actually till it was subverted by Mr. Lincoln.

How subverted, you may enquire? In this respect:

By suspending the writ of *habeas corpus*, a privilege which the Constitution expressly declares shall be suspended only by act of Congress.

By abridging the liberty of speech and the freedom of the press, which the Constitution expressly declares shall not be done even by act of Congress, much less by executive decrees.

By using millions of the public money without warrant or authority of law, and lavishing it on favorites and parasites.

By arresting citizens without warrant of law and imprisoning them without a trial, or even informing them of the charges preferred against them.

By usurping and exercising the functions of the judiciary and subjecting courts and judges to the domination of the military arm of the government, and preventing citizens from obtaining redress of grievances in the tribunals constituted for that purpose, and by preventing courts and judges from performing their constitutional duties, and by disregarding the decrees of courts when these decrees conflict with the will of the Executive.

In what respect then fellow-citizens, does our government as administered by Mr. Lincoln and the party with which he acts, differ from the Absolute Monarchy of Russia; differ from the scarcely less Absolute Government of Austria, France, Spain, Prussia or the other monarchies of Europe or even of Asia. Of what use is it to have the name of Constitutional government when its administrators are not only permitted to become despots and tyrants, but encouraged and approved in their grossest outrages.

What will this lead to?

Read history, if any one of you doubts, fellow-citizens, to what usurpation of power by Rulers leads. You will look in vain for any other result than to a change of Government, not only in policy, but in principle and system, wherever the people permitted the relations established between themselves and the Government to be violated. Rome in her palmiest days was a Republic. She became an Imperial despotism. How? First by usurpation of power by the Rulers of the Republic. Second by the acquiescence of the people in these usurpations. The Rulers forged the chains to bind the people into subjugation; the people, as we are doing in this country, stretched out their hands to be manacled, and bowed their necks to the yoke. Where now is the Republic of Rome? Where even is Imperial Rome? Naught of it is left but desolation, ruin, and scarcely enough of its crumbling dust to remind the world of what it was.

Look, too, at the history of the Republics of

Greece and of the other powerful nations of antiquity, and of the Middle Ages. What has become of them and why did they fall? While the people held their public servants to a strict accountability, and were vigilant in their watchfulness of their rights and liberties, these old nations flourished and prospered as did our own while we American citizens held our public servants to the terms of the Constitution, under whose authority and by virtue of whose provisions they exercised the functions of Government. And just as we have relaxed our vigilance and become as our ancestors of other Nations did, indifferent and even regardless of what befell us and our Government, our public servants have taken advantage of this indifference, and arrogated to themselves powers which the Constitution not only refused to give them, but positively withheld. What then is to prevent our fate as a Nation being that of Rome, Greece, Venice, and the other free, prosperous, powerful Nations of antiquity and of the Middle Ages? Reflect on it, fellow-citizens, and you must conclude with me, that the only way to prevent the desolation, destruction and ruin of our country, is to select other public servants to administer our Government, men whose political antecedents are well known to be such as are in conformity to the Constitution, and who will take the Constitution—the will of the people, not their own will, for their rule of Government. Should the people fail to do this, all will soon be lost. Our Constitutional Government will become a Military despotism in name, as it has become already in fact. Laws will be promulgated by Military power, taxes will be imposed by Military orders, property will be confiscated by Military decrees. Life, liberty, property, individual rights will exist only as Military ordinances prescribe. The Military power, instead of being as the Constitution made it, a subordinate and subject power, to be used only to aid the civil power in the enforcement of the laws, will become the dominant party in the States and Nation, and every civilian will be compelled to hold the position of serf to this stratocratic domination. Now is the time, if ever, to prevent this state of things. Let the Government be administered much longer with the acquiescence of the people in its present course, and there will not be power enough left in the people to prevent its entire subversion, and its revolution into a Military Despotism.

Look to this, fellow-citizens, before casting your vote at the next election. This state of things concerns every one of you as much as it does or will concern me. If you want to be serfs and hold the relation of subject to a Ruler, vote for the Abolition and Republican candidates for office; if you want to preserve Constitutional Government and Constitutional liberty, vote for the candidates who advocate and who have always advocated the doctrines which I enunciate to you in this Address.

4 *Strong Government.*

I am in favor of as strong a Government as is needed to give security and protection to person and property, and to maintain its legitimate authority, but I am opposed to the establishment, in these United States, of a Government which can be used by partisans for the oppression of their fellow-citizens; to a Government of arbitrary power such as Abolitionism has instituted, and which has superseded the Government given us by our forefathers. Do you imagine, does any one of you imagine for a moment that you are living to-day under the Government of Washington, Jefferson, and their patriot successors? The nearest approach to a precedent for the Administration of Mr. Lincoln, was that of the elder Adams; but even he, Monarchist as he was, did not dare to subvert the Government to the extent of ignoring the Judiciary. He had an act of Congress to fall back on for his alien and sedition decrees, while the present Executive acts not only without an act of Congress, but in direct contravention of the acts of that body.

A strong Government is not a tyrannic or despotic Government, but one which rules by and with the will of the people, legitimately manifested. The object of all Governments is to give greater security and protection to life and property than each individual could of himself bestow or exercise for the defense of his neighbor or himself. The Government of the United States, as administered by Abraham Lincoln, puts every individual at the mercy of the malice of his neighbor, and in place of protection to life, liberty and property, which it was designed by the Constitution that the Government should give even to persons guilty of the most atrocious crimes, until conviction, the Government of Mr. Lincoln condemns and punishes persons on the mere accusation of their personal and partisan enemies.

The Administration in Rebellion Against the Constitution.

I charge the President of the United States and his advisers and coadjutors with being in rebellion against the Constitution and people of the United States, and I hold myself personally responsible, not only for this charge, but to make it good, in any Constitutional tribunal which has jurisdiction of the affront. The incarceration in this prison of some two or three hundred American citizens, by an arbitrary order from the War Department, is, of itself, a sufficient proof of the truth of the charge, and of the guilt of the President and his advisers and coadjutors; but there are many other acts, equally atrocious, equally outrageous, equally violative of personal rights, of public interests, and of the Constitution of the United States, all tending to prove the utter disregard of the Executive for the obligations and restraints of the Constitution, equally demonstrative of a design to change our former system of Government, equally conclusive that the Administrators of the Government are traitors in the loyal and moral sense of the term.

Reflect, fellow-citizens, on the events of the year and half past, and let your unbiassed, untrammeled, unprejudiced judgment be influenced by your understanding, by facts, by truth, and what other conclusion can you come to, than that our once free, constitutional, enlightened and liberal Government has been overthrown, and that they by whose act it has been done are traitors, deserving of a traitor's doom. I am for holding every one of them, from the President down to his lowest minion, responsible for his misdeeds.

Arbitrary and Illegal Arrests.

Of the hundreds of persons who have been arrested and imprisoned illegally and arbitrarily by order of the War Department, not a single one of the number has been found guilty of any crime. The fact is, the Administration has not dared, in a single instance, to give a trial to one of these State prisoners, knowing full well that no crime was committed by any one of them, and that a prosecution would only end in the discomfiture of the tyrants who have used and attempted to exercise arbitrary power. I am one of the victims of this tyrannical despotism. I have pleaded in vain for a hearing or trial, but it is refused me. Why? Simply because the tyrannical usurpers of power have not the means, even by the use of perjured scoundrels who are used as tools by the Administration, to convict me no more than my fellow prisoners, of any crime.

Think you, fellow-citizens, that if it were in the power of the Administration or the Abolition Republican party to convict me of any offense whatever that they would delay to bring me to trial? Do they not want to convict me if they had an opportunity or the means to do it? If this were not their design, why have they brought me here? They hold me here without a trial, because they know full well trial must result not only in my acquittal of every charge of disloyalty, but prove that the cause, and the only cause of my arrest, was my devotion to the Constitution and the well-being of my country, whose peace has been broken, whose interests have been sacrificed, whose happiness has been destroyed, by the traitor faction which succeeded in the last Presidential election, in acquiring the reins of power.

Fellow-citizens, the party, the power, the Administration which dares to violate the rights of persons, as has been done by the illegal and arbitrary arrests with which you have become familiar, will not hesitate, if need be, for the accomplishment of their designs—the perpetuation of their rule—to despoil the people of their property, to subject them to an arbitrary domination of which the violation of our Constitutional liberties and rights, is but a foretaste.

For myself, I ask no favor from the Administration. I have petitioned for justice, and it has been refused me. Nay, more, I have been refused a copy of the charges preferred against me. I am still as ignorant as I was the morning of my arrest of what I am accused. Now why am I kept here? Simply and solely to prevent me from having such intercourse with my fellow-citizens of Iowa, as would afford me an opportunity to expose the corruptions, the imbecility, the profligacy, the treason to the Constitution, of the Administration, and the partisan fanatics who uphold and guide its course.

Remember, fellow-citizens, that it is not an individual who is involved in this illegal and arbitrary course of the Administration. Acquiesce in the assumption and exercise of arbitrary power, approve of the violations of your Constitution, of the subversion of your Government, of the deprivation of your rights, of the sacrifice of your interests, and in what respect do you differ from the most servile serfs of the Despotic Governments of Europe and Asia? Even they pine for liberty and for Constitutional Government. Will you, who have the right to enjoy those inestimable blessings, acquiesce in being deprived of them, approve of being made the veriest serfs of a Military Despotism.

Your fellow-citizens throughout the Northern States are taking action on the course of the Administration. Loyal citizens, which include all who are in favor of preserving the Constitution, and who are determined that it shall not be violated with impunity by Abraham Lincoln or his party, no more than it shall be overthrown by Jefferson Davis and his fellow-rebels, are taking measures to preserve their liberties, to secure their rights, to prevent their Government from being revolutionized by Abolitionism, from a free Government, to a Stratocratic Despotism. Will you not unite with the patriots throughout the North to effect these objects?

The Administration and the Rebellion.

The Administration has had its own way now since the 4th of March, 1861. All the men and all the money it asked for have been freely placed at its disposal. Never before did any nation pour out its treasures so lavishly on the demand of any government. Never before did any people, in such numbers, place their services at the disposal of any ruler. More than a million and a half of citizens have voluntarily enlisted in the Federal army and navy. The treasure of the nation has been exhausted to supply the army and navy with munitions of war, and recourse has been had to the issue of Government promises to pay to the extent of hundreds of millions of dollars.

And with what effect? What has the Administration effected by the immense sacrifice of the lives of not less than 250,000 of American citizens, and by the expenditure of some fifteen hundred millions of dollars, every dollar of which is to-day a mortgage upon every man's property and every man's labor for generations to come? How much nearer is the Administration now to the successful suppression of the rebellion than it was a year ago? How much nearer is it to a restoration of a Union than it was then? It is, my fellow-citizens, farther off than it ever was from the accomplishment of these objects. It is not in the power of this Administration, or the party which dominates over the Government, to put an end to the rebellion or to restore the Union. And why? I will tell you by an illustion. If you desired to convert Pagans to Christianity, whom would you send to do it? Would you send Christian missionaries, or Infidel scoffers? So if you desire to suppress the rebellion and restore the Union, whom will you depute to perform that service? An Administration which was placed in power on the principle that free and slave States could not live together in peace, keep a party in power which scoffed at those who devoted themselves to the preservation of the Union, and derided them as " Union Savers ?" As well might you send

Infidels to convert Pagans to Christianity as hope to put down the rebellion and save the Union by means of the Administration and of keeping the Abolition-Republican party in power.

It is my deliberate conviction, fellow-citizens, that the rebellion cannot be put down, that peace can never return to our country, that the Union can never be restored while the Abolition-Republican party has control of the Federal Government. If you think otherwise, keep this party in power still longer. If you think with me, elect such public servants as will administer the Government, as will have the confidence of the people at large, and as will conform their acts to the Constitution of the United States. It is for the people to determine whether or not the rebellion shall be put down, whether or not peace and prosperity shall be again the portion of the American people, whether or not we shall again be one nation and one people.

These events can never occur under the domination of Abolition-Republicanism. The Government must be administered, to be done successfully, on the principles which brought the nation into existence, which stimulated its growth in wealth, its increase in population, its power in war, its prosperity in peace.

With the rule of Abolition-Republicanism, you can have domestic war to your hearts' content; you can have a dismemberment of the Union; you can have a national debt such as burdens no other country on the face of the globe; you can have such onerous taxation as no other people ever experienced; you can have all the afflictions of fanaticism, despotism, tyranny and ignorance which characterized the most odious government of which history makes mention. Continue the Abolition-Republican party in power, elect to office the candidates presented for your suffrages by this party, and you will have just such a government and just such effects of bad government as you have been experiencing for a year and a half past. Your fathers, and even yourselves, execrated such governments as those which bring calamities upon the people and oppress them unnecessarily. What is there pleasant, agreeable or profitable in the state of things in which you now live that you should desire to continue its existence?

The Administration and the Union.

The Union can never be restored, fellow-citizens, under or by the Lincoln Administration, nor by the party which elected Mr. Lincoln to the Presidency. The people of the Southern States have no confidence in the Administration, and they will never voluntarily make any agreement with it, or with the party which they believe to be the cause of the war. Neither has the Democratic party of the North confidence in the Administration. How can the loyal citizens of the North believe that an Administration which suspends the Constitution, which arrogates to itself powers which the Constitution expressly withholds from every branch of the Government, how can they believe that an Administration which is thus disloyal to the Constitution can be trusted with the restoration of the Union?

And how can the Abolition-Republican party be in earnest in its professions of loyalty to the Constitution and devotion to the Union? It acquired power on the principle that the Constitution was a covenant with death. It acquired control of the Government on the principle that the Union was a league with hell. Has the party in power changed its principles? If it has, where is the evidence of this change, in word or act? If it has not changed its principles, how can this party be in favor of restoring the Union, or of preserving the Consiitution?

Has the Administration abjured the principles on which it was raised to power? If it has, where is the evidence of this change, in its declaration or acts? Is there any evidence of such a change? None whatever. On the contrary, have we not evidence daily in the suspension and abrogation of the Constitution in relation to loyal citizens of the United States, that the Administration regards the Constitution as of no binding force, as a thing of no validity as between citizens and the Government.

What confidence then can can there be that the Administration will be able to restore the Union, when it is evident that it has no respect for the Constitution except as the Constitution favors its policy and conduct?

Whoever of you, then, fellow-citizens, is in favor of restoring the Union, should favor also a change of Administration, a change of Congressmen, for it is only by effecting such a change that the Union and peace can possibly be restored. Under the existing Administration, there can be neither Union nor peace, nor prosperity nor happiness; neither can there be the exercise of the Constitutional rights of the people of the North.

All this must be as apparent to every one of you as it is to me, and to me it is as clear to my mind as the noonday sun is to my sight.

What has the Party in power done for the Country?

Now I ask you this question, fellow-citizens, to bring to your recollection the miseries which the party in power has brought upon the country. Need I recount those miseries to arouse your patriotism and to excite your indignation? Look back to the period, not long since, before this party had acquired influence in the country, and control of the Government. How stood we then, in relation to each other as a people, and in relation to the world as a Nation? At peace among ourselves; in the enjoyment of a prosperity unexampled in the world's history; reveling almost in the bounties of nature; acquiring wealth with a rapidity unprecedented by any other people of which we have any knowledge; and rivaling all cotemporary nations in the majesty of our power and in the splendor of our National glory. How stand we now, under the influence of less than two years of Abolition-Republican rule? Our domestic peace has been changed by the "Irrepressible Conflict" to fratricidal war. The enjoyment of our prosperity has been turned to the bitter cup of adversity, which we are forced to drink. Our bounteous plenty is wrested from us by the Administration policy which makes our productions valueless, and which imposes on the necessaries of life and the implements of labor, husbandry and manufactures, taxation beyond our ability to pay. Our Constitutional rights of security to life and person and protection to property, are abrogated. If these be the first fruits of Abolition-Republican rule, what might we anticipate the full crop of its domination to be in its effects upon the country, the government; upon persons and property? You, fellow-citizens, as well as I, judge. Reflect, then, in time. Judge before the time might come when your judgment may lose its effect, and act while you have the right of suffrage left as a means to redress grievances and to manifest your will as American citizens. In a little while the right of suffrage will be among the things that were, unless you restore the other rights which have been already violated.

Principles of the Abolition and Republican Party.

The fundamental principle of the Abolition and Republican party, is embraced in the doctrine enunciated by Lincoln and Seward, that the Free and Slaveholding States could not agree in peace under the same government, and hence they proclaimed the "irrepressible conflict" as the watchword and rallying cry of their party. They determined that the States South as well as North should abolish slavery, or leave the Union; and no sooner was the election of Mr. Lincoln to the Presidency known to be certain, than the Abolition and Republican party began to lay their plans for the abolishment of slavery, or failing in that, the dismemberment of the Union. This was the only alternative they presented to the country.

What is the IRREPRESSIBLE Conflict? Does not every intelligent citizen know the meaning of this "Irrepressible Conflict?" Does not every one know that it means no Union with Slaveholders? that it means disunion and separation, rather than the Union as our fathers made it? Now the whole end, aim and object of Abolitionism and Republicanism was and is to change our form, system and principles of Government, not by Constitutional means, but by the exercise of arbitrary power. The first step was to secure the National Administration, this done, the Army and Navy—the whole power of the Goverment would become subject to the domination and subservient to the designs of Abolitionism and Republicanism. The "Irrepressible Conflict" could then be not only inaugurated, but carried into practical effect.

A party avowedly sectional in its conception, and whose first lispings were derision of national men of all other parties as "Union Savers," succeeded in acquiring control of the Government

With the "Irrepressible Conflict" as a fundamental principle, the whole force and power and influence of the Government was to be directed to the attainment of Abolition ends. As a consequence, an inevitable effect, a necessary concomitant of the "Irrepressible Conflict," the President's

Emancipation Scheme

is proclaimed as an Administration measure of the Abolition-Republican party. And what is this scheme? It is briefly to emancipate the four million (4,000,000) slaves of the South without compensation to their owners. Now, fellow citizens, what will be the effect pecuniarily, morally and socially, of the emancipation of these slaves? Let us consider it together, you in your homes in Iowa, I in this old building, in which a Patriot Congress once legislated for the well being of our then happy country. I will make suggestions for your consideration. Reflect on them, and use your judgment and understanding and your suffrage, as you may be convinced of what is right.

Emancipation in its Social Aspects.

Suppose these slaves are freed, what would we do with them? The general understanding among Abolitionists and Republicans is, that such of them as please to do so, might come North, and mingle among the white race. Are you in favor of this being done? I tell you candidly that I am not; and why? Not because I would treat the unfortunate negro cruelly or unjustly, or even harshly, but because the incorporation of persons of the negro race among the white race will be productive of evils for which not all the good that philanthropy can accomplish, will be able to compensate. Socially, the races can never be equal, while by being brought in contact with and in proximity to each other that portion of the white race dependent upon daily labor for the maintenance of life will be brought down from its present condition to the degrading servitude of the black race. Perhaps this is what the Abolitionists desire and design by favoring emancipation.

Need I suggest to you, fellow-citizens, the other evils which will be engendered in society by the contact and proximity to each other of the white and black race. Those of you who have not reflected on the question in this aspect had better lose no time in giving it your serious consideration. Imagine what a state of society you would have when crowds of debauched negroes gather in your towns and villages and hamlets, and on the highways and byways of travel, and imagine these places to be filled by negroes of the most degraded character, and you will have some idea of the state of society to which Abolitionism invites you.

Colonization.

But the President proposes to colonize the negroes. How and where?. If we must pay for colonizing them besides, so much the worse. There is not money enough in the country, nor property enough to raise it on by mortgage and taxation to colonize the slaves. The thing is wholly impracticable, and no statesman of ordinary common sense would think seriously of getting rid of the black race in that way. It will not, it cannot be done, but the attempts to do it will involve the country in debt, and keep it excited and convulsed with the discussion of the question. Let us get rid of it by scouting the whole scheme of emancipation and colonization, and by insisting that the negroes shall be left where they are till the South itself chooses to be rid of them and to find some other place for their future abode than the United States. I need not say to you that I am opposed to emancipation and colonization otherwise than by the action of the Slave States. I am both opposed to paying for the colonization of these slaves, or suffering them to run loose in the Northern States.

Inequality of Taxation.

Another unjust principle of the Abolition Republican party is the inequality of taxation which it imposes upon one section of the country, and the discrimination it makes in favor of other sections. Need I remind you that the Western States, you among the people of the West, are taxed onerously, unequally and unjustly, as compared with your fellow-citizens of New England. Your means, for example, is in lands principally and farm stock, except what might be invested in merchandize and manufactures, while a large portion of the means of New England, New York, and Pennsylvania is invested in Government securities. Now, these securities, bearing interest which you will be taxed to pay, are exempted entirely from taxation, while your means invested in farms, stock, merchandize or manufactures, must pay an onerous and burdensome tax. So again, you are not a manufacturing people, while the people of New England, Pennsylvania, and to a large extent those of New York are. Now, what does Abolitionism and Republicanism do for you? It first legislates a heavy tariff upon such commodities as you most use, thus compelling you to pay an average of forty per cent. more for many of the necessaries of life and implements of husbandry than you would pay under other circumstances. This tariff is put on to put money into the pockets of eastern manufacturers at the expense of the people of the West. I refer you to the Federal tax bill for the proof that every article of New England manufacture, on which a tax is imposed, is protected by having a higher tax imposed upon similar articles of foreign manufacture.

Frauds on the Government.

Need I remind you, fellow-citizens, that under the Lincoln Administration, and by the collusion of some members of the Cabinet, frauds have been perpetrated on the Government by which not less than a hundred millions of dollars in the aggregate have been stolen from the Treasury. The VAN WYCK REPORT made to Congress by a Committee, a majority of whose members were Republican members of Congress, shows conclusively, by sworn testimony, that these frauds were perpetrated for the benefit of partisan friends of the Administration. It has transpired, through a debate in Congress, that thirty millions of dollars disappeared unaccountably from the Treasury by the action of the War Department, or more likely by the order of the Secretary of War, Cameron, yet, instead of holding Cameron to an account for this high-handed and outrageous act, he was transferred from the War Department to represent the American people at the Court of a friendly power, and the President of the United States avowed himself responsible for the delinquencies of his Secretary, but gives no satisfaction to the Government or people for the frauds which the Secretary committed.

Nor has any of the numerous Government swindlers been held to account for their acts, while loyal citizens, whose only offense is that they complained of these frauds, are being arrested and incarcerated arbitrarily and illegally.

Political Generals.

One of the causes, if it be not the principal and only cause why the war has not been brought to an end long ago, with comparatively little loss of life and treasure, is the appointment of mere politicians and partisan favorites to the chief commands of the army. Fremont, Banks, and Cassius M. Clay, from the Abolition party, and Butler, Dix, and others, from the Democratic party, were appointed Major Generals, not because they knew anything about the art of war, but because they were presumed to have political influence. Now, what has been the result of these appointments? Neither of these generals has fought a battle successfully. Under Fremont's military administration, Missouri was lost. Banks was driven out of Virginia by Stonewall Jackson. Butler sacrificed his men at Big Bethel, and made his name infamous at New Orleans, besides bringing upon the American name the reproach of the civilized world, and Dix is doing a service which could be done as well by a sub-lieutenant. The officers of the army who have had experience are placed under the command of those and other political Generals, and the result is very naturally what the army has experienced in defeat and disaster. This is but one of the numerous blunders of the Administration by whose means not less than two hundred and fifty thousand citizen soldiers of the Northern States have been sacrificed to death, or live tortured by wounds or loss of limbs, besides involving the people in a debt which will grind both the present and future generations to the dust merely to pay the interest on this onerous burden. Is this not so, fellow-citizens? Which of you doubts it? If any one of you does, happy for you it is, perhaps, that your credulity exempts you for the time being from experiencing the sad reality which has become the inevitable doom of the American people.

What is to be Done?

I will tell you what I think should be done, fellow-citizens. If it be desirable to restore a constitutional government to this country, the first thing to be accomplished is to restore to authority in the Government public servants who have some respect for the Constitution, who are in favor of a restoration of the Union, and who will subject themselves, as all others do, to the dominion of the laws. Abolitionism must be put down in the North, before Secessionism can be put down in the South; for while the cause of Secessionism exists in one section, the effect of Abolitionism will exist in the other section. I propose, then, that we put Abolitionism out of power in the North; and this being done, Secessionism will fall in the South without the loss of life or treasure to put it down.

Who favors the War?

Those who favor the continuance of the war, take notice, are interested persons. First, those who have commissions in the army, or who are connected with the army in some profitable occupation, as Quartermasters, Sutlers, Commissaries, and Contractors. Second, those who are engaged in furnishing material of war, commissary stores, clothing and other equipments for the army. Third, those who expect commissions in the army, or who have a prospect of, and expect to receive, contracts.

These classes of persons and their adherents and friends form the war party of the North. There are, it is true, many patriotic citizens who believe that it is only by the prosecution of the war that the Union can be restored, but the influential portion of the war party is composed of men and women who profit directly and personally by the existing state of things.

Reduce the Salaries and Expenditures.

I propose to reduce the salaries of officers of the army. You know, fellow-citizens, as well as I do, that most of those who have been appointed officers in the army from among ourselves are persons who could scarcely make a decent living at any business. Now those persons receive salaries varying from a hundred dollars a month and rations, to more than twice that amount, besides the opportunities they have, which many of them profit by, to rob the Government and plunder from the enemy. If you elect me as your Representative, I shall introduce a bill in Congress, and vote for its adoption, reducing these salaries to such an extent as to save at least twenty millions of dollars per annum to the people. I shall also introduce and urge the enactment of bills restraining the lavish expenditure of the public moneys, for punishing frauds on the Government, for holding public officers, from the President down, to a strict accountability for public moneys, for equalizing taxes according to the means of the people to pay those exactions, and for reducing both the expenditures of the Government and the taxation of the people, both of which have been enormous, to the lowest possible amount consistent with the public welfare, the necessities of the Government and the interests of the people.

Fellow-Citizens: I have been one among you for nineteen years, during which time I have held such a relation to you as enables you to judge of my fitness for the position to which I am nominated as a candidate for your suffrages.

Submitting these questions to your judgment, and relying upon your intelligence and patriotism,
I remain, very respectfully,
Your fellow-citizen,
D. A. MAHONY.

EFFECT OF THIS ADDRESS ON THE TYRANTS AND THEIR SATELLITES.

As soon as the foregoing address was published, a copy of it got into the prison by some means, and was heard of by the tyrants. Lieutenant Miller was sent to me, by Judge Advocate Turner, to inquire whether I had not made a speech against the Administration, which was published in the newspapers.

I replied, that I had never made a speech in my life that was worth publishing; that, in fact, I was no speaker, and never had made what could be called a speech.

The lieutenant looked at me very incredulously, as much as to intimate that he did not believe me; but I told him the truth, nevertheless. A few days afterwards Lieutenant Miller approached me in the yard, and, after bidding me good day, said, "I was mistaken the other day, when I intimated that you had made a speech." Without waiting for him to say any more, I replied, 'Yes, I knew you were mistaken.'

"But," said he, "you did something worse; you wrote an address, and wrote it since you have been here. Did you write the address, published over your name, to the citizens of your Congressional District in Iowa?"

'Yes, Lieutenant,' I replied. 'I did write that address, and I did send it out from here, notwithstanding the efforts made to prevent me from communicating with my friends and fellow-citizens. It was not enough,' I continued, 'that the tyrants sent and keep me here, in violation of law and of my rights as an American citizen; they attempted to deprive me also of the right of communicating by letters with my fellow-citizens, but I was determined to exercise that right the best way I could, and I have done it. Now let the tyrants make the most of it.'

I expected nothing else but to be put in the guard-house, as several of my fellow-prisoners had been for less offences than I gave, by this plain talk; but to give the lieutenant credit for his treatment of me, he left me without saying a word. It was well, however, that I was not subjected to the indignity of being put in the guard-house; for, in anticipation of such an occurrence being the effect of my Address coming to the knowledge of the tyrants, a determination was agreed on by a sufficient number of the prisoners to resent, in a manner that would be felt, any improper treatment to which I might be subjected in consequence of my writing the Address. Perhaps this resolution was known to our keepers, as they knew most of what transpired by means of the spies and detectives they kept among the prisoners. Be that as it may, I heard nothing more about the Address from any of our jailors.

August 21*st*, 1862.—My incarceration in the Old Capitol took place on the 21st of August, 1862. I was placed with my companion and fellow-victim from Iowa, Mr. Sheward, in Room No. 13, which was occupied besides us by two Virginians and Dr. Stanley, of Chigago.

After being introduced to our room-mates, Sheward and I, according to custom, registered our names. This was done with a lead pencil on the walls. I registered mine

D. A. MAHONY, of Dubuque, Iowa. A victim of partisan malignity, and of the despotism of Abraham Lincoln. August 21st, 1862.

Mr. Sheward registered his in almost a similar manner. The walls were covered almost with similar inscriptions, written generally in a large, bold handwriting, so that there could be no mistaking the names, or misapprehending the sentiments expressed in connection with them.*

My first day in the Old Capitol was spent in "learning the ropes." This we had to do from our room companions, who had been there a few days before us, for no officer of the Old Bastile came near us to give any instruction as to how we were to act or information respecting how our necessities were to be relieved or our wants supplied.

One of our Virginian room-mates seemed to be quite ill, but the ministrations of his companions in the form of large doses of whiskey, had the effect of relieving him sufficiently to give him an appetite, after satisfying which he relaxed again into apparent unconsciousness of being and indifference to transpiring events. Dr. Stanley suggested that the sick man's whiskey be diminished in quantity, which was done, with a very visible and good effect.

As my bed was more that two feet too short, and otherwise uncomfortable, consisting of a very meagre portion of old straw in a dirty tick laid on an elevated floor like a quarter deck on a ship, I did not sleep much. Neither, indeed, did any of my companions, although they all had what are called bunks to lie in. During the night, the challenges of the guards and their never ceasing repetition of all right, No. 5, or all right No. 6—an unusual language for a civilian to hear—aided in keeping us new-comers awake. Our reflections, too, on our situation, had more influence over us than sleep, courted as it was by the fatigue of our long journey from Iowa, and by the want of repose, which we had not enjoyed for several days and nights. The struggle between the weakness of our bodies and the disturbed condition of our minds, kept us in a continued state of agitation. The morning of the 22d of August dawned at last, and we felt that we had spent the first night in the Old Capitol.

August 22d.—We received a visit this day from our Harrisburg neighbors, of No. 10. They were in expectation of having a hearing, and were preparing for the ordeal.

Dr. Stanley addressed a note to the British embassy, stating that he was a British subject, and asking the interposition of the British Minister in his behalf. Mr. Sheward wrote to the Secretary of War, enquiring why he had been arrested and demanding a trial. I addressed a similar letter to the Secretary, but neither of us got any reply. Indeed, we were told that it was useless for us to write letters; nay, that the more letters we wrote to the authorities, the worse it would be for us. But we who had not yet experienced the full measure of the despotism and tyranny of the ruling powers, could not understand the objection there was to our stating the grievances to which we were subjected.

I wrote a letter to my wife, which, as it refers to my arrest and to the course I had pursued previously, I give it here from the original:

Old Capitol Prison,
Washington, D. C., Aug. 22.

My Dear Wife:—I arrived here yesterday, and have spent my first night in prison. I am still as ignorant of the cause why I am here as I was the day of my arrest. This prison is full of persons, some rebels, some citizens of the loyal States, who, like myself, are loyal men, but who have the misfortune of being Democrats. I cannot imagine what benefit it will be to the Government or to the country to arrest and imprison such citizens as myself, who never thought of being disloyal. I do not blame the ruling powers for it so much as I do my accusers, who, I learn indirectly, are some of my personal and political enemies at Dubuque, and in other parts of the State. Senator Grimes, a political opponent but personal friend of mine, told me before I left Burlington that a concerted and systematic effort had been made to effect my arrest, and here I am, the victim of the base conspiracy.

I have not heard a word from home yet, and do not know when I shall, even if you have written, as it is almost impossible to get a letter here, I am told.

There are five of us in one small room; two of them are Virginians, who claim to belong to the Southern Confederacy. One is a Dr. Stanley, from Chicago, accused of being a secessionist; and Mr. Sheward, of Iowa, and myself, who are Union men, but not in the Abolition sense.

Last night I slept, or rather, kept awake on a straw mattrass, laid on a floor which is elevated above the principal floor. The bed and floor are about two feet too short, so I have to lie crippled up all night. Our fare is pretty good for prison life. The bread, especially, is good, and that is all I care much about.

I do not know how long I am to be kept here, or whether I shall be removed to another place; but meantime, write to me here, and have the *Herald* sent to me directed Capitol Prison, Washington, D. C. I might get a look at it occasionally.

You cannot imagine how anxious I am to hear from you, and to know how you are getting along, and how you bear the affliction of my arrest and imprisonment. If the Secretary of War only knew how basely false are any charges against me involving my loyalty, he would have the miserable wretches brought here and punished who have caused my affliction. But as things are now, the Secretary cannot know the truth. He is more apt to listen to and to believe accusations against his fellow-citizens than he is to presume, as he ought to, that men are loyal till they are proved otherwise. Now this arresting of Northern men is going to do a great deal of harm. It will exasperate many persons against the Administration, and might lead to the very worse results. I hope our friends in Dubuque, and in Iowa generally, will bear to the last extremity before manifesting any opposition to the course which the President thinks it proper to adopt. Although I taught this doctrine through the *Herald*, I am strangely accused of advising opposition to the course of the Government. But it is useless to write you such things as this; I do it because my thoughts run in that direction, and I feel indignant at being here without cause.

I have nothing of interest to write you. When I get more acquainted with my fellow-prisoners, I might give you some account of them. Tell Mr. Hutchins that there is a brother of Judge Love, of Iowa, here. He was a Union man till all his neighbors became otherwise, and even now, I believe he is disposed to be so, but refuses to take the oath of allegiance. He is quite an old man, as are many others of the prisoners.

I am badly off for underclothes, but you need not send any, as it would cost more to get them on here than they are worth. I procured some things at Davenport which will keep me along for a little while—perhaps long enough to see me through my troubles.

Give my love to all our friends, and kiss the little ones for me. Tell them to be good children till papa comes home, and pray that this may be soon.

Your letters to me will, of course, be examined, so write nothing which you would not have others see.

Your affectionate
D. A. MAHONY.

Mr. Sheward and I spent the day learning what we could of how to get along in the Bastile. We found that the building was crowded in every part of it. Even the yard was full, literally, of prisoners; and it was so littered up with tents, of which there were five, and straw, and filth, that there was no room to move about. The weather, too, was intensely sultry. Nothing but the Providence of God preserved the prisoners from the natural effects of the filth, heat, and their crowded contact with each other. The first time I had occasion to obey the calls of nature, I was so disgusted with the sight of the place provided for that purpose, that my stomach sickened and I was compelled to turn away.— Oh! reader, reader, could you but know, as we prisoners of State experienced it, what it is to be subjected to the horrors of the Bastile, you would not endure for a day the despotism which degrades American freemen to a far worse condition than the most criminal felon who has ever been convicted in our courts is subjected. I dare not picture the shameful and disgusting sight of twenty prisoners together obeying the calls of nature in an open shed, exposed to the observation not only of their fellow-prisoners, but to the negro women who worked in the prison and to the occupants of a building near by. The accommodation of this horrid place was a sort of trough, all above ground, to hold the excrements, on the edge of which a person had to perch himself to obey nature's call. In this position might be seen at all times of the day, from a dozen to twenty persons. The stench of the place was so sickening that no one could endure it without vomiting the first time he entered the place. How little, thought I, do the American people know of these outrages. But did they even care?

Our meals were served us in room No. 10 by a contraband named Bob, who was blessed with a good share of human kindness. He took a great deal of interest in our welfare, and procured us whatever came in his reach that was fit to eat. Indeed, we had reason to believe that he shared with us some of his own rations. Our breakfast consisted of bread and what was called coffee, but which smelt like stale dishwater. Dinner consisted of bread and what the prisoners called mule meat. It looked, when cooked, like a piece of thick sole leather, steeped in grease and fried. Of course, but little of it was eaten. Our supper was the same as breakfast. By some management, Dr. Stanley, who was in the Old Capitol before Mr. Sheward and me, had made arrangements to procure butter, and owing to this we had butter for our bread—a luxury we found it to be, under existing circumstances.

During the day, as the prisoners had permission to go in the yard at meal times, I went down among the rest, and was introduced to a number of my fellow prisoners, both from the North and South. There were not yet very many prisoners of State from the North; but from the South, especially from the northeastern counties of Virginia, there were quite a number. Most of the southern political prisoners were men of property, and the principal object in arresting them and sending them to the Old Capitol, was to plunder them of their personal property. This they had all experienced. Not only were their negro servants run off, but they were robbed of their cattle, horses, hogs, sheep, grain, hay, and their household furniture. Everything that their patriotic accusers could make a dollar of, or that they could use in any way, was appropriated without ceremony, and even many articles of value which could not be easily moved were wantonly destroyed by the Union "Patriots."

Among the victims who suffered largely from the patriotic cupidity of the satellites of the Administration are the following, whose names I took at the time of my first interview with them: Rev. R. C. Leachman, Prince William County, Va., whose servants to the number of twenty-six were run off, and whose property was stolen and destroyed. John A. Hamsin, of the same county, lost eight servants, and all his personal property. William D. Bartlett lost eight servants. E. Nutt lost thirteen negroes, and all his personal property was plundered by King's Division. William R. Detherage lost four negroes and other property. Meredith Knightmay's premises were entirely devastated. Thomas B. McKay lost seven negroes. B. Hicks lost six negroes, and his property was devastated.

Nearly all the Southern citizens who were in the Old Capitol had the same tale to tell. Most of these gentlemen were Union men, not only up to the time of the secession of Virginia, but even up to the day when their property was plundered by the Union army. The universal testimony of these gentlemen was, that very little distinction was made by the Union soldiers between Southern Union men and Secessionists. If any of the former had property that the soldiers wanted, it was found to be an easy task to accuse them of being disloyal, and no further proof of the charge was ever required. Their property was at once seized and " confiscated," i. e. stolen, and that was the last the owner ever saw or heard of it. To prevent their making any noise about it, they were sent up to the Old Capitol, where, if they were not rebels before, they were made so in that best of institutions for transforming so called Union men into anything opposed to the tyrants who have subverted the Government and made it odious to freemen, North and South.

Aug. 23d.—Returned the call to-day of the Harrisburg Editors in room No. 10. Found them more comfortably located and situated than we in No. 13. They had provided themselves with cooking utensils, and their friends sent them provisions. I observed, also, that their bedding was tolerably good. On inquiry, I learned many things from them which I found to be useful afterwards, among other items, that if a person did not ask for what he needed, he would be apt to do without. The prisoners were not treated so much according to rules or orders, but as they became importunate and demanded what they needed.

The two Virginians were removed from our room to-day, and two victims from Illinois, Dr. Hewitt and John W. Smith, or, as he was called, the Wandering Jew, were brought to No. 13 in the place of those taken away.

We were now five northern men together, and all from the West, strangers to each, notwithstanding that we all were, we have soon become on the best of terms. "A fellow feeling" made us not only wondrous kind, but moulded us into one mind on everything connected with our condition. We almost lost our respective individualities in relation to our mutual benefit, and it was only when one indulged in his peculiar vein of humor or told a story, or acted some part characteristic of himself, that we felt ourselves to be distinct individuals, so blended did we all become in one heart and mind.

The same routine of life was gone through with to-day as on our first day in prison. We began to experience the inconvenience and subjection of confinement. Most of our time was spent in sitting near the barred window of our apartment, looking out on the busy world and reflecting on our situation and the condition of our unfortunate country.

August 24th.—Heavy firing was heard in the distance last night breaking upon the stillness of the Sunday morning. The Confederate prisoners seemed to be well advised by some means that a battle was going on near Warrenton. Pope had superceded McClellan in command of the army of the North, or as it was called, of the Potomac. This gave the Confederates much encouragement. It was known among them in prison that McClellan had been not only deprived of his command, but that he was actually degraded, being left nominally in command of an army, but deprived of every man down to his personal staff and a corporal's guard.

This being Sunday, the prisoners were informed by the Superintendent that there would be preaching in the yard and in Room No. 16. In the yard a Secesh preacher prisoner would preach the Lord God according to Jeff Davis, and in No. 16, an Abolitionist named Spears, according to Abe Lincoln; the prisoners could take their choice. Most of the prisoners went to the yard, not so much to hear the preaching, but to take a little out-door exercise. This, however, could not be indulged in to any great degree, as the yard was filled already by its permanent occupants and by the litter which I have refered to already. As I mean to devote a special notice to this first Sunday in the Old Capitol, I will pass on to the next day.

August 25th.—Nothing of special interest or worthy of comment occurred to-day, except that firing was again heard in the distance, and there were exciting rumors of movements of troops which it was expected would result in heavy and decisive battles Of this the Confederates seemed more aware than we Northerners. They had some means of information which was not vouchsafed to us, and it turned out that they were generally correctly advised both of transpiring events and of anticipated and projected movements.

August 26th.—Dr. Stanley, Mr. Sheward and I, were removed to No. 10, that occupied previously by the Harrisburg Editors. This was a far more comfortable room than 13, being considerably larger, having two windows towards the street, and being better provided with sleeping accommodations, including one sheet to each bunk. We felt comparatively well off in these new quarters. There was a fire-place and grate in the room, so that we could, if permission were given us and we desired to do so, cook our own victuals.

The excitement in the city become intense and visible to us prisoners. Rumors reached the Old Capitol that Pope was retreating before Stonewall Jackson towards Washington. The hopes of the Confederate prisoners, civilians as well as military, beat high in anticipation of the success of the Confederate arms and the consequent capture of Washington as they expected would be the result of a decisive battle between their army and the Union troops under Pope and Banks. The fact that Gen. McClellan was not in command of the Federal forces gave the assurance of success to their side, as they knew that Generals Lee, Jackson, Longstreet and the two Hills were in command of the Confederates, with a veteran army though less in number than that of Pope, Banks and Sigel, on the Federal side. Every gun heard in the distance renewed the agitation of the prisoners and increased the excitement in Washington.

The day was passed in speculations as to the result of the anticipated battle, and the general impression was from the information which reached the Confederate prisoners, that Pope would be defeated, as it was now known he had been a few days before when he lost some of his personal baggage, and was forced to retreat from the line of the Rappahannock.

August 27th.—The excitement in Washington became more and more intense, as the news of Pope's defeat on the Rappahannock, and his subsequent and consequent retreat towards Washington became confirmed. The attempt to keep the public mind in ignorance of the real condition of the army, and the disaster which befell it a few days before, only tended to stimulate the prevailing excitement, and to cause such distrust of the statements made by the War Department as not only to disbelieve any thing emanating from that quarter but to think that the very contrary of its statements were true.

Rapid and heavy firing was heard distinctly during the day, and there was no doubt that a battle was being fought not far distant.

The news boys were not allowed to come with papers in the evening, as usual, but by some means information was received that the Federal Army, under Pope, was being driven towards Washington in confusion. The Confederates, both military and civilians, were quite elated at the news, and we Northerners felt chagrined at the defeat of the Federal Army, and exasperated at the imbecility of the Administration, its conduct of the war, and its tyrannic course towards ourselves.

The continuous firing, heard distinctly all day, kept every one in the Old Capitol absorbed in one thought, the battle which was going on. How was it going to terminate in relation to the armies engaged in it? Which would conquer? If the Confederates, would they press their advantages towards Washington and capture the city? If the Federals, would it end the war? Such were the speculations all day. The firing ceased gradually towards evening, but was renewed at intervals during the night.

August 28th.—The firing of heavy arms was renewed this morning, and at a distance which judged by the sound was much nearer than it appeared for some days past. It was evident by the excitement observed in the city through the prison windows that a general alarm pervaded the people. Numbers were observed leaving by the Bladensburg Road. During the day news came of another defeat, amounting to a disaster to the Federal army, at Bull Run. The loss of the Army was estimated variously at from eight to twenty thousand. Excitement, confusion and alarm reigned in Washington. The prisoners of the Old Capitol participated in the general feeling. Some of them were so nervous under the apprehension that the city would be shelled next day by Stonewall Jackson, that they could not sit down or stand still. We, Northerners, were speculating on our probable fate. Would we be made prisoners by Stonewall Jackson, or released on parole, or discharged unconditionally, and if we should be released, would we be again subjects to the despotism of Abraham Lincoln. These questions were discussed in every aspect they could be made to assume.

August 29th.—The news of yesterday's battle was published to-day, but was not allowed to come to the prison through the news boys. A copy of an evening paper containing the news was however smuggled in by some means. During the day it was understood that an order from Gen. Halleck pressed all the vehicles of the city which could be used for conveying the wounded from the battle field, and long lines of carriages were observed wending their ways along the streets towards that locality. The actual occurrence of the battle seemed to relieve rather than to excite the public mind. It acted as a sort of relaxation to the strained stretch to which the people were subjected for several days. The alarm was by no means less than it had been, but the people went more gently and methodically about their business, and were preparing to leave Washington.

I addressed a letter to the President to-day, informing him of my arrest, and demanding a trial; also suggesting that the course of the Administration in making these arrest in the arbitrary manner in which they had been effected would only tend to raise up the people in hostility to the Government.

I told the President that he had no more right in law to cause my arrest in Dubuque, Iowa, and brought to Washington for trial or to be imprisoned without trial, than I had to order his arrest in Washington and have him taken taken to Dubuque, and imprisoned there. The Superintendent told me after reading my letter that I had better not send it as it would do me no good and would probably do me an injury, but I persisted nevertheless in having it sent. If the President did not receive it, it is because it was suppressed by his subordinates; if he did receive it, he had my opinion of his arbitrary cause and of its probable effects upon the people of the North.

August 30*th.*—A few prisoners captured at the late battles were brought to the Old Capital to-day: they told us more about the battles than the newspapers were allowed to publish, and we were therefore better posted than our fellow citizens who were allowed to call themselves freemen. These prisoners alleged that Pope's defeat was a perfect one; that he had lost all his stores, ordinance and commissary, that his army was completely demoralized, and that it was determined not to fight under such a General. We learned from other sources of information that the Army demanded the recall of Gen. McClellan. Pope was evidently played out. He commenced as a braggart and ended as most braggarts do, in being discomfited.

The excitement of these days made us prisoners almost forget our situation, except in connexion with our prospect of being released by the Confederates.

Our Fredericksburg neighbors were almost in ecstacies at the success of the Confederate arms. They became more confident of success than ever before, and more unsparing of their sarcasm and sneers at the Northern army. Several of them had sons in the Confederate service, and although they were anxious of their fate, as they were likely to have been in the late battles, yet their chief thoughts seemed to be directed to the success of the Confederate army. No sacrifice was too great to make, to effect that paramount object. And yet these Fredericksburg civilians were all but one of the nineteen, Union men, till the course of the Administration and of the Federal army in Virginia, forced the conviction on their minds that the Southern leaders understood better than others did the true character of the party which had succeeded in acquiring control of the Government. These once Union men were now the most inveterate rebels, not from choice, but in self defence.

August 31*st.*—Hundreds of the inhabitants of Washington left the city yesterday, and more are leaving to-day, in apprehension that the city will be taken by the Confederates, who are understood to be but a few miles distant. Rumor says that they are as near by as Munson's Hill, and that they are preparing to shell the city. The Capitol is to be converted into a hospital, for the purpose, it is suspected, of preventing its destruction in case the Confederates should get near enough to fire upon it. The yellow flag which will be hoisted on it, will be a safer protection than the stars and stripes. Alas! to what straits is our once great and glorious country reduced, when it is obliged to have recourse to the protection of a signal of distress to protect its capitol from the destruction threatened by some of its own children.

This is Sunday, but it does not look like the Sabbath, either out doors or in the Old Capitol. Troops and people are in constant motion. The wounded in the late battles are being brought in by the hundred, and numbers of stragglers are passing by, apparently fatigued. Not one of them has his arms with him. Crowds of contrabands are also seen passing by, some with bundles of clothes, others with baskets containing food, eggs, &c. Perhaps they are not all runaways, but they look very much as if they were.

Sept. 1st.—The road towards Bladensburg was thronged all day with vehicles carrying household goods and their owners away from Washington. It is understood that the city is invested by the Confederates, and apprehensions are entertained by the citizens and by the Federal authorities, that an attack will soon be made upon it. Rumor says that Gen. McClellan will be placed in command of the army for the defense of the Capital. The Confederates in the Old Capitol are praying that this might not be so, as they fear that if McClellan should be placed once more at the head of his army, the drooping spirits of the demoralized troops will be revived, and discipline restored. Something must be done soon, or the Capital is lost.

Sept. 2d.—The news of to-day was the order of the President placing Gen. McClellan in command of the army for the defense of the Capital. It read as follows:

HEADQUARTERS OF THE ARMY,
Adjutant General's Office,
Washington, Sept. 2, 1862.

By direction of the President, Major General McClellan will have command of the fortifications of Washington, and of all troops for the defence of the Capital.

By order of the Secretary of War:

E. D. TOWNSEND, Assist. Adj. Gen.

The *Intelligencer* referred to this order, in the following brief but comprehensive article:

"GEN. McCLELLAN IN COMMAND.—The subjoined order, containing the official notification of the command assigned to Gen. McClellan for the defense of the National Capital, will be received with general satisfaction. The fortifications which surround this city were constructed mainly under his eye; and the greater part of his army which may be soon expected to make them the base of both defensive and aggressive operations, has learned to put all confidence in his skill and bravery as a commander. In this confidence the great mass of the loyal people of the United States fully share; and the bare announcement of his appointment to this high command, inspires a sense of security from apprehended dangers."

This order, from what we could hear in the Old Capitol, did more to restore confidence, allay excitement and quiet apprehensions in Washington, than if a hundred thousand new troops had been added to the army. The Confederates in the Old Capitol lost heart as soon as this order was read. The Federal army was no longer, they admitted, without a leader; and they knew that with such a leader as McClellan was admitted to be, the army would soon become efficient and be prepared to resume the offensive instead of remaining as it was, for a week or two past, in the face of the ragged Confederates.

It was alleged that immediately after the result of the battle of the 28th of August became known for certain at the War Department, General Halleck went to the President and told him that either General McClellan or Stonewall Jackson would have possession of the city in twenty-four hours. The President could take his choice. Reduced to this alternative, Mr. Lincoln was compelled to recall General McClellan, whom he degraded and humiliated but a few days before, at the instigation and under the influence of the partisans who wield the President at will.

September 3rd.—Last evening about one hundred and seventy deserters from the Federal Army were brought to this prison. Superintendent Wood, who is a character in his way, refused to receive them at first, swearing out at them and at their guard that this prison was intended for gentlemen, and not for such infernal villains as those deserters. "G—d d—n them," said he, "take them down to the Navy Yard, and shoot every d—n son of a bitch of them." They were taken away somewhere or other, but returned again with an order from head-quarters to Superintendent Wood to receive them. They were accommodated to lodgings on the brick pavement in the yard, and to such shelter as the few tents which have stood there for some time could afford. This morning, after breakfast, we had an opportunity to see them closely, and to converse with them at a distance of some five feet between us. It was amusing to hear the conversations between them and the state and rebel prisoners. The latter taunted the deserters in every conceivable manner which could provoke a person of feeling. The deserters generally gave as a reason for their abandonment of the army that they enlisted to fight for and save the Union; but they found out that it was not for the Union but for the slaves of the South that the war is waged. Many of them declared that they would join Stonewall Jackson's standard if he should make his appearance here. Some one intimated that they would be taken back to their regiments, when one of the deserters replied, "Yes; and so may a horse be taken to water against his will, but will he drink?"

The guards were trebled last night in the prison yard and around the building. Every one of us who happened to be obliged to visit the water closet, as such a place as we have of this kind is called by courtesy, were escorted to the place by a guard with musket shouldered. It was evident that apprehensions were entertained by the authorities that an attempt would be made to break prison, not by the state prisoners, who would not leave if they could, but by the rebels and deserters. These deserters are a hard-looking crowd. They are mostly from New York, but among them are natives of other States, and of Ireland and Germany. Their conversation is both amusing and disgusting. Most of them evidently were swells, rowdies or burglars before they joined the army, and it has not improved their morals nor their manners to have been in the service of Uncle Samuel, or honest Old Abe.

September 4th.—After breakfast this morning the prisoners, as usual, went to the yard for a few minutes' recreation. The deserters were drawn up in line preparatory to be marched off to breakfast, they being left for the last to eat. I was able to take a good look at them in this position, and to study their characters by the expression of their countenances and their antics. Some of them are quite cheerful, others are much cast down. A few Yankees among them have become quite patriotic, especially when the officer of the day is within hearing distance. One of the rebel prisoners taunted a deserter of this class with having skedaddled near Richmond. The deserter had been boasting of what sort of a reception Stonewall Jackson would receive if he should make his appearance in this city.

"What! from such fellows as you?" said the rebel.

"Well, if I couldn't do it," said Yankee deserter, "Pope can."

"Pope," replied the rebel; "isn't he the General

who told his men that he meant to keep his headquarters on horseback, who then threw away picks and shovels, and who was never to be seen by the enemy but with his face towards them?"

"Well," said deserter, "what has he done?"

"He has shown his —— to Stonewall Jackson."

Thus ended the conversation between the two disputants. Turning my eyes from the party, I noticed one of the lieutenants not far distant, for whose ear the Yankee deserter's part of the conversation was evidently intended.

I went down at bedtime to see how the deserters were disposed of for the night. Along the walk to the privies was strewn some straw on the brick pavement. Lying upon this as close as they could pack themselves side by side, were most of these wretches. Some few of them were enveloped in a kind of blanket, others had no other covering than their clothes and heaven's canopy. The moon was shining brightly, revealing every face and form of this abandoned crowd of human beings, some of whom I learn will be shot, others imprisoned, and some few sent to their regiments. I hear it said that among the crowd are a few who were never in the army, and who were brought here only for the purpose of palming them off as deserters, so as to make five dollars a head on the transaction, this being the price the Government pays for capturing this class of soldiers. The only noticable incident which occurred to our observation to-day was the challenge of one of the guards beneath our room window on the pavement below to the ladies who stood at a corner chatting nearly a square distant, but in sight of the prison. The guard called at them to go on, and they not complying readily, the fellow raised his musket to a ready, and threatened them with its contents. The ladies did not wait for further admonition, but walked off. No one dares to walk in the direction of the prison without being brought to a halt by the guard, and if any sign of recognition or sympathy is made by any one passing the streets, the offender is arrested at once, and put in the prison. Some of our Federal prisoners who were subjected to the rebel treatment down in Dixie complain bitterly of the course pursued towards them. With how much more reason may we state prisoners complain of the treatment to which we are subjected by our Abolition persecutors?

Sept. 5th.—A number of gentlemen from Illinois arrived here to-day under arrest. Among them are Judge Duff, of Benton, Judge Mulkey, of Cairo, and A. P. Corder, Esq., a District Attorney.— These Illinois prisoners—Judges, Attorneys, Doctors, respectable farmers and all, as they are, were obliged to feed like hogs at the trough under the hospital, with the herd of cowardly deserters, and filthy and ragged rebels. This was the most degrading subjection to which the Prisoners of State were reduced, because it was one which even the spirit, no matter how brave in fortitude, could not resist or overcome. Hunger will compel even a proud, defiant spirit to eat one's bread wherever he can get it. But what a sight was this in the United States of America to see a throng of freemen,— freemen ! no, not freemen any longer, but men who, but a short time before were freemen, some of them administering justice from the Bench, others who were advocates of justice at the Bar, others in the practice of the humane and honorable profession of medicine—to see these men in a crowded throng, coatless, rushing to be first at the trough set by the Government for the victims of despotism to eat at, so that a clean tin plate and knife and fork could be procured—this would surely provoke the indignation of the American people, unless they have lost all sense of that propriety and dignity of character for which they were once distinguished and characterized.

Sept. 6th—To-day, for the first time, we are put on cracker rations. This, we are told by our little bird, is owing to the arrival here of Burnside's corps d'armee, which has to be furnished with bread rations. Loud and terrible are the curses of the State Prisoners generally at being subjected to this old cracker ration. One of my room companions, Mr. Sheward, swears that the barrel from which the crackers given to us to-day were taken, was marked 400 B. C.—an indication of their age which the reader will understand without explanation.— The crackers were indeed old and hard. I would not complain of their hardness, for I happen to have a good set of teeth—but they beat me in the age. Our first meal of them did not lessen their number very perceptibly, especially as Mr. Sheward begged a piece of bread from one of the contrabands, who appear to be better supplied than either the State Prisoners, or the prisoners of war. We are promised bread for to-morrow by Superintendent Wood, who appears to be determined that we shall not want for this necessary article of food.

Near bed-time, the Superintendent came along with a bundle of clean sheets on his arm, the first indication since we came here that our bed clothing was ever to be changed. In room 13, where we had been first quartered, there was but one of the bunks which was furnished with a sheet. I had none, nor blanket either, while in that room. But in Number 10, where I am now, the room was better furnished, owing I presume to the exertions of the editors of the Harrisburg Patriot and Union, its former occupants. The bunks here had a sheet a-piece, and by watching our opportunity, Mr. Sheward and myself managed to procure another one each. To be sure, from all appearances, they had never been subjected to contact with soap and water—but no matter, they were sheets, and we were glad to have them. Under these circumstances, it was both a relief from filth, and a luxury to be presented with a clean sheet a-piece.

This evening we indulged in venting our indignation on our Abolition persecutors and on the Administration. We reflected upon the once happy condition of the American people, and of their proud position as a free nation, enjoying their natural and political rights under the protection of the Government of their own institution. But alas! how changed is all this now! Instead of the Constitutional Government instituted by the State and People, power has been usurped and exercised by the Administration to restrain the freedom of speech and of the press, to incarcerate freemen for exercising their rights, and for performing their duty as American citizens, and to perpetuate the rule of fanatic partisanship over our once free, happy, and prosperous country. And strange to say, the people bear it all, submit to it all, hold out their arms to be manacled by the tyrants in power, and bend their heads that the yoke may be put on without trouble to their tyrant rulers.

Sept. 7th.—This is Sunday, the third since my arrest, the second of my arbitrary and illegal imprisonment. I slept late. The luxury and comfort of a clean sheet might be the cause of it, or, more likely, it may have been owing to the fact that I begin to feel dull and heavy at my incarceration. I opened my eyes and saw the breakfast things on the table— a plate of the same crackers which had been furnished the night before—a plate of what we call mule beef, and which we seldom eat, three small cups, a cup of sugar, camp knives which stain any thing they touch, forks to match, and a teapot of what is called coffee, but which looks as if the cof fee-slops of some hotel table were all put together and boiled over. Well, there is no help for it. We are now under Abolition rule, and whoever the tyrants in power single out as victims of persecution must submit, it seems, to be deprived both of their rights and liberties and subjected to such treatment as these hell hounds choose to inflict on him. How long is this to last? How long will the American People suffer themselves to be thus humiliated, degraded, persecuted—their rights violated, their persons outraged, their interests sacrificed, their country given over to desolation and spoliation? Will they wait till there is nothing left to save, till all that is dear and valuable to them as men, as Americans, as freemen, shall have been sacrificed to the fanaticism of the day? The time has come to answer. Soon it will be too late either to answer or to act.

Before dinner a copy of the Philadelphia Sunday Mercury made its way into the prison. Some one told me it contained an article reflecting on the despotism of the Administration. I hunted round for the paper, found it, and read it with avidity and gratification. It commented on the arrest of Charles Ingersoll, of Philadelphia, as unjust and unwise—two truths which the ruling powers should understand and appreciate. The same paper contained a patriotic address from Mr. Hughes, Chairman of the Democratic Central Committee of Pennsylvania, in which he recommends that the 17th of September be commemorated as the day of the adoption of the Constitution of the United States. This number of the Mercury contained also an article from the Dayton (Ohio) Empire, which did the State Prisoners good to read. The Empire, it appears, had been reproached with being a " stickler for the Constitution," as all of us State Prisoners are, and taking this reproach for its subject, it showed what the

Constitution is, what it was designed to be, and how it is violated and disregarded by the Administration and the Abolition-Republican Party.

We had not seen so much sound doctrine since our incarceration in this place as was contained in this one number of the Sunday Mercury.

Dinner was late to-day. Some of us felt weak for want of food; and when dinner came, although it was composed of the old hard biscuit or crackers which were sent up to us for supper the night before, and the old beef which goes among us by the name of mule beef, still we ate heartily. We are without butter to-day, as we were for supper last night. For neither love nor money could we procure a pound of butter. The Prison Commissary refused or neglected to purchase any, and so we were obliged to do without. After dinner, as we generally do, the State Prisoners took a turn in the yard, which by the way is now crowded with the deserters I mentioned before. The place is made disagreeable by their uncleanliness. Poor wretches cannot help being filthy, as most of them have no change of clothes, and they have to sleep, as I remarked before, on loose straw strewn on the walk or pavement along the yard fence. It appeared as if an examination was going on respecting them, as Lieutenant Miller was calling out the names of some of them, and these, in their turn, were being taken into the official's headquarters. A good deal of badinage was kept up between the candidates for examination and their fellows whose turn had not yet come for this ordeal. One fellow inquired of another, "Jim, when will you be hanged?"

"Hanged, the devil," replied the fellow addressed as Jim; "I expect to be shot."

"Shot, eh, my laddie?" said the other; "I thought they hanged deserters."

"That's what they'll do with you," returned Jim.

"Is it?" said the other. "Then I hope you'll come to see the rope put on."

A general ha! ha! was indulged in by the crowd of deserters, showing how indifferent or callous they were of their fate, and how little they dreaded being convicted or punished for their alleged crime. One of these deserters is said to have offended in this way six times over, and he threatens to do so again if he should have a chance.

This is Sunday evening—the close of a long, dull Sunday for us State Prisoners. A Yankee Abolition preacher named Spears and his wife were sent here to-day to preach their abominable trash to the prisoners. Of course I did not go to hear them, but am told by some of my companions, who went to gratify their curiosity and to indulge their sense of the ludicrous at the expense of these Abolitionists, that the exercises commenced by an address from Mrs. Spears, who is one of the strong-minded women we hear of. She appeared before the audience with a forefinger to her nose, and eyed the crowd as no woman can or could but an Abolition she-male. She did not talk long, as the crowd did not appear disposed to listen to her farrago.

Sept. 8th—The prison is full of rumors this morning of the advance of the Confederates into Maryland. The Confederate prisoners here are almost beside themselves with joy. They cannot, indeed they will not, try to contain themselves. They hurrah for Jackson through the barred windows, and sympathizers can be seen passing along the streets almost every minute, who make some sign to the prisoners of their feelings. This has to be done unknown to the guard who are pacing the pavement below; but no vigilance can detect these sympathizers, who elude the most watchful of the argus-eyed patrols.

A new arrangement has been made to-day by

which the Prisoners of State are allowed to take a half hour's recreation by themselves in the yard, after meals. This is an improvement in some respects over the arrangement existing heretofore, which gave only a half hour's recreation at meal time to all the prisoners, rebel, military and State, at the same time. The objection to the latter arrangement was, that the yard is too small to give so many persons an opportunity to move about. The consequence was that the whole crowd of prisoners, sometimes nearly six hundred in number, were huddled together as closely as they could comfortably stand. The new arrangement will give us a chance to walk about.

I received an intimation in writing to-day from the Provost-Marshal, that the names of my correspondents must be written in full to their letters, or that I should not receive them hereafter. This was caused by my wife having failed to write her name in full to a letter received by me to-day. Only think of it, ye American freemen and freewomen, that it is in the power of a petty official, or of any person in office, to prescribe how a wife shall subscribe her name when addressing her husband, who happens to be a victim of the persecution of Lincolnism.

Sept. 9th.—Another lot, over ninety in number, of alleged deserters was brought here last night. I happened to come in contact with two of them this morning, and learned from them that they were both wounded at the battle of Seven Pines, and both are disabled. The object in arresting them was to make five dollars a-piece on them. These two men told me that most of their companions are wounded soldiers who have not yet got well enough to go back to their regiments.

Among the Confederate prisoners brought here yesterday is one who is almost barefooted. One of the guard asked him if that was the way the rebel Government treated its soldiers. The Confederate prisoner replied, "We do not fight for pay or clothing, and we will fight you barefooted till hell freezes over." This ended the conversation.

We had the best dinner to-day that was given us since our incarceration. The meat was tolerable, and it was pretty well cooked. We ate of it heartily. Indeed we needed a hearty meal, as we were becoming weak for want of nourishing food.

Col. Kohler, a Federal officer, imprisoned here, was allowed to visit our room to-day. Among other things which he told us about the war, was this: When his regiment, the 12th Pennsylvania cavalry, was at Manassas some weeks since, Gen. McDowell ordered the regiment to do some work on the railroad. The Colonel protested against his cavalry being employed in such a service, especially as there were some hundreds of negroes at the place, fed by the Government. These negroes were furnished with fresh bread every day, while the soldiers were supplied with crackers half the time which were so old and hard as to become unpalatable. Many of the soldiers picked up and ate bread which had been thrown away by the negroes, so abundantly were the contrabands furnished with bread rations, while the soldiers, who were fighting the battles of the country were obliged to pick up on the highways the leavings of these negroes. This is one of the beauties of Lincolnism.

Several prisoners have been brought here to-day from the neighborhood of Fredericksburgh. Among them were some negroes, one of them, a large, intelligent spoken fellow, was very anxious to see his master, who, having been paroled, was not brought to the prison. I asked this slave whether he would go back to his master. "Yes, sir," said he, "I don't want to stay here; my master always treated me well, and I don't want to leave him." "But," said I, "they will keep you here, or send you north." "Well, massa," said he, "if they won't let me go home, I can't help it; but, if they will let me away, I will go with my master." In connection with this, I may say, from conversations I have had with nearly every one of the male contrabands around the premises, that every one of them desires, and designs, if he should have an opportunity, to go back to his master. Most of them were brought here against their will, and, if left free to choose, they will go back to their old masters, in preference to remaining here or going north.

September 10*th.*—Dr. Broaddus, one of the Fredericksburgh hostages, who left here nearly two weeks ago to effect an exchange of himself and companions, returned this morning with the glad tidings to his comrades that he had been successful. These men have been kept here nearly a month as hostages for seven Union men who were imprisoned by the Confederate Government for some alleged crime or other. These hostages are almost beside themselves with joy at their deliverance from the restraints and hardships of this Republican Bastile. The Confederates have fared vastly better, however, than most others, as their friends and sympathizers in Baltimore and Washington furnished them not only with most of the necessaries of life, but with luxuries also. They received, at one time, three barrels of bottled porter, ten pounds of tea, piles of clothing, groceries, &c. They lived, indeed, like fighting cocks, but not at the expense of the Government. They cooked most of their own victuals, and ate their meals in their rooms.

Some two hundred more deserters from a Pennsylvania regiment arrived here this evening. They say that the bounty promised them has not been paid, and therefore the contract between them and the Government has been violated. They give the guard and officers a great deal of trouble. They are a set of dare-devils, and will do mischief, if they be left without restraint. The guard is much more afraid of them than they are of the guard.

Troops have been moving about all day. We hear that heavy bodies are going out to meet Stonewall Jackson, who seems to be a terror to the Federal army.

Two more prisoners have been domiciled in our room to-day, making our number six in a room where there is a place for five only. One had to take the floor for it. The atmosphere became so foul, after lying down, that we had to open the windows and door of our prison room to breathe pure air.

September 11*th*.—I find that the two hundred deserters referred to in my notes of yesterday are Philadelphians. They are a hard set of fellows, but they have been badly treated. The bounty promised them as an inducement to enlist has been withheld, which is the cause of their mutiny, they being in reality mutinous in their conduct, and are deserters. The moral effect on them of withholding their bounty has had the worst possible effect on their military spirit. I never saw a more insubordinate harem scarem set of fellows in my life. They do almost what they please. Poor fellows, they had the yard for their bed last night, without a particle of covering save their uniforms; still they appeared lively this morning and in right good spirits. They appear to be perfectly indifferent to any fate that might befall them, but swear they will not fight till their wrongs are redressed, and their rights respected, and the obligations of the Government due them performed.

September 12*th*.—We had a sensation to-day, on a small scale. Dr. Hewitt, a next door room companion of ours, came rushing into our room and told us, in an excited manner, that an investigation was going on down stairs with a view to ascertain who are Knights of the Golden Circle, and that it is determined to have every member of the order executed immediately. He said the investigation was being conducted by a committee in the hall of the Old Capitol. A rush was made for the scene of operations, and on coming in sight of the premises, one of the most ludicrous scenes was presented to our view. Several of the prisoners were stripped to the buff, with their shirts in their hands, examining them closely. Their fingers were busy dragging the "Knights of the Golden Circle" from their hiding places, and no sooner were they caught than summary execution was inflicted on them between the thumb nails of the executioners. The reader can imagine far better than I can describe this scene. It was one of the most ludicrous imaginable, however, and provoked such a roar of laughter as was never before heard in the Old Capitol. This search for these "Knights of the Golden Circle" is being extended to every room in the Prison. Thousands of these miscreants have been discovered and summarily executed; but, like the martyrs, who are said to be the seed of the Church, the blood of these killed lice seems to generate a thousand others for every one that is slain. Lice, bugs, or, as they are called here, chinches, and mice, hold almost unlimited sway in this once Temple of American Patriotism, now converted into a loathsome prison house.

One of our prison companions, Dr. Hewitt, of Springfield, Illinois, became so infested with the prison lice, that to get rid of some of them, he bundled up his under-clothes and threw them into the privy sink. Up to this time, going on the fourth week of the incarceration of Mr. Sheward of Iowa, and myself, we have been furnished with one clean sheet and a clean blanket, our other bedding being in use not only by ourselves since our incarceration, but from its appearance, ever since the prison was opened, and by every sort of persons, clean and filthy, sick and well.

The Superintendent is not to blame for this, for, according to his own statement, which I believe to be true, the prisoners are better treated then the powers above him desire. General Mansfield, who I am informed, was once Military Governor in this city, ordered that all the prisoners should have nothing else but soldiers' rations, concluding like all other fanatics, that every person accused no matter how or by whom of disloyalty, is *ipso facto*, a traitor who should be treated accordingly. Hence, he ordered that the prisoners should be kept in close confinement, and if I have not misunderstood my informant, handcuffed, and kept on crackers and water. Is not this the decent, proper treatment to which American citizens should be subjected on the mere accusation of some malicious personal enemy or partisan adversary. This Administration in its treatment of political prisoners has cast in the shade some of the blackest crimes of the French Jacobins, which have caused these miscreants to be execrated by even the barbarians of later days. It would make the blood of every American, whose blood retains the semblance of American manhood, rise to see some hundreds of his fellow-citizens in this prison of all ages and conditions in life, rush from their dens to the pen where they are fed. The sight and place is so loathsome to many of them, that they pick up a piece of bread and a junk of what we call mule meat, from its color, texture, taste and toughness, and break for the yard or for their dens to eat it in communion with their own thoughts. I met yesterday, Judges Duff and Mulkey of Illinois, each with a piece of bread and a tin cup, of what is called by courtesy, coffee, in his hands. They had been to the prisoners feed pen, and though hungry enough to eat, they could not stomach their food until they found relief for their senses of sight and smell in the open air. I have not as yet been in this feed pen, happening to be placed on the first day of my incarceration on the third floor of the prison, where the occupants are allowed to eat their meals in their rooms. But I see enough of this place without going into it, and it excites my indignation every time I see my fellow-citizens and fellow-prisoners, some of them among the most distinguished men of the country, and all entitled to the respect and consideration of American freemen, subjected to such outrages as those inflicted on them here, for having, at the very worst, exercised the right recognized to be inherent in every American citizen and guaranteed by the Constitution—the Constitution! faugh, who cares now about that—to be one of the characteristics of an American freeman.

Picture to yourself those Capitol Prison scenes, American reader, and be you a partisan the most virulent, a fanatic the most violent, and what excuse will you make consistent with your ideas of free government for the outrages to which we, your fellow-citizens, have been subjected. These outrages will excite the emotions of American freemen, and a verdict, a judgment will be rendered, aye, and execution of sentence will be inflicted on the tyrants, the despots and their aiders and abettors, who have subjected us to these cruel indignities.

The Confederate prisoners to the number of forty brought here lately, were all clothed to day, the means being furnished from a secret fund contribution by Southern sympathisers in this city. After the gentleman who had been made the means of contributing to the comfort of these Confederates had left the prison, one of them remarked to another, "It is a good thing for us that we have been taken prisoners and brought here. We shall have a rest and get some clothes and shoes which we need badly. After some days' rest and recuperation, we will be exchanged and then we shall be able to fight the damned Yankees like damnation." This was said in the hearing of several of us State prisoners, but not designed for us to hear.

And by the way, does it not look like child's play to bring prisoners of war to this place, to be recruited in strength, clothed, and then exchanged after being made far more formidable, not only in physical strength, but in valuable information, derived from Northern Union men, who have been exasperated almost to hostility against the government by the illegal and arbitrary course of the Administration towards themselves, and who have become disgusted at its imbecility, vascilation and want of statesmanship in its conduct of the war. Prisoners as we are, we feel that the Administration is not equal to the emergency. We see it here as if we were at liberty, and perhaps with a clearer perception and with a better understanding of the "situation."

Sept. 13th.—The two hundred Zouaves who were brought here a few days ago have been taken away from here to-day. The fact is they became so unruly towards the guard, and so familiar with the other prisoners, that it became necessary to remove them. The report among them is that they are to be sent to the Rip Raps, and that an orderly sergeant of their number is to be shot. It is doubtful whether anything like extreme measures will be resorted to in their case. The fact is the army is demoralized, and it will not do under existing circumstances to be to severe with the malcontents.

I ought to have noticed under the head of yesterday's date, that we had a visit from Supeintendent Wood last night. He gave us his views at considerable length on the cause of the war and its probable termination. His opinions and our own differed so slightly that it occurred to me to observe that it was very singular that we held the relation of prisoners of State to the government and the Superintendant that of a government employee, while our opinions on State affairs are so slightly different. It only shows what kind of rulers we have in these unfortunate days of the Republic. Call yourself a Republican and you can be a traitor with impunity; but avow yourself a Democrat and no act of patriotism will save you from the imputation of being a traitor. Who does not perceive this to be a fact.

This has been rather a dull day in prison incidents. We were made aware this afternoon that a government detective had been placed in the next room to us to watch our movements and to report our conversation. This is not the first time we have had similar intimations of an effort to entrap Mr. Sheward and myself. Our partisan persecutors— the Administration tyrants, finding no evidence against us to warrant them in their course towards us so far, are resorting to desperate and contemptible means to criminate us. They will fail signally. It is they, not we, who are traitors to the country, and our worst crime is that we have proven them to be so in fact.

Sept. 14*th*.—Sunday has come round again, but in prison it is much like other days. Those who are so fortunate as to have a change of shirts, put one on, and look clean for one day in the week. In the afternoon it was announced that there would be preaching in the yard, and in Room No. 17, the room which was formerly used as one of the legislative halls of Congress. In making the announcement that preaching would take place, Mr. W., who is as good-natured and accommodating as a man can be in his position, announced as usual that those who wanted to hear the Gospel preached by a Secessionist, could be accommodated by going down into the yard—and those who preferred to have it preached from a Union point of view, could do so by going down to No. 17. As I did not care to hear the Gospel through either a Secession or an Abolition preacher, I remained in my room. My room companions went to hear the preaching—but they soon came back disgusted. The so-called Union preacher was a Boston Abolitionist, whose God is an Abolition Deity—whose Bible teaches nothing but Abolitionism and New England morality, and who would not go to heaven with a Southern man.

Firing has been heard here all day. No doubt a battle is progressing in the direction of Harper's Ferry.

Sept. 15th.—Our prison Superintendent came near getting into a scrape to-day. He was walking along the street, with a lady on his arm, in the vicinity of the prison, when a black fellow taunted him with being Secesh. Mr. W. wears a suit of gray, the Confederate color, which was the probable cause of his being taken for a Secesh by Mr. darkey. Mr. Wood only smiled at the darkey's impudence at first, but as the fellow persisted in his impertinence, W. dropped the lady for a moment, and making for the darkey, knocked him down by a well-directed blow in the face. Darkey ran off a little distance, pulled out a formidable looking knife, and called out to W. that he was a d——d son of a female dog. This was too much for W., who although a rank Republican, is no worshipper of negroes. He made for Mr. darkey on a run— reached him—and in an instant had the fellow on his back, notwithstanding the knife which he had to defend himself with. When he attempted to rise, Wood gave him a kick, which he repeated several times over—and having tired both hands and feet on the darkey's body, he made the fellow get up and walk over to the prison and into the guardhouse, where he is now. The whole scene which I have described took place in view of the prison.— Those who saw it were considerably amused at the incident.

Prisoners are being brought here every day, and others are taken away. Not many State Prisoners, however, have been released since I came here.— The number here now is larger than it has been for some time. Every effort the State Prisoners make to have their cases heard seems to be futile. There is an evident determination on the part of those who have assumed authority in the matter, to give no satisfaction to the prisoners, nor to give them the least opportunity to be heard in their defense. A reign of terror and of despotism is as firmly established here as in any city on the globe.

Judge Mason, Mr. Sheward's counsel and mine, sent us a note to-day informing us that he could find no one who assumed the responsibility of our arrest, and yet that he could not effect our discharge. This shows how matters affecting the rights of persons who happen to have fallen into the hands of the Abolition Philistines are regarded by those who have, for the time being, become invested with power temporarily. No one seems to be willing to shoulder the responsibility of our arrest, yet no one is willing to give us a hearing, or to discharge us from this prison. Is not this a pretty condition of things for our country to be placed in? Is not this a position to be subjected to which we State prisoners will be warranted in demanding satisfaction, and if refused, in obtaining it as best we can. Wo, I say, be to some of our persecutors—to some of the despots who have exercised towards us arbitrary power. Their lives would be but a small atonement for the injuries and outrages they have inflicted upon most of those who have been in this loathsome den. If Secretary Stanton and Judge Advocate Turner, and General Wadsworth and Provost Marshal Doster, do not receive the punishment their treatment of the Prisoners of State deserves, it will be because there will not be any power either of law or of physical force to inflict it on them. Secretary Stanton, to illustrate his connection with the arrests, suffers his subordinates to use his name for the arrest of some one who becomes obnoxious to the Abolition-Republicans of his neighborhood, but when the attention of the Secretary is called to the arrest of the victim, who meanwhile is brought here from home and business, the Secretary knows nothing about it. Judge Advocate Turner, on being requested to give a prisoner a hearing, excuses himself by alleging that he has no orders from the Secretary of War, and the Secretary of War declares that he appointed Major Turner, Judge Advocate, for the sole purpose of hearing the statements of the prisoners. So, between these officers, with an occasional intimation that it is General Wadsworth, or General Halleck, or some other dignitary who has control of the matter, we Prisoners of State, or rather, victims of Abolition outrage, are kept here for weeks in atonement for the crime of disagreeing with the Administration.

Sept. 16.—Instead of continuing the events of Old Capitol life in the form presented up to this period, those worthy of most notice will be given under appropriate headings. In this form the reader will have a better idea of Old Capitol life, and what it is to have our country ruled by a Military Despotism.

HOW FREE CITIZENS BECOME TRANSFORMED INTO SERVILE SOLDIERS.

One day after the President's Proclamation of the 22nd of September, I was walking in the Old Capitol yard, and met one of the 135th Pennsylvania Regiment, a company of which was performing duty at the Prison. During a brief conversation between us, he intimated that he for one would not continue in the service or obey any order designed to carry into practical effect the President's Proclamation of Emancipation. I doubted that he would disobey any order of the kind referred to, but he persisting in his own opinion of what he would do. I put this case to him to show how a citizen loses not only his own will but his judgment in becoming a soldier. Suppose, said I, that Lieutenant Miller would order you to go up to Room No. 16, to-morrow morning and take with you a file of soldiers and bring me down into this yard and shoot me, would you not obey the order, although you may be fully aware that I had no trial, and consequently that no sentence had been pronounced upon me? The soldier hesitated a moment, but admitted when he replied that he would obey the order of the lieutenant. "Now then," said I, "do you presume to think that you will not obey an order to enforce the Proclamation of Emancipation?" The poor fellow had not a word to say.

The fact is, that soldiers are mere machines; they have neither will nor judgment of their own, except to follow the inclinations of their passions, which are often indulged by their officers to win the soldiers over to the behests of power.

Of all other forms of despotism, the Stratocratic is the most odious and intolerable. Indeed there is no other despotism but that which is sustained by military force and power; for without this security to sustain and protect rulers in their outrageous acts their tyranny would not be endured for a single day. Hence the first step towards establishing a despotism, is to raise a subservient army. Our tyrants have profited by the example and experience of others in this respect.

APPLICATION FOR TRIAL—NO TRIAL GRANTED.

The cases of Messrs. Mahony and Sheward, of Iowa, are so connected together by circumstances, that they will be so referred to, except where there is something distinct and peculiar in them. On the second day after reaching the Old Capitol, Mr. Sheward addressed a note to the Secretary of War, requesting to be informed of the charges against him, and to have a trial set at as early a period as possible for a hearing, to which no reply was ever made by the Secretary. At the same time I wrote a letter of similar effect to the Secretary, and to the President of the United States, in which I took the position that my arrest was illegal and arbitrary, and that if such violations of the Constitution were continued, there would probably be a revolution in the Northern States. I advised the President, as a friend of the Government, to desist from making arrests in an illegal manner, and to conform to the well known and long established customs and forms prescribed by law and practiced universally under Constitutional Governments in dealing with political offenders.

In my letter to the Secretary of War, I took the same ground, and reminded the Secretary that if he (the Secretary) should be judged by charges made against him without trial or investigation, he would be subjected to a punishment which he might think to be arbitrary, unconstitutional and oppressive.

These letters had no other effect than to gall the tyrants to whom they were addressed, and goad them into a still more virulent determination to treat the prisoners without mercy. Every effort of the prisoners to be informed of the charges against them, to have these charges investigated, and to have a judgment of some kind passed upon them, were in vain.

Judge Mason, who volunteered to act as counsel for the Iowa prisoners, made application at the War Department to have a copy of the charges against these prisoners furnished to them, but in vain. The following statement, prepared by Judge Mason, will show what disposition there was among the officials, to give the prisoners a hearing, as it will convince every reasonable person that there was some other motive for arresting and detaining these offenders against the Administration, than the well being of the country.

STATEMENT OF JUDGE MASON, FOR MAHONY AND SHEWARD.

WASHINGTON, Aug. 25th, 1862.

HON. E. M. STANTON, SEC'Y. OF WAR:

SIR: On the 14th instant, D. A. Mahony, the senior editor of the Dubuque *Herald*, a daily paper, published at Dubuque, in the State of Iowa, was arrested by an officer professing to act by your order, and on the 17th David Sheward, the editor of a weekly paper called "*The Constitution and Union*," published at Fairfield, in the same State, was arrested in like manner. Both of these gentlemen were brought to this city by the United States Marshal for the State of Iowa, and on Thursday 21st instant, were lodged in the Old Capitol prison, where they now remain.

Learning from the officer by whom they were brought hither, that the charges on which their arrest and detention were founded, were filed in the office of the Provost Marshal, I called at that office on the 23rd, as the friend and counsel of those prisoners, and requested permission to see those charges. This was refused me, unless I could bring an order from the War Department granting such permission.

I then applied for this purpose to the Hon. P. H. Watson, Ass't. Secretary of War, who declined granting me that privilege, it being contrary, as he stated, to the rule observed in such cases. He however intimated to me that if I could present a case, showing that they were not guilty, it would be considered. I am now endeavoring to avail myself of this privilege.

I feel, however, no little awkwardness in making an effort to show the innocence of these prisoners, as I have never before made or witnessed such an attempt, especially, as I am not permitted to know what is the accusation against them. I mention this, not by way of raising any legal technical question to the course which has been pursued, but because I am assured by both the prisoners that they have never been informed of the cause of their arrest and detention, and have no suspicions of that cause, except such as have been created by floating rumors, or irresponsible newspaper paragraphs. I have, however, addressed myself to my task in the best manner I could.

Having obtained the necessary permission, I called to see the prisoners. My interview being limited by the officer in charge to precisely fifteen minutes, I could do nothing more than obtain brief verbal information from them. In fact I was informed that I would not be permitted to take a written communication from them, addressed even to the War Department, without presenting a previous order to that effect.

Both these prisoners most positively assured me that they had never uttered a disloyal word; nor harbored a disloyal thought; that although they frequently had occasion to differ with the Administration in regard to measures of policy they had endeavored to confine themselves within the limits of legitimate discussion, and had never, as they believed, transgressed those limits, that they had never said or done anything intended to discourage enlistments in the army, or which, as they believe was calculated to produce that result; that they had always been in favor of fully maintaining the Constitutional power of the Government under which they lived; that they were entirely opposed to disunion in any of its forms, and to all those acts and things which were calculated to produce or promote any such result, and that when they had occasion to differ with those who now control the Government, it was because they conscientiously believed the course they were pursuing was calculated to produce the very result which all were desirous to prevent.

I assure you, sir, that I fully believe the statements made to me by these gentlemen to be true. I have been well acquainted with them both for many years, and I feel sure that they are men of integrity. If desirable, I will, with your permission, obtain their affidavits to statements substantially like that above set forth, to be filed in your office, and used as you shall direct.

With regard to one of those gentlemen, (Mr. Mahony,) I can speak with more confidence, founded upon my personal knowledge. In October of last year, in my presence, and in that of many other persons, he expressed a willingness to raise a regiment of Irishmen in Northern Iowa, and was only prevented from making the effort (as I believed) by an unwillingness to ask from the Governor of Iowa what the latter was in the habit of regarding as a great favor, and which would therefore probably be refused to a political antagonist.

His daily paper has been sent to me for the last nine months, and although many of the numbers have failed to reach me, I think I may safely say that his paper has not, as I believe, expressed any sentiments for which he should be visited by the material displeasure of the Government. His views will undoubtedly be deemed very erroneous by many of his fellow-citizens; I myself differ very materially from him in many of the opinions he has expressed. But in a country where so wide a latitude has always been given to the right of free discussion—where even error of opinion has been justly said to be safely left essentially untrammeled so long as truth was free to combat it, I trust there has been nothing said by him that should call for the interposition of the Head of the War Department of the Government. I have never believed his errors fraught with danger to the country.

In order to show the grounds of the opinion above expressed, I send herewith several numbers of the Dubuque HERALD, which will speak for themselves. They consist of the 9th and 24th of July, and of the 3d, 5th, 7th, 9th, 10th, 12, 13th, and 14th of August, which last was printed on the day of his arrest. I have preserved no file of these papers and those I now send comprise every one that, after a careful search, can now be found. I think they will give you a just idea of the general course of the editor. I particularly refer you to the leading editorials in the numbers of the 3d, 7th, and 10th of August—not because I suppose you will fully approve of all you there find, but because they lay bare the views and feelings of the editor more completely than any of the other numbers. For a similar reason I forward you also the Burlington *Argus*, of the 19th inst., containing a letter from Mr. Mahony, expressive of his views and opinions at that time.

With regard to Mr. Sheward, I have not the same kind of testimony. His is a weekly paper of limited circulation—confined, as I believe, almost entirely to a single interior county of the State. I think I have not seen a number of it for the last three months, and have not one within my reach.

What either of these gentlemen have said or done outside of their respective newspapers, I have no means of knowing, except by their own statement, as I have seen neither of them since October of last year until I saw them in prison. But from the facts above above detailed, I feel authorized to express the belief—which I do, most unqualifiedly—that neither of them has done any act which would call for their arrest or incarceration for a single moment; and I fully believe that your Department has been imposed upon by the hasty zeal of some persons, or by some other cause which I do not feel justified or inclined to suggest.

But although you may think me mistaken in this respect, I respectfully submit whether these prisoners are not entitled to be informed of the nature of the accusation against them and to have an early opportunity to convince you of their innocence.

I hope, however, they will be at once permitted to return to their homes, strengthened in that loyalty to the Government which can best be created and preserved by a reliance on its justice, and a trust in the continuance of all those safeguards with which the Constitution and the Laws have so carefully endeavored to protect the liberties of each and every citizen.

Yours, very respectfully,
CHAS. MASON.

It will scarcely be credited by the American people that a prisoner in the custody of the Government, on the application of himself and of his counsel to be informed of what crime he is accused, and to have a hearing or trial so as to determine whether he is guilty of any offense or not, would be answered in the tyrannical manner stated in the foregoing appeal to the War Department.

"Let them prove themselves innocent,". was the mandate of Assistant Secretary Watson.

"Innocent of what?" enquired Judge Mason. "How are they to know of what they are to prove themselves innocent?"

But appeal and remonstrance was alike in vain. All that Judge Mason could get for an answer to his application for charges, for a trial, for an investigation was, "Let them prove themselves innocent," and from that day till the day the prisoners were discharged on the 11th of November, after being nearly three months incarcerated, they were neither informed of the nature of the charges against them, nor had they ever, even on the day of their release and discharge, any trial, investigation of the charges against them, if any were made, or examination, although there was not a week passed that they did not plead for a hearing, trial, investigation, anything that would give them an opportunity to be heard in their own defense. These applications were made to every official, from the President down to detective Baker, all to the same effect, in vain. No reply was ever returned to any application or solicitation of this kind. The only official who interested himself to obtain for any of the prisoners a hearing, was the Superintendent of the Old Capitol, whose humane impulses would, despite his partisan prejudices, influence him to act in their behalf.

A PROPOSITION TO TAKE BONDS FOR THE RELEASE OF PRISONERS.

About the middle of September, Superintendent Wood came to me, and said that my friends in Dubuque had sent a bond signed for my release, and that if I would sign it I would be discharged forthwith. I enquired what the bond was, and who had directed or authorized it to be given on my account.

Mr. Wood replied that the bond was in the penal sum of $10,000, and conditioned upon my preserving the relations of good citizenship towards the Government.

"That would imply," said I to Mr. Wood, "that I have heretofore not complied with what is due from me as a good citizen, which I do not admit till I be tried and convicted of some offense against the Government. I know my own heart, Mr. Wood, and I know that there is not a more loyal and devoted friend of this Government living than I am. Therefore, I will give no bond which would imply or admit in any way that I have been guilty of any offense against the Government, and though I desire beyond anything else now to be released from this Bastile, not so much on my own account, bad as my health is, but on account of my suffering wife and children, I will stay here and rot before I sign any bond such as that you propose."

I was surprised how it came that any such thing as a bond of the kind referred to was gotten up without my knowledge or consent, and on after enquiry I found that there was nothing of the kind. The proposition was made me to ascertain whether I would agree to anything of the kind, and then when my consent should be obtained, the bond would be sent to my friends for their signature.

Writing to my wife about this matter under date of September 22d, which letter passed through the hands of the Judge Advocate, I said:

" I hear that some one has sent a Bond here on which to obtain my release. While I am much obliged to my friends for this proof of their regard and confidence, I shall *never* sign any Bond which would imply that I have been guilty of any crime or offense towards the Government. I offered my services, as thousands in Iowa have done, to maintain the supremacy of the Government and to put down the rebellion; and I would give my life to maintain the Constitutional authority of the President or of any other officer or branch of the Government, just as readily as I have offered myself a victim to partisan malice and arbitrary power, for defending the Constitution from violation and the Government from subversion. Hence, why should I give any Bond for my future course? I shall not do it, be the result what it might."

This ended the Bond business, so far as I was concerned. Several others gave the required Bonds. Indeed, all others did to whom the proposition was made, so far as I was informed.

MILITARY COMMISSION FOR THE TRIAL OF POLITICAL OFFENDERS.

The purpose of the Secretary of War, a purpose no doubt determined on by the Administration, after due consideration—to try the Prisoners of State by a Military Commission, was so far carried into effect as to have the Commission constituted for that purpose. This was done about the middle of September, by an order of the Secretary of War, naming Generals Hunter, Cadwallader and others, for that purpose. Application for a copy of this order at the War Department, did not succeed in obtaining it; and if the original can be destroyed, there is not much doubt it will be done. "Why?" the reader may enquire; because as soon as the result of the October elections was known, this Commission which was to try the Prisoners of State, was used for another purpose, and this was done to cloak the real designs of the Administration in constituting the Commission. The result of the October elections deterred the Secretary of War from carrying into effect his design to try by his Military Commission civilians who had had no connection whatever with the army. Had the elections gone in favor of the Administration, these Prisoners of State would in all probability be not only tried by this Commission, but convicted on the secret testimony obtained against them, and executed, as was no doubt the design of the Administration. The Military Commission was so constituted that any verdict desired by the Administration was likely to be obtained, when it affected only the liberty and life of one who believed that it was to the Constitution and the Government instituted by it, that he owed allegiance and duty, and not to the enemies of both.

The fact that a copy of the order containing this Commission was refused to be given, shows that it is designed to keep a knowledge of its existence and of its objects from the public. But the order was published in the newspapers at the time it was issued, and although the writer has not been able to reproduce it here, there is no doubt of the fact of its having been issued, and there is as little doubt in the mind of the writer of its design and object.

Thanks, under Providence, to the manifeststion of popular indignation against the arbitrary, despotic and tyrannic course of the Administration for preserving the Prisoners of State from becoming lifeless victims of partisan malignity and of the tyranny of arbitrary power. The will to deprive them of life as they had been deprived of liberty, was not wanting; and nothing but the dread of popular retribution deterred the tyrants from consummating their designs.

MY FIRST SUNDAY IN THE OLD CAPITOL—THE GOSPEL ACCORDING TO JEFF DAVIS, AND ACCORDING TO ABE LINCOLN.

While I sat musing on my situation, the first Sunday I spent in the Old Capitol, I was startled by the extraordinary exclamation which rang through every room in the Bastile, "All ye who want to hear the Lord God preached according to Jeff Davis, go down in the yard; and all who want to hear the Lord God preached according to Abe Lincoln, go down to No. 16."

"What in the world does that mean?" inquired one of us.

By the time the inquiry was made, Superintendent Wood made his appearance at the door of our room, repeating the invitation to us which had been given at every room as he came along.

"Suppose," inquired one of us, "that we do not want to hear the Lord God preached according to either Jeff Davis or Abe Lincoln, what then, Mr. Wood?"

"Oh," accommodatingly replied the Superintendent, "you can stay in your room."

Mr. Wood the reader had as well be informed, is an infidel, or pretended to be, and he was no doubt sincere in his professions. So that it was not so much for any respect for Jeff Davis or even for Abe Lincoln that he invited the prisoners to hear the Lord God preached according to either of their standards, but out of pure disbelief in the Gospel itself, and to show his contempt both for the word of God and pity for any one who was so credulous as to believe in it.

And yet withal, Mr. Wood had a good heart when his better feelings were not thwarted by his prejudices, and especially by his partisan failings. When the dictates of humanity and the interests of party conflicted with each other, the struggle for mastery was often strong and violent in Mr. Wood. The partisan generally had the best of it in the outset, but in due time passion became gratified, reason asserted its influence, and the finer feelings of the heart took possession of the man and influenced his actions.

But to the preaching. Although none of us cared to hear the Lord God blasphemed by a Jeff Davis or Abe Lincoln preacher, we all availed ourselves of the opportunity to take an airing in the yard. The preaching according to Jeff Davis was done by a hard shell Baptist, who delivered a sensible discourse on the causes which produced the existing difficulties. He attributed the war to the fanaticism, zealotry and bigotry of New England. To her temperance lecturers, her tract distributors, her missionary societies. These, he argued, were one of the exciting causes of the war as well as Abolitionism. New England, he said, assumed that all the rest of mankind and especially the people of the Southern States were living in ignorance of the knowledge of God, and of the words and works of God, and she felt herself called on to be not only the instructress of all the world, but the guardian of the weak and chastiser of the wicked. Hence she sent her lecturers through the country declaiming against the immoralities of the South, when it was a statistical fact that there was more immorality in herself than in any other portion of the Union. She scattered her religious tracts throughout the South, not for the purpose of teaching the reader how to know and love God, but in a latent, insiduous manner, to teach the slaves how to become disobedient and rebellious towards their masters. Such was the conduct of New England, said the preacher according to Jeff Davis, towards the South, and it was such conduct which resulted in provoking the South to resent the injuries sought to be inflicted on her. If there was not much Gospel truth in the sermon, there was a considerable amount of fact in it, and the conclusions drawn by the preacher were such as accorded with the judgment of the audience.

As soon as the preacher was through with his discourse, the Superintendent, who liked neither the religious nor political sentiments of the speaker, called his attention to another text of Scripture, which says, "I did not come to present you with peace but with a sword." The sermon or discourse was founded on the beautiful hymn of the Angels, "Glory to God in the highest, and peace on earth to men of good will," and it was both to show there was a contradiction in the word of God and to confound the preacher, that his attention was called to the other text: but the preacher was not at all disconcerted; on the contrary, he turned the tables upon the unbeliever and instrument of arbitrary power, showing him that the sword Christ referred to, was the word of God, which he was using with effect on just such persons as he and those in whose employ he was, and who become the instruments of despotism and tyranny. The audience could scarcely refrain from applauding the preacher, for the aptness of his application of the text which, it was expected, would disconcert and confuse him. Thus ended the preaching of the Lord God according to Jeff Davis for that Sunday.

The preaching of the Gospel according to Abe Lincoln was done by an Abolitionist named Spears and his wife. Spears very charitably and disinterestedly (he was looking after a chaplaincy which he soon after secured) volunteered his Sunday services to carry the glad tidings of the gospel according to the fashion of the day, to the inmates of the Old Capitol. He was accompanied by his wife, one of those lank, skinny, cadaverous she-males to which nature in some of her freaks or blunders gave the sex of woman. Mrs. Spears not only spoke through her nose as most of her kind do, but when she did speak, she put a finger to her nose as if to make her nasal twang more perfect in her estimation, and more disagreeable to her hearers. She, of course, spoke first. It was with much difficulty that her audience refrained from a burst of laughter, so ludicrous was her *tout ensemble* and so impudently presumptuous was her address. She spoke but a few minutes, being satisfied no doubt that her efforts were not appreciated.

It was next the turn of her spouse who was a good match for her in every respect. He was an Abolitionist and a Preacher on the same principle that one is a shoemaker or other tradesman, it paid; and although he was but a very indifferent exponent either of Abolitionism or of the Gospel according to Abe Lincoln, he made up in presumption what he lacked in ability. This sermon, if such a farrago of cant and nonsense as he uttered could be so called, was a mixture of scripture quotations jumbled together without application, and of suggestions to the prisoners that there was hope even for them in the Kingdom of Christ. The hypocritical knave! just as if the meanest person in the Old Capitol was not an Angel of light compared to him, who volunteered to give spiritual comfort to the inmates of the Bastile, only that attention might be attracted to his disinterested (?) services, and that he might be rewarded with what he was seeking to obtain, a chaplaincy to one of the City Hospitals, which of course, he succeeded in securing.

HOW THE PRISONERS WERE FED.

Prison fare in the Old Capitol—and it appears to have been much the same in Forts Lafayette, Warren and Delaware—consisted of bread, generally good, salt pork, and occasionally, fresh beef. The pork was of poor quality, and was worse by being badly kept and illy cooked. The beef was of such a quality that it was seldom eaten by those who had any means of procuring better, and who had the permission to do so. It was in appearance, when cooked—fried it generally was—like a piece of thick sole leather steeped in grease and subjected to the heat of the fire in an iron utensil. Those that had good teeth could masticate it with an effort, but, even then, they could not swallow it.

Under these circumstances, Prisoners of State and others who could afford it, clubbed together and formed messes in their rooms, and by the aid of Corporal Brown in the Old Capitol, procured such edibles as they could prevail on that functionary to purchase for them. The principal mess of this kind in the Old Capitol among the Prisoners of State was in Room No. 16. It included Judges Duff and

Mulkey, of Illinois, also Dr. Ross, Rev. Samuel H. Bundy, A. P. Corder, John M. Clemenson, D. H. Dowell, and some others of that State. Rev. J. D. Benedict, Dr. T. T. Ellis, T. T. Edgerton, Esq., and —— Hill, of New York, D. A. Mahony and David Sheward, of Iowa, Dr. Moran and B. F. Brown, of Frederick City, Maryland, Geo. W. Wilson, Esq., of Upper Marlboro, same State, V. R. Jackson, Esq., of Washington City, and, from time to time, some others.

Of this mess, Mr. Sheward of Iowa was chosen by unanimous vote, commissary and purveyor, and Dr. Ross, of Illinois, and D. H. Dowell, of Missouri, assistants. Each member of the mess paid when called on by the commissary his portion of the week's expenses for provisions. This, of course, did not include tobacco, segars, and such other luxuries as individuals chose to indulge in. When meats were procured, through the gracious aid of Corporal Brown and the permission of Superintent Wood, the cooking was done by one of the contrabands of the establishment, who was always paid, of course, for his services.

Before this mess was formed, the Prisoners of State fared pretty roughly. Mahony and Sheward, of Iowa, were obliged to ask it as a favor of their friend, Judge Mason, to procure them some food that they could eat with an appetite. That gentleman did so, readily, willingly, cheerfully, and with a heart feelingly sensible of the indignities to which his fellow-citizens of Iowa had been subjected.— Other prisoners were similarly favored by their acquaintances and friends. Colonel Young, of the Federal Army, was indebted to his wife for most of what he eat. So was A. R. Allen, Esq., of Washington City, who was imprisoned by General Wadsworth for arresting a fugitive slave, complying, as he did, with all the recently enacted laws in performing that duty. So, too, did V. R. Jackson, Esq., of Washington City, depend upon his wife for his food, the prison fare being such that he could not eat it with any appetite. Of course, those who were far away from friends, and who had no means to purchase anything else, were obliged to eat Old Capitol fare or starve.

It is but just to say of Superintendent Wood, that it was no fault of his that the Prisoners of State fared so badly. General Mansfield, when Military Governor of Washington City, gave orders that these prisoners should be fed on side pork and hard biscuit, the worst that could be procured. Mr. Wood remonstrated with the Military Governor on this order, saying that these prisoners were not convicts, that they were under no sentence of any tribunal, judicial or military, but were merely held to await a trial, and that most of them were gentlemen who were not used to such hard living as he prescribed.

"Damn them!" was General Mansfield's reply—"they are all traitors, or they would not be there," meaning in the Old Capitol. "They shall have nothing else but what I have ordered; that is good enough for them."

Superintendent Wood became indignant at this, and told General Mansfield to his face that these prisoners were just as good men as he was, and he be d—d if they did not have bread at least to eat while he was Superintendent of the Old Capitol. And he made his word good, for on being refused bread for his prisoners by General Mansfield, he engaged the bakers near the prison to furnish all the bread he needed.

I might say here, that when the prisoners heard of the death of General Mansfield at Antietam, they hoped he would realize in the new existence to which he was introduced what it is to be a tyrant towards his fellow mortals in misfortune. This was the most charitable feeling entertained towards him. It might be inferred what those wished him who suffered their feelings to be influenced by his infamous course towards the Old Capitol Prisoners. It was established as a sort of rule in the prison, that whoever was released should send something in the shape of food back to his fellow prisoners. No one could know better the needs of the prisoners than those who had been subjected to the prison treatment. In accordance with this rule, Messrs. Kugler and Wright, of New Jersey, sent from home a box containing several pounds of fresh butter, tomatoes, and sauces. These were most acceptable to the mess, as it was then of Room No. 10. When the Prisoners of State were all placed together in Room 16, their means and opportunities of providing themselves and of being provided by their friends with such things as butter, meat and other necessaries were more abundant and frequent, and there was more system in their arrangements, so that they generally fared pretty well during the month of October, and till the Prisoners of State were discharged early in November. This faring better, however, was due to their own means, and to the favor of their friends and released fellow prisoners, and it ought to be added creditably to Superintendent Wood, that he gave the prisoners permission to provide themselves with such food as they could eat, and to receive such as might be sent them.

Appreciating the acts of generosity of released prisoners and friends, votes of thanks of mess in Room No. 16 were passed to Mrs. A. R. Allen and Mrs. V. R. Jackson of Washington City, to Messrs. Geo. W. Wilson of Upper Marlboro', Md., and —— Hill of New York, and of mess in Room No. 10, to Judge Mason of Iowa, and Messrs. Kugler of

Frenchtown, N. J., and Wright of Milford, same State. A copy of the preamble and resolutions of thanks adopted in one of these instances is appended:

Whereas, The Government of the United States, under the Presidency of Abraham Lincoln, has been used for the oppression of loyal citizens of the Northern States who have presumed to differ with the Administration on questions purely politic or political; and

Whereas, Among other grievous acts violative alike of the rights of persons and the Constitution of the United States, and of the Constitutions of the several States, numerous persons have been arrested by arbitrary and illegal means, under the orders and directions of the War Department, and these persons deprived not only of the privileges of the writ of *habeas corpus* guaranteed to them by the Constitution, except when suspended by act of Congress, but also of the right to consult with counsel and to communicate with their wives and families, except in the presence of minions of the Administration, or subject, as in the case of correspondence, to the supervision and approval of petty clerks who earn the favor of their employers by the rigor of their scrutiny, the harshness of their judgment, and the insolence of their official conduct; and

Whereas, The undersigned and many hundreds of others have been made the victims of the arbitrary power referred to, and some of us deprived of and denied for months our personal and constitutional rights, by being incarcerated in what is called the Old Capitol Prison, at Washington, and subjected to such treatment therein as is prescribed for military prisoners, except as we ourselves have been able to procure by our own means or the favor of friends such necessaries and comforts as are absolutely essential to the preservation of health; and

Whereas, Among our fellow-prisoners incarcerated with us for some time, on some flimsy pretext which when investigated was found to be devoid of crime or offense, were George W. Wilson, of Upper Marlboro', Maryland, and —— Hill of New York; and

Whereas, These, our fellow-prisoners, did not forget us in the re acquirement of their liberty, but on the contrary, recollecting the meagre fare furnished to us by those who have deprived us of our liberty, have sent us a bountiful repast, which for several days made us feel not only that we were not forgotten by the world beyond these prison walls, but made us comparatively insensible to the hardships to which we are here subjected; and

Whereas, Such an act of kindness, regard, and consideration deserves to be commemorated in such a manner as to show some appreciation of it on our part,

Be it, therefore, and it is hereby

Resolved, That the thanks, heartfelt, sincere, and grateful of us prisoners of despotism, confined in room No. 16, in the Old Capitol Building, is hereby expressed and tendered to our late room-mates, Messrs. George W. Wilson and —— Hill, for the bountiful supply of creature comforts furnished by them, and for the goodness of heart which prompted them to remember us, their fellow-prisoners, in the enjoyment of their newly-acquired liberty.

The prisoners generally lived or languished on the Old Capitol fare, the only redeeming quality of which was good bread; thanks to Superintendent Wood for that. The eating place was on the ground floor of a frame building extending eastward from the prison proper. The second story of this building was used for hospital purposes; the first, for eating in, negro quarters, washing rooms, &c. The eating room could accommodate at one time as many as a hundred persons. There were two tables running the length of the room. Each eater was furnished with a tin plate, tin cup, knife and fork, of camp quality. Plenty of bread was furnished to each person, and more than enough of meat, for but few persons could eat that which was furnished generally. Soup was given out occasionally, made of dessicated vegetables, and once in a while boiled rice also was served up. Potatoes, a few times a week, formed a part of the fare.

When there were more prisoners than would fill the eating room one time, when the meal was called by the proper officer, a rush would be made by the whole crowd to be at the first table. This was owing less to the desire to be first to eat, than it was to avoid eating and drinking from the same unwashed plates and tin cups, and the used knives and forks of the first set. Sometimes there would be half a dozen sets to eat—all of those who came after the first set being obliged to eat off of dirty plates, and drink out of the dirty cups of their predecessor eaters. This became so disgusting to all but the roughest specimens of humanity in the prison, that it was a general practice of those of refined tastes and delicate stomachs to take the bread and meat in their hands and eat them in the yard, or in their rooms.

Most of the Prisoners of State were obliged to go with the crowd of deserters and criminals of the Federal Army, and lousy confederate prisoners of war to this feeding place. There were but few who had not to go through this humiliating and disgusting subjection to arbitrary power, tyrannically exercised the first days of their incarceration.

Can any American, innocent of crime, who has been subjected to this outrage, ever forget it, aye, or ever forgive the tyrants by whom it was perpetrated. No being of sensibility inferior to God in perfection, can he so charitable as to forgive the tyrants Lincoln, Stanton, and their associates in despotism; who have thrown down the security and trampled under their heels the guarantees of the Constitution to American citizens, and outraged in person and property the victims of their displeasure.

BELLE BOYD—DEFEAT OF BANKS ATTRIBUTED TO HER STRATEGY—ARRESTED AND TAKEN TO THE OLD CAPITOL—SUBJECTED TO SOLITARY CONFINEMENT—MAKES THE ACQUAINTANCE OF A CONFEDERATE OFFICER—ROMANTIC SEQUEL.

Among the prisoners in the Old Capitol when I reached there was the somewhat famous Belle Boyd, to whom has been attributed the defeat of General Banks in the Shenandoah Valley by Stonewall Jackson. Belle, as she was familiarly called by all the prisoners, and affectionately so by the confederates, was arrested and imprisoned as a spy. She was said, by the confederates who professed to be acquainted with her family, to be the daughter of a respectable Presbyterian clergyman at Martinsburg, Virginia, and the sister of Mrs. Faulkner, whose husband was the late United States Minister to France.

The first intimation some of us new comers in the Old Capitol had of the fact of there being a lady in that place, was the hearing of "Maryland, my Maryland," sang the first night of our incarceration in what we could not be mistaken was a female voice. On enquiring we were informed that it was Belle Boyd. Some of us had never heard of the lady before, and we were all enquiring about her. Who was she, where was she from, and what did she do. The most satisfactory account represented her as being a young lady of about nineteen years of age, of lithe body, and of a pleasing, though not what is called either beautiful or handsome countenance.

When Banks was down the Shenandoah Valley, Belle conceived the idea of playing the part of Delilah on him. To accomplish this purpose she gave out invitations to the Federal officers in camp, including General Banks, for a ball to come off some days subsequently. This done, she took a fleet and long-winded horse, starting late one evening, and rode by morning sixty miles across the mountains to where Stonewall Jackson was encamped. She informed that wary officer of her plans, of the situation of the Federal troops, their disposition in camp, the number and position of their cannon, and, in short, of everything she knew about Banks' army. The night of the ball was fixed for just the time it would take Jackson to march his "foot cavalry," as his infantry were called by the confederates, to Banks' camp. Belle's arrangements being all made with Jackson, she rode back the same day, making the hundred and twenty miles in twenty-four hours. This, to some, will appear incredible, but Belle Boyd is said to have no superior, man or woman, as an equestrian in Virginia.

On the night of the ball, Belle lavished her blandishments on General Banks especially. She had procured a large and elegant secesh flag, with which she covered the person of the General, and by her familiarity made him oblivious, it would seem, to all else than the attentions of his fair entertainer. Meanwhile Stonewall Jackson had made a successful march, and knowing from Belle's information, the weak points in the Federal camp, attacked Banks corps so suddenly and with such boldness that it was thrown into confusion. A panic succeeded, and Banks suffered not only an overwhelming defeat, but a disaster which has never been repaired, as ever since the Shenandoah valley has been in the virtual, if not in the actual, control of the Confederates.

Subsequent to this, Belle Boyd went to Washington, where being well known, she had the *entree* to the best society of the Capital. But she did not mean to spend her time uselessly. Virginia had claims upon her services, and to requite these claims she conceived the idea of sketching the fortifications over the Potomac. It was not difficult at the time, especially for a young lady, to procure a pass to cross the long bridge. Furnished with this, Belle crossed the river on her reconnoisance, but being less cautious than she was zealous, she was detected in the act of making a sketch of one of the forts by which Washington is defended on the South. She was immediately arrested, and taken to the Old Capitol, the only one of her sex in that Bastile. Belle was put in solitary confinement, but allowed to have her room door open, and to sit outside of it in a hall or stair-landing, in the evening. Whenever she availed herself of this privilege, as she frequently did, the greatest curiosity was manifested by the victims of despotism to see her. Her room being on the second story, those who occupied the third story had a good opportunity to indulge their curiosity, especially as there were no guards at that time in the third story of the building, a favor for which the other prisoners were indebted to the fact that it was on the third story, the civilians from Fredericksburg, who have been referred to already, were confined. Were all the prisoners on that story Northern political offenders, they would not have thus been exempt from the surveillance and annoyance of the guards. Thanks, therefore, to the gentlemen from Fredericksburg for the enjoyment of a moderate degree of liberty in the Old Capitol.

But we must not lose sight of Belle Boyd. I heard her voice my first night in prison singing "Maryland, my Maryland," the first time I had ever heard that Southern song. The words, stirring enough to Southern hearts, were enunciated by her with such peculiar expression as to touch even sensibilities which did not sympathize with the cause which inspired the song. It was difficult to listen unmoved to this lady throwing her whole soul as it were into the expression of the sentiments of devotion to the South, defiance of the North, and affectionately confident appeals to Maryland which form the burden of that celebrated song. The pathos of her voice, her apparently forlorn condition, and at these times when her soul seemed absorbed in the thoughts she was uttering in song, her melancholy manner, affected all who heard her, not only with compassion for her, but with an interest in her which came near on several occasions bringing about a conflict between the prisoners and the guards.

Fronting on the same hall or stair-landing on which Belle Boyd's room door opened, were three other rooms, all filled to their capacity with prisoners, mostly Confederate officers. Several of these were personally acquainted with Belle, as she was most of the time and by nearly every one called. In the evenings, those prisoners were permitted to crowd inside of their room doors, whence they could see and sometimes exchange a word with Belle. When this liberty was not allowed, Belle contrived to procure a large marble, around which she would tie a note written on tissue-paper, and when the guard turned his back to patrol his beat in the hall, she would roll the marble into one of the open doors of the Confederate prisoners' rooms. When the contents were read and noted, a missive would be written in reply and the marble similarly burdened as it came, would be rolled back to Belle. Thus was a correspondence established and kept up between Belle and her fellow-prisoners till a more convenient and effective mode was discovered. This occurred soon after some of us were transfered from room No. 13 to No. 10. One day Mr. Sheward and I were rummaging in an old dirty, doorless closet in No. 10, when we discovered an opening in the floor, and looking down perceived the light in the room below which happened to be that occupied by Belle Boyd. Here was a discovery. No sooner was it made than we set to writing a note which was tied to a thread and dropped down through the discovered aperture. It happened to be seen by Belle, who soon returned the compliment. Thenceforth, a regular mail passed through the floor in No. 10, and though Lieutenant Miller and Superintendent Wood prided themselves on being well informed of every occurrence which took place in the prison contrary to the rules, with all their vigilance aided by the presence, as they admitted, of a detective in every room in the prison, except that of Belle Boyd, they never discovered this through-the-floor mail. It would be not the least interesting chapters of the history of the Old Capitol, to give in it the letters to and from Belle Boyd. But the time for this is not yet.

Belle usually commenced her evening entertainment with "Maryland, my Maryland." Although the words of this celebrated song have been published frequently and extensively in the Northern papers, some might see it for the first time by reproducing it here.

INCIDENTS IN THE OLD CAPITOL.

"MARYLAND, MY MARYLAND."

AS SUNG BY BELLE BOYD IN THE OLD CAPITOL.

The despot's heel is on thy shore,
            Maryland!
His torch is at thy temple door,
            Maryland!
Avenge the patriotic gore
hat wept o'er gallant Baltimore,
Tnd be the battle queen of yore,
            Maryland! My Maryland!

Hark to a wandering son's appeal,
            Maryland!
My Mother State, to thee I kneel,
            Maryland!
For life and death, for woe and weal,
Thy peerless chivalry reveal,
And gird thy beauteous limbs with steel,
            Maryland! My Maryland!

Thou wilt not cower in the dust,
            Maryland!
Thy beaming sword shall never rust,
            Maryland!
Remember Carroll's sacred trust,
Remember Howard's warlike thrust,
And all thy slumber'rs with the just,
            Maryland! My Maryland!

Come! 'tis the red dawn of the day,
            Maryland!
Come with thy panoplied array,
            Maryland!
With Ringgold's spirit for the fray,
With Watson's blood at Monterey,
With fearless Lowe and dashing May,
            Maryland! My Maryland!

Dear mother! burst the tyrant's chain,
            Maryland!
Virginia should not call in vain,
            Maryland!
She meets her sisters on the plain,
"*Sic Semper*," 'tis her proud refrain,
That baffles minions back amain,
            Maryland!
rise in majesty again,
            Maryland! My Maryland!

Come! for thy shield is bright and strong,
          Maryland!
Come, for thy dalliance does thee wrong,
          Maryland!
Come to thine own heroic throng,
That stalks with liberty along,
And gives a new Key to thy song,
          Maryland! My Maryland!

I see the blush upon thy cheek,
          Maryland!
But thou wert ever bravely meek,
          Maryland!
But lo! there surges forth a shriek,
From hill to hill, from creek to creek;
Potomac calls to Chesapeake,
          Maryland! My Maryland!

Thou wilt not yield the Vandal toll,
          Maryland!
Thou wilt not crook to his control,
          Maryland!
Better the fire upon the roll,
Better the shot, the blade, the bowl,
Than crucifixion of the soul,
          Maryland! My Maryland!

Hear the distant thunder hum,
          Maryland!
The Old Line's bugle, fife and drum,
          Maryland!
She is not dead, nor deaf, nor dumb—
Huzza! she spurns the northern scum!
She breathes—she burns—she'll come, she'll come,
          Maryland! My Maryland!

The singing of this song often brought Belle in collision with the guard who passed to and fro in front of her room door. This occurred especially towards the close, where particular stress was laid upon the sentiment

"Huzza! she spurns the northern scum!"

which was sang by every rebel voice within hearing. The guard would tell Belle to hush up. Belle would reply, "I shan't do it," and then repeat

"Huzza! she spurns the northern scum!"

and suiting the action to the word, she would seize a broom and apply it to that part of the floor trod by the guard. This, of course, was provoking to the guard; but was such a place the proper one to imprison a female, and especially one who, whatever may have been her offense, was in the estimation of the world, a lady.

Belle was allowed to go in the yard on Sundays, when there was preaching there. On these occasions she wore a small confederate flag in her bosom. No sooner would her presence be known to the confederate prisoners than they manifested towards her every mark of respect which persons in their situation could bestow. Most of them doffed their hats as she approached them, and she, with a grace and dignity which might be envied by a queen, extended a hand to them as she moved along to her designated position in a corner near the preacher. We northern Prisoners of State envied the confederates who enjoyed the acquaintance of Belle Boyd, and who secured from her such glances of sympathy as can only glow from a woman's eyes.

Belle's situation was a peculiarly trying one. If she kept her room, a solitary prisoner, her health and probably her mind would become affected by the confinement and solitude, and if she indulged herself by sitting out side her room door, she became exposed to the gaze of more than a hundred prisoners, nearly all of them strangers to her, and many of them her enemies by the laws of war. Nor was this all. She could not help hearing the comments made on her and the opinions expressed of her by passers-by, some of them complimentary and flattering, it is true, but oftentimes couched in expressions which were not what she should hear. The guards, too, were sometimes rude towards her both by word and action. One time, especially, one of the guards presented his bayoneted musket at her in a threatening manner. She, brave and unterrified, dared the craven-hearted fellow to put his threat into execution. It was well for him that he did not, for he would have been torn into pieces before it could be known to the prison authorities what had happened.

Bell was subjected to another worse annoyance and indignity than even this. Her room fronted on A street, and as was usual with all the prisoners whose rooms had windows opening towards the street, Belle would sit at her window sometimes and look abroad upon the houses, streets and people of the city named after Washington. It happened frequently that troops were moving to and fro, and it was on such occasions especially that Belle, prompted by that curiosity which seems to be a law of nature in mankind, would look through her barred window at the soldiers. No sooner would they perceive her than they indulged in coarse jests, vulgar expressions and the vilest slang of the brothel, made still more coarse, vulgar and indecent by the throwing off of the little restraint which civilized society places upon the most abandoned prostitutes and their companions. Belle revenged herself upon them by hurrahing for Jeff Davis and Stonewall Jackson, and by such enquiries as—

"How long did it take you to come from Bull Run?"

"Are you going on to Richmond?"

"Where's General Pope's head-quarters?"

"Where did Pope leave his coat?"

"Hush up, you d—n b—h," one of the soldiers would bellow, "or I'll shoot you."

"Shoot me," Belle would reply, "go meet men, you cowards. What are you doing here in Washington? Stonewall Jackson is waiting for you on the other side of the Potomac. Aye, you could fight defenceless, imprisoned women like me, but you were driven out of the Shenandoah valley by the men of Virginia."

Did the officers of the troops passing by permit the soldiers to thus insult a female and subject themselves to such scornful and contemptuous reproof, the reader will be apt to enquire. Yes, and participate with the soldiers in uttering the most vulgar language and indecent allusions to the imprisoned woman, and that too, without having the remotest idea of who she was, or of what she was accused. It was enough for them that she was a defenseless woman to insult and outrage her by such language as they would not dare to apply in the public streets to an abandoned woman who had her liberty. And these men were going forth to fight the battles of the Union. They had just parted with mothers, wives and sisters. It would seem that in doing so, they turned their back upon the virtues which give beauty to woman and dignity to man.

Who would suppose that it was but yesterday, or a week ago, those soldiers, who are howling through the streets of the Capitol the most execrable language, parted from the tender embraces of a wife, sister or mother. Yet so it was in most instances, Some of them, it is true, had been campaigning, and not a few of them, as Belle Boyd properly inferred, had been with Pope at the second battle of Bull Run, and were now returning from the Arsenal with new arms to supply the place of those thrown away in the rout of the 28th and 29th of August. It was not so much wonder that such soldiers as these, both officers and men, would turn aside as they passed by the Old Capitol and insult a defenseless woman with the language of the brothel. They seemed to be more adept in that than they were in fighting rebels. When these marching soldiers provoked Belle too much, she would stick out her secesh flag through the window, and leave it there till they had all passed by. Their imprecations would then be lost on her, for she would retire from the window, out of sight and hearing.

During Belle's stay in the Old Capitol, a young officer of the Confederate army, a fellow-prisoner of hers, named McVay, cultivated an acquaintance with her which had been formed on a previous occasion. Lieutenant McVay was wounded in one of the battles before Richmond, and being left for dead by the Confederates, was taken prisoner by the Federal forces. His condition was such that he could not be removed far, and on the application of some friendly acquaintances of his, he was paroled and taken in care by them. Contrary to their expectations, he survived his dangerous wound, grew better, and finally recovered. Being under parole he did not feel at liberty to go at large, nor to return to the Confederate service. His place of residence being near Alexandria, and within the Federal lines, lest he might be presumed to have returned to his allegiance to the Federal Government, and lest he might be suspected of occupying an equivocal position, he gave up his parole to General Wadsworth, Military Governor of Washington, and desired to be considered as a prisoner of war. Wadsworth at first refused to so consider and treat him, but sent him to the Old Capitol. Meantime he renewed, and, as has been said, cultivated an acquaintance with Belle Boyd, which ripened, it was generally understood, into such mutual regard as ended in an engagement to unite their persons in connubial life. The marble which was spoken of in another part of this narrative played an important part in the courtship of these young lovers. McVay's room opened on the same little corridor or hall as that of Belle Boyd's, and the marble with its freight of billets deux could be rolled from one room to the other. The patience of the guard as well as his vigilance was often taxed by the rolling of this marble. As soon as he would hear the sound, he would turn suddenly around, but not in time to discover what was the cause of his annoyance. The marble always reached its destination, and never failed to carry with it safely its precious burden.

At the general exchange of prisoners which took place in September, Belle Boyd was sent to Richmond. As soon as it became known in the Old Capitol that she was about to leave, there was not one, Federalist or Confederate, Prisoner of State, officer of the Old Capitol, as well as prisoner of war, who did not feel that he was about to part with one for whom he had at least a great personal regard. With many it was more than mere regard. There was more than one McVay who aspired to the enviable position which the handsome, dashing, and gentlemanly Confederate Lieutenant succeeded in acquiring. Every inmate of the Old Capitol tried to procure some token of remembrance from Belle, and there was scarcely one who did not bestow to her some mark of regard, esteem or affection, as their sentiments and feelings influenced them severally, and as the means at their disposal afforded them an apportunity to manifest their sensibility. While every man who had any delicacy of feeling for the apparently forlorn prisoner, rejoiced at her release from such a loathsome place, and from being subjected, as she continually was, to insult and contumely, there was not a gentleman in the Old Capitol whose emotions did not overcome him as he saw her leave the place for home.

WRITING ON THE WALL.

When the Almighty became so provoked and indignant at the wickedness of the King of Babylon, that he could not suffer himself to be outraged any longer, He wrote the mysterious sentence of the King's punishment on the wall of his dining hall. Whether it was in imitation of this that the Old Capitol prisoners wrote their condemnation of Abe Lincoln and of his fellow-tyrants on the walls of their prison, the writer cannot say, but certain it is that these prison walls were almost literally covered with sentiments expressive of the indignation of those who were deprived of their liberty and other rights by the infamous tyrants at Washington. It was the custom of the prisoners to write their names in pencil on the wall of the first room in which they were incarcerated, adding the date of their arrest, the alleged cause of it, if suspected or known, and then adding their opinion, sometimes in doggerel, of their tyrant rulers. It is easy to see that by degrees, a little being added by every new comer, the walls would soon be covered with writing. This was the case, and it became so offensive that whitewashing was restored to, to mutilate it. Nor was it writing alone with which the Old Capitol walls were disfigured, speaking Administratively. Various designs of flags, caricatures, &c., were conspicuously displayed on these walls, some of which laid considerable claim to artistic merit. As most of the prisoners were Confederates, the devices on the walls were generally such as signified the feelings and sentiments of the people of the South. Rebel flags, both of the Southern States and of the Confederation, were displayed profusely, and in one room was a nearly full sized figure of Stonewall Jackson on his war charger. Thrown in among rebel songs, rebel sentiments and flags, a Northerner would occasionally have a fling at the Administration in some of his sentiments. The following are copied from the walls of room No. 10.

> In fancy free my mind doth roam
> From prison walls to distant home,
> No prison walls my thoughts can bound,
>   No tyrant's power can make me fear.
> Though hireling bayonets me surround,
>   What I was free, I still am here.
> I still am free by truth and right,
> A prisoner, not by law, but might,
> The victim of a despot's will,
> I'm doomed a felon's place to fill.
> I'm called a traitor, base pretense,
> I love my country, my offense.
> O, Country, once how happy thou,
> But where are all thy glories now?
> Where that liberty, thy boast,
> Where that Union, once our toast?
> Liberty in shackles weeps,
> While her avenger rashly sleeps.
> Avenger, says't thou? Where are they
> Who once o'er this broad land held sway,
> Where are the freemen who would not brook
> The rule of scepter, crown or crook?
> Degenerate they in every state
> Which made their fathers good and great.

Another was as follows:

AN APPEAL TO FREE AMERICANS.

> Freemen, ye sleep while the Nation is dying,
>   Arouse from your stupor, ye sons of the brave,
> See, in the Bastiles your comrades are lying,
>   Shall tyranny trample them down to the grave?
>   No! you reply,
>   Freemen will die
> Rather than one shall live as a slave.

> Come then to the rescue, let each one be striving
>   For who shall be foremost in Liberty's cause,
> Down with the Bastiles! see, the tyrants are flying,
>   Who outraged their country, its honor and laws.
>   Victims of might,
>   Servants of right,
> The tyrants are worsted, join us in applause.

At the bottom of this was signed the name of the writer, so that there could be no mistaking who was the offender. This was but one of the many evidences written on the walls and uttered in the hearing of those whose duty it was to convey the information to head-quarters of the spirit which still animated the emaciated bodies of the political martyrs. They could be imprisoned by the might of the tyrants, they could be treated with indignity without having the physical strength to resent it, they could be almost starved to enforce submission, but it was not in the power, mighty as it became with a million of armed men at its back, for the Administration to shackle the spirits of the freemen whose bodies the arbitrary decrees of Lincoln and Stanton subjected to Old Capitol Prison outrages.

NO. 10 AND ITS OCCUPANTS.

About the end of August, Messrs. Stanley, Sheward, and Mahony were transferred rrom No. 13 to No. 10, in the Old Capitol. No. 10 was a sort of privileged room. There were no guards to interfere with one's recreations and amusements, and the victims of Lincolnism in this room were not obliged to feed at the pen down stairs, but were brought their meals, such as they were, by a contraband.

Soon after the introduction of the aforenamed victims into these new quarters, two gentlemen from New Jersey were brought in to keep them company. These were Joseph Kugler of Frenchtown, and Joseph W. Wright of Milford. They were not kept long in subjection, as influential persons at home, and the Governor of their State, it was understood, interposed in their behalf. As soon as they reached home they sent their fellow victims in No. 10 a box of such delicacies as a small crock of fresh butter, some of the largest and finest tomatoes that even New Jersey could produce, and various other things which, added to the Old Capitol fare, made living tolerable for several days. The thanks of No. 10 were voted to our New Jersey friends.

After the release of these victims, Dr. Marshal of Snowhill, Maryland, Aquila R. Allen of Washington City, John Apple of Philadelphia, Hugh Ardley of some place in Western Virginia, Warner Perry of ———, Penn., and a policeman named Newell, of Washington City, were occupants of this famous room.

Dr. Marshal was furious with indignation the day he was brought in, and for some days afterterwards he chafed like a caged lion, and could not understand how it was that those of us who had been subjected for weeks already to the arbitrary despotism which ruled over us, could endure it so complacently. We told him he would be cooled down after living on prison fare for a few weeks, as we had done. But he scarcely did. His indignation was never relaxed. Every time his thoughts ran on his arrest and situation, he gave loose rein to the feelings excited by the outrages to which he had been subjected.

The night on which the Doctor was arrested, one of his servants, a slave, went to him and told him that if he would only say the word, the servants, slaves, would soon dispose of the officers who were then in the house. The poor, faithful slaves could not see what massa had done wrong to be thus torn away from home, and taken he knew not where. Little did they think that it was on their account, and others such as they, that these outrages were committed on free white men.

AQUILA R. ALLEN was serving his second term in

O. C. P. at this time. His offence was the arrest of a fugitive slave, according to law—and to Gen. Wadsworth belongs the credit of imprisoning Mr. Allen for this performance of, to him, his duty. As this case is referred to elsewhere, I will not repeat it here.

JOHN APPLE, after living for some time in the Hospital for want of room in the prison proper, was quartered in No. 10. He became one of the most useful members of our mess. He had some acquaintances in Washington, through whom he procured various necessaries of life which were not furnished by Uncle Abe, and he had an aptitude for "learning the ropes" about the Old Capitol, which he never failed to turn to good account for the benefit of "our mess." Through his exertions and the favors of Mrs. Allen, and the management of our commissary department by Mr. Sheward, we lived some of the time in No. 10 like "fighting cocks." But it was either a feast or a famine with us. For two or three days at a time we had plenty —then again we would be reduced for some time to Lincoln fare.

As there were no guards in No. 10, a good deal of "skylarking" was indulged in. As we could not sleep at night with the torments of the vermin, we often had to get up and pass away the time as best we could. On one occasion Sheward and Apple proposed to Mr. Crolly to have a dance. Mr. Crolly I ought to have said, was an old bachelor who had been engaged for many years as a railroad contractor in Virginia.

On the breaking out of the war, the State of Virginia was largely in his debt. It so happened that at the time of the battles before Richmond, Mr. Crolly was at that place endeavoring to procure a settlement of his account with the State, which he effected, so far as to ascertain how much was due him, but did not get the money. After obtaining the settlement, Mr. Crolly returned to his home in Western Virginia, then in the possession of the Federal army and recognizing the authority of the Federal Government. Mr. Crolly being an industrious man, determined to turn his attention to merchandizing, and for that purpose he went to Baltimore late in August to purchase goods. While there he fell in with an Irishman, a countryman of his own, who it turned out was in the employ of Baker, chief detective of the War Department. This fellow soon found out that Crolly was a goose pretty well feathered, and learning from Crolly some of his antecedents, had him arrested, and taken before the Provost Marshal at Baltimore. After hearing the case, Crolly making an honest statement about himself, the Provost Marshal discharged him. But his quondam friend, the detective, was determined he should not get off in that way, so he procured an order from Washington for Crolly's apprehension. This time he got into Baker's clutches, and from his grasp there was no escape but by the relaxing power of money. So Crolly was thrust into the Old Capitol, and became a roommate of No. 10. From a fancied resemblance which he bore to General Jackson, he was at once dubbed by that cognomen, by which he was known among us in the Old Capitol.

Mr. Crolly was now an old man, not less than sixty years of age, but he was straight as a shingle, and prided himself a good deal on his accomplishments, among which was that of dancing.

"Can you dance, Jackson," enquired Apple, putting his head out of his bunk on the occasion referred to.

"Huh, in faith I can," was the reply.

"What can you dance?" enquired the mischievous Apple.

"Anything at all you wish," replied Jackson.

By this time, every one in the room was sitting up in bed and a light had been struck.

"Sheward," enquired Apple, "can you whistle."

"Yes," replied Sheward, "what do you want me to do?"

"Jackson here says he can dance, and I just want to see if he can. If you will whistle I'll beat juber for him, and we'll see whether he is playing off on us or not. Jackson," continued Apple, "come down here and let us see what you can do."

"Jackson," who was thus adressed was in the bunk over Apple, and without more ado, down he came, in his night shirt and drawers, straightened himself up and took the position to begin. Sheward whistled, Apple beat juber, Crolly danced with a vim, and the rest of the crowd roared with laughter. Crolly's feet were applied to the floor so vigorously that the rickety old building fairly shook, and in a few minutes a crash was heard below.

"To bed with you, ye devil," was shouted at Crolly, and to bed he jumped as nimbly as a youth of sixteen. He was scarcely there before the corporal of the guard made his appearance.

"What the h—l and d———n are you fellows doing up here?" enquired the corporal.

"Why, what's the matter, corporal?" said one, in a voice as if of one just disturbed from sleep.

"The whole ceiling under here has just fallen down on Colonel Kohler, and he is d———n near dead."

"How did it happen, corporal?" was the enquiry.

"Happen," said the corporal, "why you fellows have been making a noise up here; that's how it happened, and there's the devil to pay."

"Corporal, just look here," said one. "Do you see this man dying on the floor," pointing to Warner Perry, whose bedstead was the floor. "Every time he rolls over this house shakes. Perry," addressing the gentleman on the floor, " won't you roll over to let the corporal see how it is."

Mr. Perry who weighed fifty pounds either under or over three hundred, I forget which, gave a roll and sure enough the building shook. "There, corporal," continued the spokesman, "if anything has happened down stairs, it came of leaving that man sleep on the floor."

"Da—nd if I don't believe it's so," said the Corporal, and off he went satisfied that nothing wrong had occurred in No. 10. But we who knew better were all anxiety to learn whether any harm had befallen our friend Col. Kohler. Our fears were relieved by his appearance among us next morning by special permission. His first salute to us was, 'what the devil were you fellows about last night?" Seeing that he was not hurt we told him the whole story, and he enjoyed it as much as we had done.

A large piece of the ceiling had fallen down, but fortunately missed both the Colonel and a Major who was his room mate.

In No. 10, as in the other rooms during the hot weather, a portion of every night was spent in killing vermin. The sight of a party of men in their night clothes with a candle in one hand, and the other occupied in destroying the tormentors of their rest was ludicrous in the extreme, and the conversation which accompanied the operation was not less amusing. Nothing short of a representation of such scenes could do them any justice or give the reader more than a faint idea of the reality.

NO. 16, AND ITS INMATES.

Towards the latter end of September, those of us who had been left in No. 10 up to that time, viz. Allen, Sheward, Apple and Mahony were transferred to No. 16, with the promise that the change was made preparatory to releasing us soon ; but this was not the design or the cause of our removal.

The real cause of removing us was that the rooms on the third story were to be used to keep some prisoners who were expected soon in solitary confinement.

When we were placed in No. 16, the following named persons were there before us, and were our room-mates till they were discharged, and some of whom remained till the 11th of November.

ADDRESS OF PERSONS CONFINED IN ROOM NO. 16, OLD CAPITOL PRISON.

John H. Mulkey, Circuit Judge, Cairo, Ill., Attorney.
A. D. Duff, C. P. Judge, Benton, Ill.,   "
J. Blanchard, Murphysboro, Ill.,   "
J. M. Williams, Spring Garden, Ill., Merchant.
A. C. Nelson, Marion, Ill., Farmer.
John M. Clementson, Marion, Ill., Attorney.
A. P. Corder,   "   " M. D.
Samuel H. Bundy,   "   " Attorney.
F. M. Youngblood, Benton,   "   "
J. R. Brown, Shiloh Hill, Ill., Doctor.
W. A. Haines, Tamaroa, Ill., Farmer.
M. L. Ross,   "   " Doctor.
W. E. Smith.   "   "   "
W. S. Hawkes,   "   " Editor.
Bedford Turman,   "   " Farmer.
O. H. McCarvier,   "   "   "
David Patten, Griggsville, "   "
P. L. Reeder, Chesterfield, "   "
Hiram A. Royse, Sullivan, "   "
D. H. Dowell, Quincy,   "   "
Samuel Stoutzberger, Rob Roy, Ind., Farmer.
H. W. Newland, Benton, Ill.   "
A. B. Hewitt, Chatham, Ill., Doctor.

Mehaffey & O'Dell, Eds. Dem. Standard, Paris.
John W. Smith, Jacksonville, Citizen.

In addition to these, a number of others were incarcerated with us in this famous rooom. Among them were:

Rev. J. D. Benedict, of Buffalo, N. Y.
T. T. Edgerton, New York, N. Y.
Dr. T. T. Ellis,   "   "
Dr. Moran, Frederick, Md.
B. F. Brown,   "   "
V. R. Jackson, Washington City, D. C.
George W. Wilson, Upper Marlboro', Md.
Edwin Henry, Flushing, N. Y.
—— Hill, N. Y.
Samuel Emmons, Philadelphia, Penn.
—— Hopkins, Washington, D. C.
Frank Blair, Jr., St. Louis, Mo.

The doings of this room, among the victims of arbitrary power, beggars all description. A faint effort at describing the occurrences of this famous locality is attempted in other parts of this book, but not till the pen of some Dickens or Thackeray can be inspired by the various recitals of each one's history will justice be done to No. 16 Old Capitol.

PRISON AMUSEMENTS AND RECREATION.

The prisoners generally in the Old Capitol were permitted to spend a half hour at each meal time in the yard, or rather so much of that time as was not occupied in eating. The prisoners who took their meals in their rooms could so arrange the time of eating as to take the whole half hour allowed in the yard, in recreation. Most of the time, however during the months of August, September, and part of October, there was no room in the yard to indulge in any exercise. The yard was lumbered up with tents during this time, and full of prisoners, both Federal and Confederate, so that all the recreation which could be indulged in, was to gather in a crowd together, and elbow one's way through it. Even this was made disagreeable by being dogged around by the detectives and spies who were ever on the alert to listen to the conversation and to watch the actions of the prisoners. No sooner would a few persons stand in a group to converse with each other, than one of these detectives, pretending to be a prisoner like the others, would approach and manifest the greatest possible interest in the subject of conversation. If it happened to be on the affairs of the Government, or the state of the country, or the outrageous course of the Administration, as the conversation often was, these spies became trebly interested. They were sure to put in a word which was calculated to draw out others. Sometimes one would forget that he was a prisoner and feeling as if he were an American freeman, would give such expression to his emotions and convictions as would thrill his audience, and load the detectives with valuable information for headquarters. Of course every conversation of this kind was carefully noted, and those who participated in them, were more vigilantly observed.

During the most of October, and up to the time in November of the discharge of the Political prisoners, the yard was comparatively clear of rubbish, so that the prisoners had, during the half hour at a time allowed them, an opportunity to stretch their legs in a walk. This they did generally in pairs, one object of which was to avoid the detectives. In this way, the prisoners who were well acquainted with each other, would take what was called their recreation. Those who were not so fortunate as to have acquaintances, fell of course into the hands of the detectives, who, through these prisoners found out what they could of these whom they could not so familiarly approach.

About the latter end of October, several balls and chains were placed in the yard. Their appearance there was regarded by most of the prisoners as significant, nothing of the kind having been seen there before. For some days no one ventured near these instruments of punishment, their very appearance in such a place being so suggestive of disagreeable emotions as to keep off the most reckless from any familiarity. At length, however, some of the younger prisoners ventured to approach and handle these iron instruments of punishment, and soon they were used by most of the crowd in gymnastic feats.

The yard recreation, though monotonous, had nevertheless some variety, as there was something new occurring every day. Very often during the time of recreation some new prisoners would be brought in. The whole crowd would gather round the new comers to learn the news, and for the time being the scene would be quite animative. If the new comers happened, as was often the case, to be prisoners of war, more reliable information was obtained from them of the result of the battles in which they participated than the Administration news agents were allowed to publish.

The scenes in the yard were occasionally enlivened by the antics of the contrabands, who were the only persons within the prison precincts who were allowed to enjoy their natural liberty. As they had a good deal of idle time, they would indulge in their favorite pastime of skylarking. The men would make a dash into the women's quarters, and after pulling and hauling at each other for some time, the women would seem to get the better of their male associates, who would be obliged to run at the top of their speed, followed by the women with brooms or some other weapon of combat. These scenes were enjoyed by the prisoners as much, if not more, than any comedy they had ever seen acted on the stage. Their effect in exciting their emotions to laughter was really beneficial, as there was little in prison life to produce such feelings.

The amusements proper of the prison were but few and simple. Most of the prisoners played cards all day long and till roll-call at nine o'clock at night. The favorite game was bluff-poker, and the stakes or chips were one-cent pieces. It was as amusing to a looker on to see with what earnestness and feeling the game was played as it was to the players themselves. For days and weeks in succession, without any other intermission than meals, sleep and Sundays, did the same set play their game of poker, killing both time and their feelings by having their mind occupied in that amusement. What could they have done to keep them from thinking of the outrages to which they had been subjected, were it not for having those cards to amuse them? Whoever invented them, no matter how much they have been made the means of doing mischief, contributed to the gratification of his fellow beings in no small degree. The writer of this is not a card-player, but he is satisfied from his own observation, that there is amusement in them for the most enlightened and cultivated intellect, as there is for the simplest and most ignorant of mankind.

Next to poker, the favorite game was muggins, or, as it was called in the prison, Old Capitol. This is not a gambling game, like the other, and though very simple, is nevertheless considerably amusing, if one might judge from the almost continued laughter and disputes of the players.

As time wore on for week after week, the prisoners became dull, stupid, and debilitated for want of bodily exercise. Judge Mulkey, of Cairo, Ill., hit upon the happy expedient of exercising his roommates of No. 16, by leading off, once or twice a day, in a march back and forth the room, followed by all his fellow-prisoners, who joined in the chorus of the songs of the Judge, to which the feet of the party kept time. This exercise would sometimes be kept up for an hour at a time, and its beneficial effects were experienced all round. Those who had previously lain in a sort of stupor all day on their beds, felt invigorated and cheerful after a few such exercises as that alluded to. Nor was it the exercise alone that contributed to this salutary effect.— The songs of Judge Mulkey were generally of such a ludicrous character that the whole crowd would be convulsed with laughter, not only at the songs, but at the Judge's manner of singing them.

One of the favorite songs was "Out of the Wilderness." A sample of two verses will satisfy the reader.

> My old horse, he came from Jerusalem,
>   He came from Jerusalem,
>   He came from Jerusalem,
> My old horse, he came from Jerusalem,
>   Down in Alabam,
> Oh, law gals, bully boys, hay.
> Oh, ain't you mighty glad you are out of the wilderness,
>   Out of the wilderness,
>   Out of the wilderness,
> Ain't you mighty glad you are out of the wilderness,
>   Down in Alabam.
>
> He kicked so high they put him in the Museum,
>   They put him in the Museum,
>   They put him in the Musenm,

He kicked so high they put him in the Museum,
  Down in Alabam.
Oh, law gals, &c.

The bumble bee he stang the rooster,
  He stang the rooster,
  He stang the rooster,
The bumble bee he stang the rooster,
  Down in Alabam.
Oh, law gals, &c.

Not many theatrical scenes could be more ludicrous than that presented by the prisoners of Room No. 16, singing this song and keeping step to the refrain, led off by Judge Mulkey. The Judge, who was the life of the party on such occasions, would be in his shirt sleeves, his hat drawn forward, and his countenance expressive of good humor, using one of his hands to mark time as he sang and moved along.

Next after him, generally, was Judge Duff, or Mahony, both the very opposite of their leader in disposition, but enjoying with as much zest as any one, his amusing songs. Indeed, it was as much, and more, for their amusement and that of his fellow-prisoners than for his own, that Judge Mulkey relaxed himself from the dignity of a Judge to the character in which he appeared in No. 16. By his ever-ready disposition to contribute to the amusement of his fellow-prisoners, he endeared himself to them by such ties of feeling as neither distance apart can sever or time destroy.

Another song, and a general favorite, was "I have a home up yonder."

"The sucker's melody," one of Judge Mulkey's own composition, was the song of all others which brought down the house. This was sung usually after roll call at night, and generally when all were in bed. It was a kind of a winding up of the day's exercises. As the song was composed for the exclusive use of No. 16, Old Capitol, publishing it is not permitted.

After the Sucker's Melody, which was generally sung in bed, "Old Aunt Rosy" was sung as a hymn, and then all would be silent for the night in No. 16, except when disturbed by the call of the guards by the introduction of a new prisoner, or by, what was frequently the case, being roused out of bed by the attacks of the chinches, as bedbugs are called in the locality of Washington.

INTRODUCING A NEW PRISONER.

It frequently happened that prisoners were brought in at night. When this was the case, the scene presented to the poor new comer's vision was anything but prepossessing. Let the introduction be into No. 16, for the purpose of giving the reader some idea of the scene presented to the prisoner's view. After passing through the ordeal of an examination of baggage, &c., if one should be permitted to have any, in the "Captain's office," the prisoner is accompanied up stairs to No. 16, by probably a sergeant or corporal of the guard, or by a lieutenant. The door of the room is unlocked by the sentinel or guard, and the light of a candle carried by the officer reveals to the inquisitive eye of the prisoner his future quarters, No. 16, containing say twenty persons. Here to the right as you enter are three or four shake-downs on the floor, each one occupied by a sleeper. To the left a little farther on, and with just space enough to walk carefully between the sleepers, are two or three more of the victims of tyranny. On tables in the center of the room are two others. These tables are used in the day time for eating on and playing cards. At night, a couple of straw ticks are laid on them and two prisoners use them for their beds. Judge Duff and Dr. Ross of Illinois occupied these tables for weeks, as their bedstead. To the left of the tables in a corner, one on the floor and the other on a cot, are two others, Judge Mulkey is the occupant of the cot and Mr. Sheward lies on the floor near him. To the right of the center of the room there are three iron bedsteads occupied by Messrs. Mahony, Ellis and Edgerton. Just beyond are beds on the floor. Every foot almost of the floor is occupied in this way while most of the bunks, of which there are twenty-one in the room, are empty.

The officer hunts round and with the aid of Commissary Brown who arrives by this time, or of his assistant Charley, a place is found for the new comer to lie down. Very likely some one wakes up in the confusion made by the intrusion of the new comer, who is at once subjected to such queries as the following:

"Stranger, it is the custom of this place to enquire of every new comer his name, place of residence, and what was he sent here for. In accordance with this custom, although you may think the enquiry impertinent, I now ask your name."

Stranger gives his name.

"Will you now please to tell us where you are from?"

Stranger complies.

"The next question we have to put, and to which we request an answer, is what have you done, or what are you accused of having done?"

This is generally a very difficult question to answer, as not one in a hundred knows what the charge is on which he is arrested. So some explanation is given, and this leads generally to such a conversation between the new comer and the other prisoners as enables the latter to form their opinion of the character of their new associate. There are but few circumstances in life in which men can be placed where their character can be sooner estimated and properly appreciated than in the Old Capitol. Nature in man has more of its influence in such a place than where one is at liberty. Except in detectives, perhaps, and such other satellites of the Administration, there is no inducement or motive for a man to be otherwise than what nature made him. His good and ill qualities become apparent at once, and it is seldom that a proper estimate was not made of a new comer in No. 16, on the first introduction.

The stranger having answered the queries put to him, if by his deportment and manner he has shown himself to be worthy of respect, he is asked whether he has had any supper; or if it be in the day time, after the usual hour of meals, whether he had breakfast or dinner, as the case might be. If he replied in the negative, Commissary Sheward rummaged his larder and produced some bread and butter (the latter purchased by the prisoners themselves), and possibly a portion of meat, of which there was some generally on hand, the purchase also of the prisoners, that furnished by the Government being seldom eaten. This, and a general introduction all round, concludes the initiatory ceremonies of a new prisoner in No. 16, and thenceforward the new comer was treated as a brother victim of the despotism which reigns in Washington. The new comer was duly informed that if he had only swindled the Government, and especially of a large sum, or ran the blockade, or done anything else contrary to law which resulted in putting money in his pocket, he was all right, and would soon be released—a part of the money he made would do it—but if he had dared to think and say that our country's liberties were in danger, then God help him. Three months, at least, would be his punishment.

CATCHING CHINCHES OR BED BUGS.

During the hot weather of August, September, and most of October, catching bed bugs was a nightly occupation in the Old Capitol.

No dodging could escape the reconnoissance of these vigilant and active marauders. Even those who slept on the tables were soon assailed with as much fury as those who remained in the bunks. The floor was the best place of all to sleep on, as it was swept every day; so that, to reach the sleepers on the floor, the bugs would have to make considerable of a journey from their "base of operations." This, however, they accomplished at about 12 or 1 o'clock, when the assault would be made in force upon their sleeping victims. About that time of the night, some one would wake up smarting from the bites which he had received, and uttering imprecations on his tormentors. Soon the whole crowd would be awake, candles would be lighted, and then for the onslaught on the bugs If the scene, as it was presented on one of these occasions, could be properly illustrated, it would cause more laughter than all the comedies played upon the stage for years. Nothing short of a tableaux vivants could give a good idea of what it was; but it would be defective without the conversation which took place on such occasions.

"Ross," one would inquire of Dr. Ross, of Illinois, " how are you making out?"

"Oh! bully," replies Ross, who, with a lighted candle in his hand, is burning the bugs out of a crack in the table on which he slept. "I'm slaying them by the hundred," continues he.

Away off, in the left hand corner, Judge Mulkey is bent down examining his bedclothes, and picking off the enemy as fast as his fingers could reach them. Sheward is near by, killing away vigorously. Judge Duff is helping Ross, his bedmate. Mahony is sitting up in bed, searching among his bedclothes for the bloodthirsty intruders. Wilson, of Upper Marlboro', Md., whose sleeping place is down near the door, right hand side, is punning on every remark made by the others. "Quinine," an alias given to a prisoner who was arrested because some quinine was found in his possession at Washington, is shaking his bed and bedclothes, and with the sole of his boot putting an end to the existence of his assailants. Father Benedict, of Buffalo, N. Y., is committing the murder, quietly, of a portion of his tormentors. Hill, also of New York, is armed with a shoe, and standing as high up as he can get a foothold, he is plying his weapon of destruction vigorously. Frank Blair, Jr., is similarly engaged.

"Oh golly!" exclaims Frank, "what a whopper I killed just now."

Instead of doing which, the mischievous Frank was throwing down every bug he caught on some of the fellows below.

"Hanged if I don't believe they are falling down from the ceiling," exclaims Quinine, who was one of the special objects of Frank's mischief.

"So I think," observes Mr. Henry, who slept in a third story bunk.

"There," says another, "one has just fallen down on my face."

It was so—the mischievous Frank was as busy as he could be in searching for them for the purpose of throwing them down on the victims of his mischievous amusement. And so, for an hour or two every warm night, the occupants of No. 16 were engaged in killing bugs. All the orders of battle which could be conceived of were given on these occasions. Pickets were set to watch the enemy, skirmishers were thrown out, bases of operation were selected, reports made of the number of captured and slain—and after an exhaustive battle, in which many wounds were inflicted on one party, and thousands killed on the other side, the assailing party being always routed, the prisoners slept upon their arms, ready at a moment's warning for a renewal of the attack.

A COMPASSIONATE CONTRABAND SHARES HIS BREAD WITH A VICTIM OF DESPOTISM.

One of the most touching incidents of my life in the Old Capitol was the compassionate regard manifested for me on more than one occasion by the contraband "Bob," who brought our meals to us while we occupied Nos. 13 and 10, in the Bastile in Washington.

Soon after the second battle of Bull Run, when Burnside's corps d'armee reached Washington it was out of provisions, and a requisition was made on all the bread that could be spared from other mouths to feed Burnside's army. Of course we Prisoners of State, victims of despotism, were among the first to be deprived of bread, instead of which old hard crackers were substituted. One of the prisoners, Dr. Ross, of Tamaroa, Ill., describes these crackers as being so hard that fire was knocked out of them when struck against each other, and cigars were lit by the sparks. This figurative language will scarcely give the reader an idea of how hard these crackers were—but it will be sufficient to say that the prisoners actually played with them like quoits without breaking them.

The contraband, Bob, took it into his head that I could not eat these crackers—so on the second day they were furnished to us the poor fellow came up stairs and approached me in an awkwardly familiar manner, saying as he came near, "Dese crackers is too hard for massa, an' I to't I'd bring him dis ere loaf o' bread"—saying which he pulled out from his bosom a small loaf of bread, a part of his own rations, and handed it to me.

I was overpowered with conflicting emotions.— My treatment and that of my fellow prisoners—our subjection to such usage as that which we were enduring, and the humanity of this poor negro—these and other thoughts crowded together in my mind, and for the moment left me without power of utterance. When I got proper control of myself, I inquired of Bob whether the servants, all colored, were furnished with bread rations. He replied that they were. It was only the victims of despotism who were obliged to put up with the cracker fare.

I will do the Superintendent the justice which I thought at the time he deserved, to say as I believed, that he did his best to have bread furnished the prisoners—and it was doubtless owing to his exertions that an order issued from head-quarters was revoked withholding bread from the prisoners altogether.

MURDER OF TWO PRISONERS IN THE OLD CAPITOL, JESSE W. WHARTON AND HARRY STEWART.

I have mentioned, in another place, the recklessness and wilful malevolence of the guards at the Old Capitol. I will cite, in confirmation of what I experienced myself and came under my own observation, two cases of murder, which occurred before my incarceration. They are related by eyewitnesses of the murderous scenes:

About the latter part of March, or the first of April, Mr. Jesse W. Wharton, a young man about twenty-six years of age—son of Dr. Wharton, Professor of Agricultural Chemistry in Prince Georges County, Md.—was wantonly murdered by a man named Harrison Baker, a member of the 91st Pennsylvania Regiment, then stationed as a guard in the Old Capitol. Mr. Wharton was formerly an officer in the U. S. Regular Service, noted for courage the most undaunted, and a liberality of heart and qualities of mind which made him numerous friends wherever he sojourned. One of the regulations of the prison was, that no one should protrude his head or limbs beyond the line of the building, when looking from the windows. On this unfortunate occasion the deceased gentleman was standing at the window of Room No. 10, and was strictly within the prescribed limits allowed, when Baker, the sentry in the yard, very insultingly ordered him away, "or he would blow his d—d head off;" when Mr. Wharton, feeling indignant, made some rejoinder, and then turning, paced the room a few times, and then quietly presented himself at the window again—some two feet or so from the window—with his arms folded over his breast, looking out. The sentinel (Baker) again, without any reason or provocation, ordered him away with a threat. Mr. Wharton, conscious of not infringing any of the rules, paid no particular attention to the leveled musket in the guard's hands, and kept his position in the room, his arms still folded; when the sentry, with the most guilty thirst for the blood of an unarmed prisoner, confined without the least chance of escape, took deliberate aim and fired his piece, the "minie" ball passing through the hand of the left arm and the elbow of the right, breaking the bone and entering exactly at the right nipple, passed out near the spine, going through the lungs.

Still erect, he gazed fixedly at his murderer a moment, then began to reel backwards, when two of his room-mates caught him in their arms and lowered him to the floor. He remained quiet until the doctors came, when he called for the Lieutenant commanding the post (Mr. Mulligan)—and he having come, Wharton bid him face him, when he clearly and distinctly, in the presence of the doctors and his fellow prisoners, accused Lieutenant Mulligan of having given the order to fire—he having heard him—and branded him his murderer, calling upon him to look upon a dying man, and hear his sentence from the chilling lips of his unoffending victim. Whatever the officer's thoughts, he exhibited no emotions but a slavish fear, and then left the room without a word, with Cain's brand upon him. The dying prisoner lingered eight hours from the time of his being shot (about eleven o'clock A. M.), and was attended by his young wife and two sisters, until his last gasp betokened him death's prisoner, and the grave his next cell.

Mr. Wharton resigned his commission in the Federal army, and was consequently arrested by the Government and confined here for fear of his going South. The sentinel who shot him was promoted.

In the latter part of May—Mr. Harry Stewart—aged about 23 years, and son of Dr. Frederick Stewart of Baltimore, was shot by a sentinel belonging to the 86th Regiment, N. Y. Vols., under the following circumstances. Mr. Stewart was a very fine young gentleman, of short but robust stature, and excellent qualities, and having been to Richmond, was arrested upon his return as a spy. The charge being a serious one, he was anxious to escape, and the sentry who shot him, having several times committed himself by introducing such remarks as would lead the prisoners to believe him open for a bribe,

Mr. Stewart managed to converse with him, when the sentinel told him positively that he would for fifty dollars connive at his escape, and permit him to pass from the second story window to the pavement below without molestation. For at least a week this plan was discussed, giving the guard ample time to revoke his bargain, if he desired, but he still encouraged Stewart in the attempt and finally fixed the night himself, he being on guard from 10 to 12 and 4 to 6 o'clock. Mr. Stewart remained up all night awaiting the signal of his co-operator, which occurred about 4 o'clock, A. M., the sentinel calling him and saying "now was his time," and to make haste. Stewart trusting to the man's honesty of purpose, swung himself by a rope from the window, and before he was three feet from the top of the window, the sentry cried halt! and before a second elapsed, instantly fired his musket, the ball penetrating the right leg below the knee, passing through the knee-bone, completely splintering it and passing out between the knee and the hip upon the inside. His friends pulled him into the room again, and before the proper applications could be administered, great loss of blood prostrated the sufferer exceedingly. About 11 o'clock the prison surgeon, Dr. Stewart came, when he determined to amputate Mr. Stewart's leg, there being no other hope. The operation was performed, before the system had rallied from the great nervous shock sustained, and the loss of blood being severe, the patient expired within an hour after the amputation. Chloroform was administered. The fifty dollars was found in the young man's pocket all ready wrapped up for the sentry, and written upon the paper containing the funds was the sentence,—"This is the money I promised you." The bribery was fairly proven, the deliberation attending the attempt to murder was apparent, and proof that the sentry called him, was ready, and yet the authorities did not even punish the guilty sentinel, but actually put the villain upon guard afterwards, though he was subsequently placed in some other position.

The same sentinel deserted afterwards and was brought back to the Old Capitol a prisoner, where he was up to the middle of November. He was one of the most villainous looking human beings that ever had the face and head of a man. He would pass for a twin-brother of Marshal Hoxie of Iowa, whom every one would call a villain from his looks.

ARREST OF SYMPATHIZING FEMALES, AND THEIR SUBJECTION TO INSULT AND OUTRAGE.

"Pass on there," "hurry on off that corner." Such and similar were the more than hourly exclamations of the guards around the Old Capitol Prison to passers by, who lingered for a moment on the side-walks opposite the prison, or who ventured to cast a look of curiosity or of sympathy towards that Bastile. It was a matter of daily occurrence for the corporal of the guard to seize his musket and run across the street to drive off any loiterer who may not be walking fast enough by to satisfy the commands of the Provost Marshal, Doster, or Military Governor Wadsworth, and it was a thing of frequent, almost of daily occurrence for the corporal of the guard to arrest, detain, and sometimes bring into the prison persons who had the temerity to look towards the prison windows, or who made any sign of sympathy for or recognition of the prisoners. The victims of this extraordinary vigilance were mostly females, who could only resent the outrages to which they were subjected by indignant looks accompanied by such gestures as one might suppose would be provoked in a spirited woman on being taken hold of by an ill-mannered corporal, or guard. It seemed to the prisoners on witnessing such occurrences, that it was done more by the guards to gratify their beastly feelings, than it was to perform a necessary duty. Certain it is, that for one person of the male kind arrested and detained in this way, there were not less than fifty females.

The prisoners were witnesses frequently to such occurrences as here stated, and of course they could only see what happened on the street occasionally, as they were prevented from standing close to the windows, and it was only during a portion of the day that they indulged their curiosity by looking out into the streets.

Almost every day a carriage full of ladies would be halted by the guards for no other apparent cause than that one of the number would turn her head towards one of the windows of the prison as the carriage drove by. Of course, rather than be shot at, the carriage would be stopped in compliance with the order to halt. Sometimes, after a long altercation between the corporal of the guards and the occupants of the carriage, the vehicle would be allowed to pass on, but more frequently, the corporal ordered the driver to about his horses and drive to the entrance of the prison where the ladies would be obliged to alight and enter. What transpired between them and the guards was not vouchsafed for the prisoners to see or hear, but after being detained for some time they would be permitted to leave, fully impressed, no doubt, with the conviction that there was a government in these United States of America, which both respected personal rights and secured every person, even defenceless females, in their enjoyment.

One day, towards the latter part of October, a lady with two little girls was passing along the street in front of the Old Capitol. When they had reached the corner, the lady stopped for a moment and turned round towards the prison. Scarcely had she stopped before the guard who was patroling in front of the prison entrance, ordered her to halt with which she of course complied. The corporal of the guard went to her, and after some conversation in which the lady evidently manifested some reluctance to accompany him to the prison, one of the little girls was permitted to go on while the lady and the other one, the larger of the two, was compelled to accompany the guard to the prison.

After being detained either in the room occupied by the guards, or in the inner room occupied by the officer of the day, for more than an hour, the young lady and her young companion were let loose; admonished, no doubt, of the wickedness of casting even a glance of curiosity at the Old Capitol Prison. Reader, do you realize that such occurrences as this took place in broad daylight, not only in the city of Washington, in the United States of America, but under the shadow of the Capitol, and in an edifice in whose halls the principles of free government were nobly vindicated and boldly enunciated by the immortal statesmen of the last generation? There, in the very precincts now used by the despots of our day for the imprisonment of American freemen, the men whom the world delights to honor and call its own taught us our rights and instructed us in the duty we should perform to preserve our liberties. Alas! how have these old walls been desecrated! Desecrated, did I say?—no, not desecrated; for what fitter place was there to imprison martyrs of liberty than the sacred premises whence the doctrines of liberty were preached to the American people, and to all the world? But these precincts were desecrated by other scenes—by a brutal and beastly set who dragged inoffensive women from the streets and subjected them to insult and outrage.

ESPIONAGE IN THE PRISON.

The Administration, not content with having deprived its victims of their rights, and with holding them writhing in its tyrannic grasp, established a system of espionage over them in the Old Capitol prison. This was done by means of detectives, who ostensibly appeared among the other prisoners as Prisoners of State. One of these detectives, it was understood, indeed one of the officers of the prison gave such information, that there was one of these detectives in every room of the Prison, and that no word could escape his hearing and no act his observation. The writer of this was in the habit of talking freely and as plainly and boldly of the course of the Administration in the prison as out of it, and therefore became a special object of this espionage. Time and again when conversing with some friends or acquaintances in the prison yard during the half hour's recreation allowed at meal time, a listener might be noticed within hearing distance catching every word that was spoken, and when he thought that he was not observed, turning his eye upon the speakers to catch the expression of their countenance and the motion of their gestures.

These detectives would once in a while be spotted and then the word would be passed round among the prisoners to look out for the scoundrel. The detective being thus observed, finding it useless for him to remain any longer, would either leave voluntarily or be sent away to make room for another more expert or shrewd than himself. It kept the prisoners in almost constant watchfulness to detect these contemptible hirelings of the Administration; but with all the vigilance that the prisoners could exert, they would of course be frequently foiled.

Lieutenant Miller, who appeared to be the principal officer of the Old Capitol next to Superintendent Wood, used to boast that there was nothing said or done in any room of the prison, that he was not aware of. This to some extent at least, was not so, for in spite of all the espionage and surveillance of the detectives, the prisoners would have communication with each other, and once in a while with their friends. It is needless here to say how: that will do to tell when Lincoln's reign of terror will have been succeeded by the mild, gentle and simple sway of a Constitutional Government, and when it will not harm any one in or out of prison to reveal by what means letters and communications were conveyed from prisoners in the Old Capitol, to their friends and families. It will form an interesting sequel to what is now published concerning Lincoln's Bastiles.

There is one incident which it might not be amiss to publish, as it shows in what estimation the detective system of the Government was regarded by Superintendent Wood of the Old Capitol. One of the Washington City Police having been committed to the prison by order of General Wadsworth for some offense or other connected with a runaway negro, the prisoner was placed in Room No. 10, where there were four other prisoners, all Prisoners of State at the time, among them Mahony and Sheward, of Iowa, and John Apple, Esq., of Philadelphia. The Prisoners of State looked with considerable suspicion on the policeman; but he told so fair a story and entered so much into their feelings and made himself so agreeable, that their suspicions became lulled into security, and they conversed as freely as ever on the state of the country, the tyranny of the Administration, the prospective result of the war, &c.

Not many days after the introduction among us

of this policeman, the Superintendent entered the room in such a moody gait and countenance, that every one was at once struck with his appearance, and their conjectures were at once excited as to what might be the matter, for very evidently there was something wrong when the Superintendent did not look pleased. After a few moments pacing of the room, the Superintendent, with an open letter in his hand, approached the policeman, and in a stern, demanding tone, inquired of him whether he had written the letter to which his attention was called. Policeman glanced at the letter, but before having time to answer, the Superintendent denounced him in such terms of opprobrium and contumely as it would be almost impossible to excel. "'You infernal scoundrel," said he, "I put you in this room among gentlemen, presuming you to be a gentleman, but you have acted in such a manner as proves that you were never in the habit of associating with gentlemen before;" and taking a rough, strong hold of the policeman with the grip and strength of a giant, the Superintendent shook him almost out of his clothes, denouncing him in the most opprobrious terms as he did so, and finishing up by saying, "You contemptible fellow, I'll put you among congenial spirits, among horse-thieves, who are the proper sort of company for such as you;" and thus saying, jerked Mr. Policeman off to another apartment devoted to what Mr. Wood called "congenial spirits," i. e., horse-thieves.

It appeared that the policeman had written to Gen. Wadsworth, Military Governor of Washington, in which he told that functionary that his room mates were all secessionists, and in which he made some disparaging remarks of his fellow prisoners.— This, from a person who did not appear to have been a regular detective in the pay of the Government, but who became a voluntary informer and spy, to effect some sinister purpose, seemed to be so mean, contemptible and reprehensible in the estimation of the Superintendent, one of nature's noblemen, that he, as has been said, summarily ejected him from the presence of the prisoners whom he sought to injure.

THE GUARD HOUSE IN THE OLD CAPITOL.

It is unnecessary to describe a guard house, sufficient to say that it is a place of punishment for drunken and refractory soldiers. It was used in the Old Capitol for other purposes. Captain Clark, a confederate prisoner of war, was put in the Old Capitol guard house by Lieutenant Miller, in command of the guard at the time. This was in September. Of course, it was a violation of the rules of war, but what of that? What cares the Lincoln Administration for rules of war when it cares nothing for the Federal Constitution.

But it was not prisoners of war alone who were subjected to the indignity of being placed in the guard house. Several Prisoners of State, and other Federal Prisoners were subjected to this punishment on the most frivolous grounds.

A Mr. Hopkins, of Washington City, who was arrested and sent to the Old Capitol for selling liquors contrary to the orders of Military Governor Wadsworth and Provost Marshal Doster, was sent to the guard house under the following circumstances:— Mr. Hopkins asked and obtained permission to send for some brandy for his own use. The permission was granted with the condition that he would place the liquor in charge of the hospital steward, which condition he complied with. On the following morning after receiving his liquor, he went according to arrangement to take a portion of it, when he was informed by the steward that Lieutenant Miller had come up during the night and taken the liquor away; adding that the Lieutenant had some brother officers for company, and as he presumed Mr. Hopkins' liquor was of good quality, he made free to take it. As might be supposed, this information was not very welcome intelligence, or pleasing to Mr. Hopkins, who left the hospital immediately to return to his room. On the way through the yard he fell in with Lieutenant Miller, who bid Hopkins good morning very cordially and familiarly. "Good morning, Lieutenant," returned Hopkins, who by this time had recovered his usual good-humored disposition. A few more words passed between them, when Hopkins ventured in the most familiar tone to remind the Lieutenant of how he had purloined his liquor, not reproachfully, for Hopkins cared but little about it, as he would give it freely if asked of him, but as one familiar and even friendly with another might intimate. Lieutenant Miller took the matter in another light, however, and seizing Mr. Hopkins by the collar, in the most ruffianly manner, dragged him to the guard house and kept him there in filth and without food till next day.— Every person in the Old Capitol was indignant at this outrage, and it would not have taken much provocation to incite them to resist it.

Sundays in the Old Capitol being observed as Sabbath to the extent of refraining from the usual amusements which occupied the time and attention of the prisoners, it was made a habit by those who were acquainted in Washington and by some of the other prisoners who had the curiosity to observe the passers-by, to look out of the windows on that day.

On one occasion, it was on the 2d of November, Mr. V. R. Jackson, a resident of Washington, was looking through the window in No 16, when some acquaintances of his chanced to ride by in a barouche. He and they recognized each other, they by bowing to him, and he by touching his hat to them. One of the guards who was on the qui vive to observe the gestures of passers by, ordered the gentlemen in the barouche to halt, which they of course did. The party were compelled to alight from the vehicle, and enter the prison, when they no doubt, to exculpate themselves, informed Lieutenant Miller that they had only bowed in return to a salute from their friend Mr. Jackson. Lieutenant Miller came up stairs immediately, accompanied with a corporal. He inquired, who was it that made a sign of recognition to those gentlemen who had just been arrested by the guard? No one answered at first; when he directed his inquiry to Mr. Jackson, asking that gentleman if his name was not Jackson, and if he was not a clerk in the Post Office? Mr. Jackson replied in the affirmative. The Lieutenant then asked him if he had not taken his hat off to the gentlemen in the barouche? Mr. Jackson replied that he was not certain that he had done that, but admitted that he had touched his hat to the gentlemen, they being acquaintances and friends of his, and he was not aware that it was forbidden the prisoners to do so. "Take him to the guard-house," commanded Miller to the corporal; and poor Mr. Jackson was seized suddenly by the corporal and taken to and kept in the guard-house till bedtime, and would probably be kept there all night were it not for the solicitation of his fellow-prisoners and the interposition of the Superintendent according to their request for his release.

Frank Blair, Jr., a son of Hon. Frank Blair, Jr., of Missouri, was put in the guard-house for going into the next room to No. 16, and was sent there another time for making a little more noise than Lieutenant Miller thought it the right of a prisoner to do. Frank was a lively young fellow, excited with mischief, and playful to a degree beyond propriety sometimes. But the guard-house was not the proper way to restrain or correct him. A kind or civil word would have done better.

Marcus Buck Baily, the gentleman who was taken in company with Miss Beukner, the quinine lady, was put in the guard-house for a similar offense to that committed by Mr. Jackson. It went hard with Buck to be treated with such indignity, he being one of the F. F. V.'s; but Lieutenant Miller was no respecter of persons. Even if Buck Baily *was* arrested in company of a niece of Post Master General Blair, it made no difference with Lieutenant Miller.

In this respect, the lieutenant was right, but it was a small business in him to outrage the feelings of gentlemen who happened to be placed in his power, by placing them in his guard-house for bowing to a friend or acquaintance on the streets of Washington through the barred windows of the Old Capitol.

Petty tyranny exercised by a shoulder strapped official was never better exemplified than it was in several instances in the Old Capitol, where besides the cases referred to above two insane men, one a man formerly well known in New York in connection with the anti-rent excitement, by the name of Burrell, was repeatedly placed in the guard-house, not to keep him from doing mischief, but as a punishment for some trifling offense. Burrell, better known in the prison as General Thunderbolt, imagined himself to be the person designated by Providence to command the Federal Army and lead it to victory. Under the influence of this hallucination, he had sought an interview with President Lincoln at his country residence, the Soldiers' Home, and being taken into custody there by some one, the

President and his friends took it into their frightened heads that Burrel was an assassin, and so the poor lunatic was sent down to the Old Capitol. It appeared that he had been down to Richmond, which circumstance gave color to the accusation of evil designs upon the President.

Whenever Burrell, or as he was better known, General Thunderbolt, happened to be in the yard at recreation time, he was the center of attraction. Insane as he was, he was as caustic in his sarcasms and witty in repartee as if his intellect were perfectly sound. One day Lieutenant Miller enquired of him what he thought of the rebel soldiers in comparison with those of the Federal Army. Said Miller, "Don't you think, General, that you could whip them rebels yourself?"

"Yes," said General Thunderbolt, "of course I could; but I'll tell you what, Lieutenant, if the Federal Army were all like you, one rebel could whip every five of you."

Of course this disparaging compliment, albeit applied by a crazy man, could not be brooked with impunity. So poor Thunderbolt was sent to the guard-house. There was another crazy fellow, an Irishman it appeared he was, whom any one might see at a glance that he was insane, yet this poor demented fellow and Thunderbolt were oftener in the guard-house than any other prisoners in the establishment. It was purely an exercise of brute tyranny to send either of them to such a place.

CARELESSNESS OR CULPABLE RECKLESSNESS OF THE GUARDS.

The carelessness of the guards in carrying their loaded arms was a matter of constant alarm to the prisoners, who lived in continual dread of having a bullet fired through the floors, or as they passed up or down the stairways. Several such occurrences, either of carelessness or of intentional mischief, took place during the months of September and October. The floors and ceilings of some of the rooms bore unmistakable evidence, in the shape of bullet-holes, that there was sufficient cause for the apprehensions of the prisoners. In one instance, this careless, or, as it seemed, intentional discharge of firearms in the prison, came near proving fatal to one of the prisoners of state. The occurrence was so peculiar, and, under the circumstances, extraordinary, that the following statement of it was drawn up at the time:

OLD CAPITOL PRISON,
Washington, D. C., Oct. 22d, 1862.

The undersigned, prisoners in the Old Capitol, do hereby testify, that on this day, viz., the twenty-second of October, 1862, at 2 o'clock and forty minutes P. M., a ball was fired through the floor of room No. 16, in which we, the undersigned, were at the time present. The ball passed through the head of the bed on which D. A. Mahony, a prisoner of state, was at the time reclining, and on which he had been lying most of the day ill. At the moment the ball went through his bed, he had raised himself up on one of his elbows to speak with a fellow-prisoner, Dr. Moran, who was shaving at the time. Had Mr. Mahony been lying down as he had been most of the day, the ball would have gone through his head inevitably. The force with which the ball was shot will be understood from the fact that, after passing through the ceiling and floor underneath room No. 16, it went through one of the slats of the bed, through two bedticks, and through a blanket of twelve thicknesses rolled up as a pillow, and through a feather pillow, and then penetrated the ceiling overhead of room No. 16.

As an evidence of the truth of all of which, we hereby subscribe our names, in presence of II n. Andrew D. Duff, Judge of the Twenty-sixth Judicial Circuit, Illinois.

JOHN H. MULKEY.
M. L. ROSS.
FRANK P. BLAIR, Jr.

This will certify, that I was present during the affair above described, and believe, if it was not designed, to be the result of gross carelessness on the part of those having the control of the guard of the Old Capitol Prison.

THO's T. ELLIS, M. D.,
Late Post Surgeon, New York, and
Medical Director.

Next morning, after this occurrence, one of the guards shot himself through the head, in front of the prison. No public mention was made of the occurrence—no more than if it had been a dog that was killed. It was said that the guard who shot himself was a brother of the one who fired through the floor the day before.

Not only were some of the guards careless and reckless, but several of them were rude and vicious to a degree bordering on brutality.

One day, Mr. Mahony was standing at one of the windows in room No. 10, looking out, in a contemplative mood, upon the world abroad. The guard upon the pavement below, observing Mr. M., called up to him to stand back from the window. Mr. M. replied to the guard, saying that he was as far back as the rules of the prison required.

"Damn you," said the guard, "if you do not stand back, I'll shoot you."

Mr. M. very complacently remained standing where he was, but watched the guard's motions closely. After two or three commands similar to that first given to stand back, the guard brought his musket to his shoulder, and was about to take aim, when Mr. M. peremptorily ordered him to shoulder arms. The guard was so suddenly startled by the command coming, as he no doubt supposed it had done, from the officer of the guard, that he quickly shouldered his musket. A shout of derisive laughter from the other window of the prison facing the guard's position, was the first conscious intimation the fellow had that he had obeyed the orders of Mr. M., instead of his commanding officer. During the remainder of his time on duty that day, the guard seldom took his eye off the window at which Mr. M. had taken his position, and Mr. M. was no less attentive, at a respectful distance, to the movements of the guard. Once in awhile some one would shout out "Shoulder arms," when the guard would turn suddenly round only to hear himself laughed at.

In striking, and to some extent pleasing, contrast with the carelessness and recklessness of some of the guards, the conduct of others was commendable. Some of them were so good-natured as to bring upon themselves the displeasure of their officers, which sometimes was manifested in severe punishment. Cases of this kind occurred during the month of October, in which two guards were induced, by the piteous appeals of some prisoners, to take a letter each, directed to the mother of one of the prisoners, a Marylander, and to some member of the family of another one. The Marylander's mother was ill almost to death at the time of his arrest, and although he had written to her repeatedly from the prison, he could get no answer; the probability being that his letters were not allowed to reach his mother. Under these circumstances, the guard at room No. 16, who was a young man of kindly heart, offered, on being informed of the case, to take and mail a letter for the Marylander. As there were always detectives on the watch for everything that might occur, no sooner was the guard relieved, than he was marched into the presence of the officer on duty, who examined him and found the letter. The poor good-natured guard was placed in irons, and kept in them for nearly a month, and the Marylander who gave him the letter was sent to the guard house and kept there for several days. The fellow was mean enough to put as much of the blame as possible upon the poor guard, by telling the officer that the guard offered to take the letter without being requested by him to do so. No one pitied him that he had been placed in the guardhouse.

MARTIAL LAW USED AS A COVER TO OFFICIAL CORRUPTION.

Martial law has its uses—old fogies will call them abuses, some of which having come under the observation of the Prisoners of State in the Old Capitol, are given here for the enlightenment of the public.

About the first of October, a young man named Samuel Emmons, of Philadelphia, was thrust into room No. 16, Old Capitol. As usual with all new comers, the Master of Ceremonies among the inmates of the room, enquired of Mr. Emmons what was his name, what he had done, &c. To all of which he gave the following account of himself, after telling his name.

He was a wagon-master in one of the brigades of the army. A soldier offered him a horse for sale, which Emmons believing the soldier to be the proper owner of, bought for some forty odd dollars. It turned out, however, that the horse was the property of Uncle Sam, as appeared more clearly by the discovery of the old gentleman's initials branded upon one of the animal's flanks. The brand however was not very perceptible to casual observation, else Mr. Emmons could have seen it and avoided the disagreeable situation in which the purchase placed him. The fact of the sale being made, was brought to the knowledge of Colonel Baker, Chief Detective, as he is called, of the War Department, and forthwith Mr. Emmons and the soldier who sold him the horse were both arrested. On an investigation of the matter, it appeared so clearly and conclusively in evidence, that Emmons had no knowledge other than that the animal was the property of the soldier who offered him for sale, Col. Baker discharged Emmons from custody. Emmons who had paid his money for the horse, on being discharged, demanded his money, which had been taken from the soldier to whom Emmons paid it. Colonel Baker told Emmons to get an order from Captain Dana of the Quartermaster's department at Washington, and he should have his money. Emmons went to Captain Dana, and obtained the requisite order, which happened to be written in red pencil. With this order Emmons returned to Colonel Baker's office, and handed the Colonel the order. Colonel Baker took it and deliberately rubbed out the writing with a piece of India-rubber, and then committed Mr. Emmons to the Old Capitol, where he was left for five weeks to meditate upon the impropriety of demanding his money from the Chief Detective of the War Department. Reader, what do you suppose the crime of Mr. Emmons was, for which he was committed for five weeks' imprisonment? Nothing more in the world than demanding his forty-five dollars which Colonel Baker had in his possession, and which he evidently meant to keep. At the end of about five weeks, Mr. Emmons was visited in prison by Colonel Baker. Whether it was understood between them or not, that Mr. Emmons was not to demand his money as the condition of his release, no one knew, but certain it is Emmons was released and discharged without any trial.

The detectives of the War Department and other Provost Marshals made rich harvests of persons who ventured to run the blockade of the Potomac by water, or who run the risk of carrying contraband goods across the lines between the belligerent armies.

Several of these venturesome persons were arrested and brought to the Old Capitol, whence after a short detention and several private interviews with Col. Baker, or Provost-Marshal Doster, or perhaps Judge Advocate Turner, they were released for considerations, the nature of which may be inferred from an instance which was related by one of the parties in the transaction.

A German Jew named William Fleidenheimer, was detected about the latter part of September, or the beginning of October, in an attempt to run the blockade, with contraband valuables of some kind. He had with him three trunks, all of which with three others belonging to another party were seized. Fleidenheimer was sent to the Old Capitol, and his trunks taken possession of by the Provost-Marshal. Fleidenheimer was subjected by the Provost-Marshal, to all the terrorism which an offense of the kind he had been detected in committing could inspire. Hanging was the proper punishment, held up to his contemplation, until the poor Jew gave up all hope of ever being set at liberty. But the knowing ones in the Old Capitol knew what all this threatening meant, and some one suggested to Fleidenheimer that there was a way by which he might not only avoid the hanging, but of acquiring his liberty. It was well known in the Old Capitol that those who happened to be really guilty of some crime, were the most likely to be soon set at liberty; for those who know themselves to be guilty were willing to purchase immunity for their offenses, and it was well understood that certain officials connected with the War Department, cared a great deal more for a prisoner's money than they did to punish his offenses.

So Fleidenheimer being properly posted, managed to understand the hints given him by some of his fellow-prisoners, and it was not long after, therefore, before a bargain was made between him and the proper person, that on the condition of his paying three hundred dollars to ———, he should not only be released but given up to him the *six* trunks taken at the time of his attempt to run the blockade. Fleidenheimer was, of course, delighted with the proposition, especially as he was to get three trunks full of goods which did not belong to him, and which he doubted not would enable him to make up the three hundred dollars exacted of him as the price of his life and liberty, so the bargain was struck. Fleidenheimer got a parole to raise the three hundred dollars among his friends in Baltimore, paid it to ———, got his liberty and the six trunks, and made, as his fellow prisoner afterwards learned, six hundred dollars of the bargain.

Now had it not been for the substitution of martial law for the Courts established by the Constitution, such cases as this to which reference is last made, would be tried in a civil court. The person who may be guilty of an offense against the established laws of the country would be punished, and the property found in his possession under such circumstances confiscated to the United States. But under martial law, as administered at Washington, it is perfectly safe for any one to run the risk of violating the laws, provided he has means to buy himself out of the custody of the War Department.

It was the universally understood opinion, amounting indeed among the prisoners of the Old Capitol to conviction, that any person incarcerated by order of Col. Baker, could regain his liberty for a consideration. In several instances which came to the knowledge of the prisoners, direct and unequivocal propositions were made to the wives of some of the prisoners, that for a certain consideration their husbands would be released. As instances of this kind, reference is made to Mrs. Dr. T. T. Ellis of New York, and to Mrs. Spahr of Washington, both of whose husbands were inmates of the Old Capitol during the month of October, and up to the middle of November, if not longer. In both these cases the writer has the testimony of Dr. Ellis and of Mr. Spahr, they both having been informed by their wives of the propositions made to them for the release of their husbands.

Another instance of the many which occurred in which martial law is used at Washington as a means by which corrupt and venal officials profit by its existence, is the following—

Immediately after the battles fought in the vicinity of Washington in August last, the city was placed under strict martial law. The sale of liquor was inhibited by the Military Governor under the penalty of confiscation. Here was a favorable opportunity for the detectives of the War Department to ply their avocation and to make a harvest. The plan of operations mapped out was for some one of the number who was best acquainted with a liquor-dealer or saloon keeper, marked out as a victim, to go and procure from him, if possible, something to drink. If successful in the application, no matter whether on the score of old acquaintance, familiarity or friendship, information was to be filed forthwith before the Provost Marshal, and then the liquors should be seized. This programme was carried into effect—and most, if not all the liquors so seized were placed under the control of the Provost Marshal, or as he is better known, detective Baker.

Some time after the promulgation of this military order, Mr. Spahr, to whom allusion is made above, was arrested in Washington city. As he happened to be a German who was used to his liquor, he suggested to the officer, a detective who had him in custody, that it would not be amiss for them to go and have something to drink before being taken to the Old Capitol, as it was not likely that while there he would be allowed to indulge in any stimulating or exhilarating drink. The officer thought the suggestion a good one, and acquiesced in the proposal. Spahr not being desirous of being the means of acquainting the detective with any of the places known to him where the military order respecting the sale of liquors was violated, suggested that the officer indicate a place where they might be accommodated—with which suggestion the officer complied very cheerfully. The two went on to find a place of refreshment—and to the surprise and amusement of Mr. Spahr, he was taken into a room back of Provost Marshal Baker's office, where there was a bar in full blast, well supplied with liquors,—liquors, by the way, as Spahr ascertained, which were confiscated from the saloon keepers in Washington city, who had violated the order of Military Governor Wadsworth. Spahr paid the reckoning at the Provost Marshal's bar, and went off to the Old Capitol full of meditations on the system of government which Mr. Lincoln had introduced instead of that prescribed by the Constitution.

These of course are but mere instances of the gigantic system of peculation, robbery and plunder, which has been established under the patronage of the War Department, and in which there is circumstantial evidence enough to lead any one's judgment who knows it, to the conclusion, that the heads of that Department participate profitably. An investigation into the detective business of the War Department would reveal such flagitious violations of law, decency and personal rights, and such corrupt and outrageous practices, having for their sole object the gratification of the lust of avarice, if not the lust of the flesh, as would place the Government, as administered under Abraham Lincoln, in disparaging comparison with the most unprincipled of any nation extant or extinct. It is due to the people that such an investigation be had, unless indeed it be dreaded by them that the revelations and developments of such an investigation might be so infamous and disgusting as to bring upon the American name eternal reproach and shame.

A CHAPTER ON LETTERS.

L-E-T-T-E-R-S-! Once a day the Superintendent, or in his absence, Lieutenant Miller, called at the rooms of the prison for letters. When the Superintendent came round, every one crowded about him, each urging some request or other. One, that his letter might be allowed to reach his wife; another, that his might be sent for certain to his mother, and so on through the whole number. The good-natured Superintendent would pretend to be bothered with them, but his heart was all the time belieing his tongue, and notwithstanding anything that he might say by word to the contrary or by gesture, were em passen that he would not comply with the requests impressed upon him, he would invariably do his best to have the prisoners' letters passed through the hands of the Provost Marshal and Judge Advocate, as the case may be.

Every letter written by the prisoners was handed to the Superintendent, or his deputy endorsed, except letters to high officials, which might be sealed. These letters were examined, probably in the prison, but certainly by some one in the office of Provost Marshal, or Judge Advocate, so that it depended upon the caprice of these officials, or of their clerks whether any one's letters ever reached their destination or not. Of course many letters of the greatest importance to the prisoners and to their families, never reached the Post Office, and it was more by the attention and favor of Superintendent Wood that letters ever reached their destination than it was from the attention given to them by any other person connected with the Government. Hence it was no wonder that the prisoners looked more to Superintendent Wood, than any one else for the favor, yes, reader, the favor of having their letters to their families sent to their destination.

Enter, reader, one of the Old Capitol Prison rooms in imagination when the Superintendent's call for letters, announces his presence for the purpose of being the bearer of those messages, which tell wives and children at home of how the husband and father is faring in the Bastile.

No sooner would Mr. Wood enter the room than a rush would be made for him by from half a dozen to twenty persons, each one eager to be first to have a chance to impress him with the importance of what he wanted to communicate, and to appeal to his feelings as a man in behalf of the missive he held in his hand.

"Now Wood, I am sure my letters have not reached home," one would urge in a voice modulated to earnest pathos, "or if they have been sent, their letters to me have been suppressed. Won't you see whether there are any letters for me at the Provost Marshal's office?"

As likely as not, the Superintendent would reply—

"There are several letters for you at the office of the Provost Marshal, but they are not examined—some of the Miss Nancy clerks up there have got to be so important in their own estimation since they have got into the position of examining letters, that they take on airs and do as they please. I cannot help it if your letters are not forwarded, or if letters to you do not reach you."

"We know that, Mr. Wood," several voices would exclaim in concert. "But," one would continue, "it is hard to be deprived of the privilege of hearing from one's home before one is convicted of any crime—and it is equally an outrage to one's family to be deprived of the privilege of hearing from him in a place like this."

"I know it is hard," would be the admission of Mr. Wood, "but you fellows had no business to be loco-focos."

This of course would be a jest so far as the Superintendent was concerned, but it was no joke for the prisoners. Their crime was truly that they were what the Superintendent called loco-focos—and for that they were kidnapped and imprisoned, and deprived of the privilege of hearing from their families, except at the caprice of "Miss Nancy" clerks in the office of the Provost Marshal at Washington.

"Wood, here is a letter—a very short one—containing nothing but to say that I am well; cannot this be sent to my wife without its being subjected to the risk of being destroyed in the office of the Provost Marshal?"

Such would be the appeal of a prisoner. Mr. Wood's reply would be much as follows—

"I cannot send any letters for you except through the Provost Marshal, or Judge Advocate Turner; but I will do my best to have your letter examined and passed."

"Here is a business letter, Wood," another of the prisoners would urge. "It is of the most vital importance to me and to my family that it should reach its address as soon as possible; why cannot it be sent immediately?"

"That I cannot answer," would be the reply of the Superintendent. "I am here to carry out the orders of the Government, and not to do my own will. The Government, or rather the officers of the Government, have their own way of doing things, and I must either obey their orders or give up my place."

"We would all be sorry that you did that," would be the sincere intimation of the prisoners.— "If you were not here, Wood, we should not receive one in ten of our letters, nor would our friends know whether we were dead or alive."

The very first letter sent out by one of the prisoners called forth the following decree:

HEADQUARTERS PROVOST MARSHAL'S OFFICE,
WASHINGTON, D. C. —— 1862.

Nothing but *family* and *business* letters are allowed to pass.

W. V. C. MURPHY.

This signature had something affixed to it which no one could make any sense of, but it was probably designed to show that this Murphy was a person of authority. Whether he was or not, it is very certain that he assumed a good deal of it in opening papers and letters, and in throwing them aside or destroying them if they contained anything which he deemed to be objectionable to his tyrant masters.

Shortly after this, the same prisoner was served with a decree to the effect that if his wife did not write her name in full, her letters would be suppressed. What thinks the reader of this petty tyranny, instituted at Washington by Lincoln's Administration. The same Murphy, whose name was signed to the foregoing, was the author of this decree also, though probably he was only the tool of some one else who owned him as a master.

Scenes similar to that described above between the Superintendent and the prisoners, were of daily occurrence. No one knows who did not experience it, what it is to be expecting a letter from home in the Old Capitol, knowing that it must first pass through the office of the Provost Marshal, or the inspection and approval of Judge Advocate Turner, before it reaches him. Meditating upon this phase of tyranny, one of the prisoners thus soliloquised:

How wretched is that man who hangs on prince's favors, but how much more wretched he whose mind swings 'twixt despair and hope while trusting to a tyrant's heartless rule.

Oh! did we Americans ever think 'twould come to this—that one man's will, and he the people's servant, should set all other rules at naught, and arrogate to his selfwill supremacy over people, Government and law.

What despot, what usurper, tyrant, did ever more than this? Cæsar, a noble despot, who gave to Rome, his country, immortality, and entwined her glory with his own ambition, lost his life for less of usurpation than our rulers have presumed. So did the kingly Charles lose his head for a far less transgression on the liberties of England. And shall it be borne now that citizen born freemen, men made free by law, shall be subjected to a worse than kingly or Imperial despotism, by a mere creature of their will and power. It shall not be, by heaven and by the blood of our ancestral sires, shed to secure our freedom's heritage; no man, much less our public servants, shall with impunity make serfs of us.

Our tyrant rulers did not hear this soliloquy, although they read something like it in some of the letters from the prisoners, written more for their eye than with any expectation that these letters would ever reach their destination, which, of course, they never did.

The tyranny which prevented the Old Capitol Prisoners from sending and of receiving letters resulted, as might be supposed, in driving them to have recourse to other means than through the Superintendent to forward their letters. It is needless to say how this was done; for although every effort to send out letters surreptitiously was not successful, several such efforts were—so that, despite the Secretary of War, his Provost Marshals, and his detective spies, the Old Capital Prisoners of State did communicate with their wives and children. O! how one's blood warms with indignation at the outrages to which he was subjected by that infamous man, Stanton, and by his villainous Assistant, Watson and his tool L. C. Turner. Were it not that vengeance belonged to the Lord God, not one of those tyrants would die a natural death. If they should do so, it will be by the mercy and favor of God, and not of that of their fellow American citizens whom they have so grossly outraged, so tyranically subjected to indignity, so heartlessly robbed of every personal right of man and of American freemen.

NELLIE GREY CAME NEAR GETTING US IN TROUBLE.

—One day in September, a regiment, which we learned was the 19th Connecticut, was drawn up in line before the west side of the Old Capitol. The prisoners in No. 16, as was usual when a regiment made its appearance in the vicinity, crowded to the large window which fronted that side of the prison. The regimental band came to the front and discoursed some of the popular airs so eloquently that the prisoners were sensibly affected; and presuming that it was as much for their gratification as it was for anything else that this musical concert was given in such a place and on such an occasion, the prisoners, at the suggestion of Dr. Brown, who was par excellence the leader of the choir of No. 16, it was determined to return the compliment, as we took it, of the regiment. So after consulting a minute as to what it were better to sing, the popular melody "Nellie Gray" was adopted, and Dr. Brown leading off, some twenty prisoners joined him in giving it the best effect. Scarcely, however, was the song commenced before the regiment appeared in considerable agitation and disorder. Orders seemed to have been given it to do something or other, as the men who had till then been at rest were handling their arms preparatory to some movement. Surely, thought we, they are not going to present arms to us. But we were soon undeceived as to the cause of their commotion. Superintendent Wood came rushing up to No. 16 almost breathless with haste, excitement and displeasure, vociferating as loud as he could find breath to do, "For God's sake come away from that window; they will shoot you." Sure enough, by that time we had perceived sufficient of the movements of the ruffians to be satisfied that such was their design. Superintendent Wood explained to us that they thought we were singing a Secesh song, "Nellie Grey" being, as they supposed, one of that character.

KIDNAPPING OF THE EDITORS AND PROPRIETORS OF THE HARRISBURG PATRIOT AND UNION.

ON the 6th of August, 1862, at about 4 o'clock A. M., Provost-Marshal Baker, of Washington City, D. C., accompanied by Captain I. Dodge, (then acting as mustering officer and Provost-Marshal at Harrisburg, Pa.,) the Chief of Police of Harrisburg, and a file of United States soldiers, arrested Messrs. Ormond Barrett, Thomas C. MacDowell, editors and proprietors of The Patriot and Union, a Democratic daily and weekly newspaper published at Harrisburg, Pa., J. Montgomery Foster, assistant editor, and N. J. Jones, local editor of said paper. The arrests of the above-named gentlemen were made at their respective homes, within a few minutes of each other. Colonel MacDowell's residence was first visited, and his arrest first made. When the object of their visit was made known to Colonel MacDowell, by the Provost-Marshal, which was done from the steps of his dwelling, where the Provost-Marshal (Baker) stood in full uniform as a captain of infantry; the door was opened, and Colonel MacDowell asked the meaning of the presence of the armed men who were surrounding his premises. Both Baker and Dodge announced that they wished to see Colonel MacDowell, and requested to be admitted to the house. Colonel MacDowell answered that Captains Baker and Dodge and the Chief of

Police might enter, but not one of the armed guard then present. This was assented to, and Baker, Dodge, and Chief of Police, B. Campbell, stepped into the parlor, where the following dialogue ensued :

Colonel MacDowell—What is your business with me, gentlemen? Provost-Marshal answered—I am ordered to arrest you, sir. Colonel MacDowell—Have you authority in writing to make my arrest? Baker—I have. Will you be kind enough to show me the authority? Marshal Baker drew from his breast a paper which he handed to Colonel MacD. which purported to be an order from Gen. W. H. Halleck, General-in-Chief, commanding Baker to proceed to Harrisburg, Pa., and arrest Messrs. O. Barrett, Thomas C. MacDowell, J. Montgomery Foster, and N. J. Jones, editors and proprietors of The Patriot and Union newspaper, and convey them to Washington City, to be tried by a Military Commission, for publishing a certain handbill discouraging enlistments, and that he (the Provost-Marshal) shall seize the presses, types, fixtures, and all the property found in The Patriot and Union printing establishment, and turn the same over to the United States Quartermaster at Harrisburg, Pa., who shall send them to Washington City. [For some reason or other the confiscation portion of the order was never executed.]

Col. MacDowell then asked permission to put up a few articles of clothing, as well as to inform his family of the necessity of his absence. An hour was readily granted by the Provost-Marshal for the purpose on the promise of Col. MacD. that he would report himself at the Mayor's office in one hour, (5 o'clock A. M.,) when the Provost-Marshal and posse left. At about 5 o'clock A. M., Messrs. Barret, MacDowell, Foster and Jones were at the Mayor's office, and at about 6 o'clock, A. M., they were marched off by the

Provost-Marshal and a file of soldiers with muskets and fixed bayonets to the depot of the Pennsylvania Central railroad, put aboard of the cars with the Provost-Marshal and guard of soldiers as close attendants.

On arriving at the cars was found, for the first time, Brigadier-General James Wadsworth, then acting as Military Governor of the District of Columbia, who, we learned, had come to Harrisburg to superintend the arrest of the editors and proprietors of The Patriot and Union; but who had taken great care not to be seen or known by any one until the arrests were made and the prisoners safely secured in the cars. General Wadsworth was in the full uniform of a Brigadier-General, U. S. A., but without side-arms.

The prisoners were taken to Washington, when we were ordered by General Wadsworth to be taken to the Old Capitol Prison by Provost-Marshal Baker and the guard. We were marched to the Old Capitol, and handed over to the keeper, Mr. Wood, who, after examining our baggage very carefully, and our persons, we were assigned a room, where we were kept, as other prisoners were kept in that place, until the 23rd of August, 1862, when we were liberated after the most consummate farce of an examination before Judge Advocate Turner, in the presence of General Wadsworth. When brought before the Judge Advocate, we demanded the affidavit upon which we were arrested—the name or names of our accuser or accusers—and the specific charge that justified the great outrage that had been perpetrated in our arrest and incarceration; but, strange to tell, both the Judge Advocate and General Wadsworth had to acknowledge that there was no written specific charge, no accuser or accusers, and after taking our respective statements under oath, in which we severally stated our unconsciousness of any crime or offense against the Government, the Constitution, or the laws of the land, we were told that we were at liberty to go whithersoever we pleased. We left Washington City on the 24th of August, 1862 for Harrisburg, Pa., which latter place we reached on the evening of the same day.

STATEMENT OF THE ARREST OF JOSEPH C. WRIGHT, OF MILFORD, N. J.

The following statement has been made by Joseph C. Wright, of Milford, N. J., of his arrest and transportation to the Old Capitol:

MILFORD, N. J., March 2d, 1863.

My Dear Sir,—You are aware that, on the 19th of August, I was arrested in the peaceful town of Milford by a military force in the hands of Deputy United States Marshal A. R. Harris and G. Dean, and after five minutes' notice was placed in a wagon and driven off to Frenchtown, four miles distant, thrust in one of the upper rooms of the hotel of the place, and there guarded by these armed men until the hour of arrival of the train for Trenton. I was then put on board (not knowing yet where I was to be taken). On my way down I asked to be shown the authority for so arresting peaceful citizens. I was told when I got to Trenton, I would be told why I was arrested and be shown the warrant. I arrived in Trenton in the evening, and I demanded again to be shown the process by which I was dragged from my home, my family and friends. I was still denied, with the promise when we reached Mount Holly Jail (County Seat of Burlington County of this State), that it would be read to me; but after getting there nothing more was said, for I saw I was only to be put off, and no time was allowed me further to insist upon my right to know by whose authority I was so arrested.

I may be getting before my statement.

After my arrival at Trenton (I was kept from all public places, or hotels), was taken to a place where private meals were served up, and given my supper; and after waiting there two and a half hours for the cars for Burlington, I was for the first time told that I was to go to Jail. We left Trenton and arrived at Burlington —was then placed in a hack and carried to Mount Holly, reaching the place at eleven P. M. I was then placed in the care of the turnkey, who showed me to a cell where I was locked up for the night. You may well imagine no sleep came near me that night. Such a place to put white men I never believed existed in any land. Nothing but a straw tick—no covering—the whole cell filled with vermin. At six A. M. was unlocked, and turned out in the yard with negroes, horse-thieves, robbers and Jackaloo the murderer. My condition was improved the next night by being given a better cell and bed. After being in Mount Holly Jail some ten days, an order came to take me to the Old Capitol Prison, Washington City, where I arrived and was shown quarters; and after remaining there eight days, through the interposition of active friends, headed by Colonel William Murphy, of the 10th N. J. Regiment, I was on the morning of the ninth day approached by the corporal of the guard and notified to pack up my baggage and report myself to Lieut. Miller, and after being conducted by the guard to his office, he notified me that my brother was in waiting for me outside, and I was at liberty to pass out, which I did after getting permission to return to my room for the purpose of bidding good-bye to my fellow-prisoners, with the injunction not to bring out any letters, as they, the letters, were considered contraband matter. This I had known for some time, as no letter of mine ever reached my family, nor did I receive any myself. I am as ignorant to-day as I was on the 19th day of August last, of what offense I was accused. I have only to refer to the fact that I was honorably discharged. I might refer to the fact that after I left the Capitol Prison, I at once called upon Mr. L. C. Turner, Judge Advocate, and demanded of him who my accusers were, and of what offense I was charged with, all of which he declined to give me. I then asked to be returned home free of expense, which he also refused. This my brother witnessed. I might write you more, perhaps, as much again, concerning myself. The message I delivered to Governor Olden, (after I reached Trenton,) at the instance of Mr. Thos. F. Knox, of Fredericksburg, Va., a gentleman of that place, then held as a hostage, (same floor with myself, Old Capitol Prison,) and who is the intimate friend of Governor Olden. But what I have already given you will fully serve to show you how loyal Democrats are treated by Mr. Lincoln and the present party in power, simply because I defended truth and principle when at stake.

Yours truly,
JOSEPH C. WRIGHT.

STATEMENT OF THE KIDNAPPING OF JOHN APPLE, OF PHILADELPHIA.

I was arrested on the 15th of August, 1862, by Deputy Marshal Schuyler. I was taken from the Jefferson House, kept by James Weston on the corner of Fifth and Poplar Streets, to the Marshal's office. I asked the Marshal what the charge was against me He told me it was for discouraging enlistments. I then asked him who made this charge against me, and he told me a man by the name of Burns. The Marshal told him to go to the Mayor and make an affidavit to that effect and bring it to him (the Marshal) and he would send it to the Secretary of War—which he did. The Secretary of War then sent a warrant on for my arrest. I employed two lawyers to get a writ of *habeas corpus* for me. They applied for it. The Marshal told them that my arrest was ordered from Washington, and I was to be tried there, and there couldn't be a writ granted for me. I was taken to Washington, and arrived there on the 16th of August, about 7 o'clock in the morning. I requested the Deputy Marshal to go with me to see Mr. Florence before he locked me up, which he did. The Marshal, Mr. Florence, and myself then went to the Judge Advocate's. Mr. Florence stated my case, and the Judge said that he had nothing at all to do with it, and said to the Marshal, you have been ordered to take this man to the Old Capitol Prison, have you not? The Marshal said that he was so ordered. The Judge then told him that he would have to take me there, for he had nothing to do with the case. I was then taken to the Old Capitol Prison, and placed in the hands of the Superintendent (Mr. Wood). I said to Mr. Wood that the Marshal had no warrant for my arrest, or no charge against me. He (Mr. Wood) said we will find a charge against you. He then sent the Marshal to the Provost-Marshal's office in the District of Columbia for a commitment for me, and kept me waiting all that time without any authority at all. He (Mr. Wood) then put me in the Hospital, where there were sixty to seventy sick men. They had all kinds of diseases. I was the only one among the lot of them that was not sick. I had to eat, sleep and everything in the same room with these people. There were sick soldiers with different kinds of diseases, brought in there every day, and most of them were lousy, and the beds full of bed-bugs. The room was lined with rats and mice, so that when you laid down they would crawl over you. The victuals that were furnished for the prisoners wasn't fit for a dog to eat. They allowed those who had money to buy their own victuals. Which I for one did.

I was kept in this hospital for about three weeks, and then was removed from there into a room with some state prisoners. The room was somewhat better than the hospital, although it was full of lice, bed-bugs, rats and mice, but it was more healthy than the other place. When we would go from our room down into the yard, we would have to examine our clothes when we came back, so as to keep us from getting lousy. I never saw a friend of mine while I was there but one person. The officers wouldn't allow any one else to see me, and when I did see this one person, I was taken from my room down into the office, in the same building, and then there was an officer drawn up between me and the person that came to see me, to hear our conversation. This officer would allow nothing of any account concerning my case to be said. I was allowed one quarter of an hour to hold my conversation. My letters which I received were examined by three or four parties, then stamped on the back and approved by the Provost-Marshal before I received them, and brought to me open. Those I sent out were examined by every officer about the prison; if the letters suited them they were left pass, if not, they were sometimes returned back and sometimes not. I remained in this Old Capitol Prison about six weeks.

I was then with 6 others taken by the Superintendent to the Judge Advocate. The Judge asked me if I was a drinking man. I told him I generally drank when I felt like it. He said the reason he asked me was because he understood that I said 150 men couldn't take me. He then asked me if I did say so? I will, I replied, tell you what I said. I said that if I was drafted, that it would take 150 such monkeys as you (Mr. Burns) to take me, for I had made up my mind not to fight for this Administration, for I considered myself a Constitutional Union man, and was willing to fight to carry out the laws and the Constitution, but not to fight to carry out the laws that these people are trying to make. The Judge Advocate then asked me if I belonged to any secret Political Order? I told him no. He asked if I would take the Oath of Allegiance. I told him I was a Democrat, and as such owed allegiance already to the Government. He then said he was a Democrat himself. I told him if he was to let me hear the Oath, which he did not do. He then said to me that I would have to give a Bond for $5000.

I asked him what the bond was for, he said to keep the peace. I then told him that I had never broken the peace yet and would not give any bond to that effect. I told him I would go back to the Old Capitol Prison again, because I wanted a trial to know why I was taken from my family and imprisoned. He then said to me that I appeared like a very good natured sort of a man, he didn't think that I would do any one an injury. So he discharged me.

Yours truly,
JOHN APPLE.

ARREST OF AQUILA R. ALLEN, JOHN H. WISE AND THEIR INCARCERATION IN THE OLD CAPITOL BY ORDER OF GEN. WADSWORTH, MILITARY GOVERNOR OF WASHINGTON.

IN the District of Columbia, where the fugitive slave law has always been enforced when occasion required, the great number of fugitives from the State of Maryland made it necessary for the Circuit Court to appoint Commissioners to issue writs and decide upon claims These writs, when issued, were directed to officers of the Court, "Constables," to serve. Before the Commissioners could issue a a writ the claimant had to make oath to his loyalty, and that he has not bore arms against the United States in the present rebellion nor in any way given aid to the rebels. After the writ was returned with the fugitive before the Commissioners, they examined proofs of the claim, and if it was found to be just, the fugitive was restored to his or her master.

Mr. Thomas E. Berry, of Prince George County, Maryland, having lost a number of his slaves, and learning that they were in the city of Washington, applied to Commissioner Phillipps for a writ, and upon his taking the oath required of him, the writ was issued and directed to Aquila R. Allen, a regularly bonded officer. In the discharge of his duty, Mr. Allen arrested the fugitive and carried him before the Commissioner. The claimants' rights being proven, the fugitive was restored to his master.

On the 11th day of August, 1862, three days after these matters had transpired, Mr. Allen and Mr. John H. Wise, another Constable (who was mentioned in the writ to aid Mr. Allen,) was arrested by a file of soldiers by order of this *law-loving Governor*, Wadsworth, and taken before him. Messrs. Allen and Wise wished to show by what authority they acted, and presented their papers for that purpose; when this *honorable! gentlemanly! estimable* candidate for the high position of Governor of New York, treated them with contempt, at the same time candidly confessing his ignorance by saying "I am no lawyer," and his disregard of legal rights, by adding, "And don't care anything about the laws," and immediately sent them both to the Old Capitol Prison. They remained in prison for doing their duty eleven days, without a trial, or any opportunity of showing that they had done no more than their official oath and bonds compelled them to do.

On the 22nd day of August following, this despotical Governor, without giving them hearing, sent an officer to the prison and released them charging them that thereafter if they captured a fugitive they should notify his High Mightiness Wadsworth, within twenty-four hours after the arrest.

On the 10th day of September following, a writ was issued by Commissioner Phillipps, upon the oath of N. M. McGregor, of Prince George County, Maryland, and it was directed to Mr. Allen, who served the writ, returned the fugitive before the Commissioner, and immediately notified his High Mightiness as required upon his release from prison On the 13th day of September, Mr. Allen was again arrested by order of this honorable, law abiding law enforcing Military Governor, and without a hearing, confined in prison until the 27th day of said month. The friends of Mr. Allen applied to Wadsworth to know what he was charged with, and Wadsworth informed them, "there was no charge against him," but still kept Allen confined in prison.

It is well enough here to say that after their first release, Allen and Wise entered suit against Wadsworth, laying their damages at $30,000. If there was no charge against Allen, the question arises in the mind of every thinking man, does not the imprisonment indicate a mean revengeful feeling.

Loyal Citizens of Washington who are not tinctured with Wadsworth's political prejudices have argued thus: It is the duty of an executive officer to see that the laws of the land are strictly enforced. Every *honest* Governor will always applaud subordinates for the faithful discharge of their duties. But Governor Wadsworth did not applaud these subordinates, but imprisoned them. The conclusion is very plain. Every Governor should know the laws, and be careful and prompt to execute them. An ignoramus and a tyrant will neither know the laws or care for them. The people of Washington thought and think that if any thing worthy of imprisonment was done it was the Commissioners that did it, and they should have been arrested, not their subordinates: and the fact that Wadsworth did not order their arrest, and selected the humble subordinates as the marks of his indignation, goes far to convince them that he would allow the wealthy principal in crime to escape, and punish the poor man, no matter how honest his intentions. The course of this man Wadsworth in his official position, has done much to cool the ardor of loyal men in Washington; they are witnesses of his conduct, and instead of being popular, he was detested, especially by the laboring classes. Could the white laboring men of New-York but see and feel the rule of Wadsworth, his friends would be very scarce amongst them. A man who would wink at the guilt of the wealthy and punish the innocence of the poor, is unfit to occupy any position in which he can exercise authority.

Aquila R. Allen and John H. Wise are poor men, bound by their oaths and heavy securities to serve the writs issued by the Court's authority.

Who would blame them for discharging their duty. Allen was one of the first four men who spoke out publicly in opposition to Wigfall, Davis, Yancey & Co. when night after night they were concocting their treason. He raised the largest company of the three months men, that first entered the U. S. Service in the City, without fee or reward or expectation of compensation, and gave his services to the Government, in the detection of those who were aiding the rebels. Some who were then the friends of the rebels, Yancey and Keitt, are now holding positions under the Government, and others appear to have extensive influence with this excellent Governor per-se; this prominent candidate for the support of those for whom, his conduct shows he entertains the purest contempt.

On the 10th of November succeeding the times referred to before, Mr. Allen arrested other fugitives according to law, and as Governor Wadsworth required him to do, although the governor had no legal right to make such an order, nor was it Allen's duty to comply, Mr. Allen informed the governor of the arrests. Wadsworth immediately sent a file of the provost guard to take the fugitives from prison and set them at liberty, thus both disregarding the Constitution of the United States, the laws of Congress, the rights of white citizens and his oath of office. Mr. Allen was again threatened with imprisonment in the Old Capitol, but the threat was not put in execution. The *Republican*, Washington organ of the administration, approved of Wadsworth's disregard and violation of law, and suggested that Allen be again subjected to the same treatment as he had been before, merely for doing his required and sworn duty. Have we indeed a government at Washington, and if so, what is it?

CASE OF DR. BUNDY.

OLD CAPITOL PRISON,
WASHINGTON, Sept. 22, 1862.

THE following are the circumstances of *my arrest:*

I am forty-two years old, was born in Smith Co., Tenn.; reside eight miles east of Carbondale, on the road to Marion, in Williamson Co., Ill. Two Government detectives came to my house on the 14th day of August, 1862, but being from home they did not see me. They had then in charge Judges Wm. J. Allen, A. D. Duff, and Jno. H. Mulkey, also Jno. M. Clemenson, and Alexander C. Nelson. Allen and Mulkey left a note for me, stating that they were on their way to Cairo under arrest; that the same officers had orders to arrest me, and requesting me to come to Cairo as soon as I could. When I reached home I addressed them a letter stating that my family was very sick, one child I feared in great danger; that under the circumstances I could not leave home, but as soon as I could, I would report at Cairo.

On the 16th one of the same officers passed again, when I happened again to be from home, but came up just as he passed out at the gate. He said that he had been sent back to arrest me, but as my children were so very sick, and he had some business at Marion, he would wait till his return.

On the next morning my dear little boy, (six and a half years old,) died, and three other children were very sick. On the following day, 18th, we followed our dear boy to the burial ground, two and a half miles off, and deposited his remains in the grave.

As we returned home we met the officer, who took me from my family into his buggy and hurried off for Carbondale. I insisted on being permitted to go and make some arrangements for my sick family, get some clothes, money, &c., but he refused, saying we must reach Cairo that night.

When we reached Carbondale the officer's hurry had passed, and he left me at the hotel and went off in town. I soon perceived that they were taking down evidence in an adjoining room, and as the windows were open I walked out and stood by one and saw and heard all that occurred within. Two notorious abolitionists, Dick Dudding, of Jackson Co., and Dr. Owen, of Williamson, were the managers: the first writing down the answers drawn out of the witnesses by the other.

All the witnesses were in the room together.— They were Owen's political allies and special friends and dependents; and he prompted and led them to make just such statements as suited him; and when anything was said favorable to the parties accused, it was rejected and not written down. The evidence of some witnesses was refused entirely, because favorable to us. Judge Allen's brother was at the hotel to cross-examine the witnesses, but was refused the privilege. I asked permission to go in, but was refused; nor were any of our friends allowed to be present, though all the abolitionists about town seemed to pass in and out at pleasure.

About three o'clock, we started for Cairo. On reaching there the officer told me to go to the hotel where my friends were, and report to the Provost Marshal at 9 o'clock next morning. I did so, and was told to return to the hotel till called for. We all remained, with all the privileges of the city, two weeks; when we were summoned to appear before the Marshal at 9 o'clock, P. M., September 2d inst., and were delivered into the custody of one Major Board, and Isaac Phillips, deputy U. S. Marshals, who locked us in the cars under guard, saying we were going to Springfield for trial, but on reaching Centralia we learned we were destined for Washington.

After the first night the trip was pleasant enough, save the repeated manifestations of petty tyranny on the part of Board, who was detested by the whole party. Mr. Phillips acted the part of a gentleman and has the good will of all.

On the 5th of September we were all installed in that great receptacle of democratic offenders, the Old Capitol Prison, where I have now been five weeks.

As I shall probably have something specially to say of this famed prison, I forbear for the present. As to the charges on which I am confined, I will say in conclusion, they are utterly false. Some of the offensive language attributed to me in the affidavits, I never used at all in my life, and part of it was a quotation from an abolitionist which I condemned and held up to ridicule and contempt.

Yet this offensive language, used by an abolition speaker at a meeting to call for volunteers in my neighborhood, and much applauded by *Union* men at the time, and which I held up to public scorn, is, under oath, attributed to me by these supple tools of Dr. Owen.

When the affidavits were read to me at Cairo, I explained that part to Major Merrill, and told him how the evidence was taken, and that I could in five days prove the facts and demonstrate that the affidavits were utterly false by fifty reliable men.

He replied that it might be so, but he had no authority to hear rebutting testimony. I have now been confined five weeks, without hearing from my afflicted family since a few days after leaving, though I have written every few days.

SAMUEL H. BUNDY, M. D.,
Marion, Ill.

Dr. Bundy, as the reader will naturally infer without its being suggested to him, was one of the most afflicted men in the Old Capitol. He had, as he states in this narrative of his arrest, been torn from his afflicted family on his way home from the burial of a dear child, and was not permitted to return to give a word of consolation to a bereaved mother, or to make any provision for the other members of his family, three of whom were then sick, one of whom as it resulted, on a death bed. Day after day and week after week did this afflicted man lie in bed agonized with the thoughts of home, from which he was prevented receiving even one letter by the damnable tyranny exercised over victims of despotism by the Secretary of War. No one could look unmoved at Dr. Bundy. He knew that he had left at home three children dangerously ill, but he was not permitted to know whether they still remained in existence or death had taken them to keep company with their little brother who was buried on the day of the Doctor's arrest. Every prisoner in the Old Capitol who knew the circumstances of his arrest sympathized with him; but sympathy only seemed to affect him the more. His sensibilities were thus excited, and the wonder is that he was not driven to madness. At length, towards the end of September, Dr. Bundy, who had become almost indifferent to existence, was taken before Judge Advocate Turner—why called Judge Advocate it is difficult to say, as he is the mere servile, subservient tool of the Secretary of War. No doubt the letters from Dr. Bundy's wife had informed the tyrants, who examined all letters to and from the prisoners, of what had occurred at the Doctor's home. Another of his children had died, and he was not informed of the affliction. Was it to spare his feelings or to lacerate them with the infliction of still greater cruelties?

When the Doctor returned from his interview with Turner, he appeared downcast and dejected. Was he to be kept still longer in subjection? was the inquiry which rose foremost in every mind. I ventured to ask him what was his fate as decided by the subservient satrap of the War Department. He replied that he was discharged. Thank God! was my exclamation of feeling. But why, said I, are you so downcast, Doctor? He made no reply, but handed me a paper, a letter it was from one of his neighbors, which related the death and burial of another of Dr. Bundy's children. My heart swelled with the emotions excited by the circumstances of the Doctor's case, and without making any verbal observation, I handed back the letter. There was not a prisoner in the room who was not filled with indignation at the villains who had been the cause of so much affliction, and who did not sympathize with their fellow victim in his mental distress and bereavement. Every one for the time being became insensible of his own sufferings, so overwhelming were those of him who was now about to bid them adieu and return to a home deprived in his absence of a darling child.

And of what, the reader will be apt to inquire, was Dr. Bundy guilty—of what was he accused? He was never informed, reader, of what he was accused, and of course was not found guilty of any offense or crime whatever. Why then was he kidnapped—why so cruelly torn from his family in such trying circumstances? Go ask the tyrants and despots at Washington. They alone can answer.

DR. A. B. HEWITT AND JOHN W. SMITH, OR THE WANDERING JEW.

A few days after being thrust into the Old Capitol, the two secesh prisoners who were in No. 13 were removed to other quarters, and their places were filled by Dr. A. B. Hewitt, of Chatham, Illinois, and John W. Smith, of Jacksonville, Illinois, more familiarly known among the prisoners as the Wandering Jew. These victims had been for some time in the hospital, where they had been placed, not for the purpose of benefitting their health, but on account of the crowded state of the prison, which was full from yard to attic.

Dr. Hewitt was a practicing physician where he lived, and had nothing more to do with politics than to read the newspapers and talk over their contents with his neighbors and patients. He was very lame in one of his legs, so much so that it was painful to see him attempt to walk. This, of course, would not have prevented him from committing treason, if he were so disposed; but unless the proof were clear that he did commit such a crime, no one but a malicious person would accuse him of such an offense. Nevertheless, it seemed that the country was not safe while he was at large, so, early in August, 1862, he was kidnapped at his home in Chatham, Ill., and transported to the Old Capitol, Washington, and for want of room in the Bastile proper, was placed temporarily in the hospital. On the 26th of August, he and the "Wandering Jew" were transferred to Room No. 13, where they remained till towards the end of September. No. 13 being needed about that time to accommodate some Federal officers accused of serious offences, the occupants of 13 were transferred to No. 16, which became famous afterwards as the abode of nearly all the Prisoners of State.

Dr. Hewitt whiled away his captivity in making finger-rings of peach stones. He labored as industriously at this employment as if it were his trade, and it was all that he did, for his temperament was such that when the peach stones gave out and he had nothing to do, his mind became affected almost to madness by being subjected to the treatment of the Old Capitol. Many a time did we prisoners of despotism wish that we could be seen by our fellow citizens in the condition to which arbitrary power had reduced us. Haggard in appearance, restless as caged wild beasts in our movements, and agonizing from the spirit which burned within us which felt that it should be free, we were such pictures of despotism applied to freemen as would have moved, had they seen us, the American people to emulate the illustrious example of the Parisians and tear open the bastiles and avenge outraged liberty on the tyrants who had dared to violate it in our persons. But good care was taken that we should neither be seen nor heard. Our persons were secured by guards, and our correspondence was subjected to the surveillance of the tyrants and their dependant underlings.

"The Wandering Jew," as Mr. John W. Smith was called in the Old Capitol, was an old man, of not less than sixty-five years of age, blind of one eye, a homeless, and apparently friendless wanderer. He was a native of one of the counties of Virginia, contiguous to Washington, but had left his native State in his youth and wandered to the West, where he spent most of his subsequent life on the frontiers. He migrated to Kansas soon after that portion of the country became organized into a territory, and engaged in merchandizing and general trading there. During the troubles in the territory between the John Brownists and their opponents, he lost his property by the theft of the John Brown and Lane gangs of marauders.

This naturally soured Mr. Smith against the Abolitionists, whom he regarded with an aversion which with him knew no bounds nor duration. The immediate cause of his arrest, so well as he could ascertain it, (for he was never informed, no more than any one else so far as known,) was his invention of a bomb for disabling locomotives while in motion without injury to the railroad trains. The object, it would seem, of Mr. Smith in this invention was to place it at the disposal of the Federal Government as soon as he had it perfected, and proper models made of it for experiment. He knew a friend at St. Louis, to whom he communicated his invention and design, requesting aid from his friend to enable him to get up a proper model, as the Ordinance Department, it appears, takes no notice of inventions whose utility cannot be practically demonstrated.

The correspondence between Mr. Smith and his friend at St. Louis was seized on suspicion of its having referred to some diabolical design on the Federal Government, and Smith himself was kidnapped at Jacksonville, Illinois, early in August, 1862, and transported to the Old Capitol. He was placed in the hospital temporarily with Dr. Hewitt and others, for whom there was no accommodation any where else, and in due time became an occupant of No. 13, and subsequently of No. 16.

It is difficult to express the sentiments of indignation and feeling of disgust at the conduct of the Administration towards this blind, feeble, penny-less, infirm, old man. When he was first introduced to us in No. 13, he had neither coat nor hat, and no change of clothes of any kind, and it was some time before his fellow prisoners who had the means to help him found an opportunity to so. Being a Free Mason of a high degree in that order, he contrived to make his situation known to his brethren in Washington, and through the kind offices of Dr. Hull, who had access to the prison, the Masons relieved some of the wants of this victim of tyranny.

When Mr. Smith was brought to the Old Capitol he was stripped naked, and his rags of clothes and *person* searched for evidences of whatever charge was made against him, or of the suspicions entertained of him. But nothing was found to implicate or convict him of any offense. Nevertheless he was kept nearly two months in the Old Capitol, and was only released at last, as were several others at the same time, to make way for some other victims. Like all the other victims, he was wantonly kidnapped and cruelly punished without cause, trial, or judgment. Papers deemed of value by Mr. Smith were taken from him when he was kidnapped, and on applying for them when he was released, they were withheld from him. These papers had nothing whatever to do with the affairs of the Government, or with politics. Mr. Smith had an inventive mind, and he was continually thinking of some improvement in implements of husbandry, domestic economy, and, during the war, of improvements in arms, projectiles, &c. He had patented several improvements in bee-hives and farm implements, but, like most inventors, realized little or nothing as the fruits of his genius. It was papers which had reference to some of these inventions which were taken from him when he was kidnapped, and which were withheld from him when he was set at liberty, confiscated, doubtless, as was the property of many another victim as prize of war, or as the reward of such services as no one who had any respect for himself would descend so low as to perform. The poor old blind man, Smith, had to beg the means to feed himself on his way home, the Government furnishing only transportation.

KIDNAPPING OF HON. ANDREW D. DUFF, ONE OF THE CIRCUIT JUDGES OF ILLINOIS, WITH SOME OTHER GENTLEMEN.

I was arrested at Marion, in Williamson County, while holding Circuit Court there, on the 14th August, 1862. Hon. Wm. J. Allen, M. C., (from old 9th district,) John M. Clementson, States Attorney for 26th Judicial Circuit, Hon. John H. Mulkey, Judge of the Court of Common Pleas of the city of Cairo, Dr. H. Bundy and Alexander C. Nelson of Williamson County, were also arrested at the same time.

We were arrested by Messrs. Scott and Woodruff, United States Detective Policemen. We went with them to Cairo on Friday the 15th; we were treated generously by these gentlemen. When we got to Cairo, we were paroled upon honor, where we remained until the 2nd day of September. On the 20th of August, the affidavits, or at least a part of them were shown to us.

Four or five of them against me were for speaking against the corruptions of the administration, these affidavits being so true in the main were suppressed, and never to my knowledge published. There was one affidavit by one G. W. Myers, corporal in Captain Creed's company of three months men, then stationed at Big Muddy Bridge, near

Carbonda.e, Illinois. This witness states that he was introduced into the K. G. C., on 10th July, (year not given,) near Marion, Illinois; that afternoon he attended a meeting three miles from Blairsville in Williamson County, where upwards of three hundred men were present; that seven or eight speakers addressed the meeting; that I was present and made a speech in which I informed the meeting that the K. G. C., would soon be armed, &c., giving no date, no names, &c., not even stating that he knew me at all.

Upon the reading of this affidavit, I informed the Provost Marshal, Mr. J. W. Merrill, that it was a lie of whole cloth, that I had never seen or heard of this man on earth before, that if he (Merrill,) would send up (being about eighty miles,) the line, and retake his affidavit, and require him to state who the speakers were that addressed the meeting, and name some of the persons present, name the day of the week, month and year, also state whether he was personally acquainted with me, if so, describe my person, &c., or else bring him down to Cairo and bring the witness to cross-examination himself. I proposed if this was done, that I would pay all expenses attending the same, knowing that Creed's company, to which this corporal belonged, left Duquoin about 15th July, for Camp Butler, Ill., where they remained till first August, and my court commenced at Vienna the fourth of August, leaving but five or seven days from tenth July to seventeenth for him to fix upon, so that he could either prove his or my whereabouts. But all this was denied me as if their object was accomplished which they desired.

On the 24th of Aug. all the evidences the other gentlemen together with this aff. and also an additional aff. (the name of affiant not given) was published by the Chicago Tribune, and then by all the Abolition papers in the West. This publication was made before any decision was made by the Provost Marshal, and was obtained from his office (and was intended to prejudice us before trial.) The name of this last affiant we have so far been unable to obtain, but is false from end to end. This affiant states that myself, F. M. Youngblood, W. Newland, and J. Crouch of Franklin County, attended a meeting of the K. G. C. two miles north of Pinckneyville, in Perry county. This is thirty miles west from Benton. As to this affiant, it is enough to state that the meeting is stated to have been on the 10th of August, 1862. My Circuit Court commenced at Vienna on the first Monday in August, being 4th August, where I remained till ten o'clock Saturday, the 9th—drove home fifty miles that night—was at home all day on Sunday—was about town and the taverns in Benton all day on the 10th. Half the inhabitants, both men, women and children, both Democrats, Republicans, and Abolitionists, saw me at all hours of the day up till dark; and on Monday morning, 11th, I left for Marion, Williamson Co., where I opened my Court at ten o'clock. All these facts I offered to prove, but was also denied. We were all started to Washington city 2d Sept., 1862. At Centralia we met with Captain Corder, also of Marion, and Dr. John R. Brown, of Randolph county, under charge of Captain Rockford. We then proceeded to Washington city under charge of Deputy Marshal Isaac Philips, who is a gentleman in every sense of the word, Major Board, (who is both a fool and a tyrant) and Captain Rockford, who is also a gentleman.

We arrived at Washington the 5th Sept. Judge Allen being very sick, was paroled and left at the

Kirkwood House, and the balance of us were committed to the Old Capitol Prison.

ANDREW D. DUFF,
Judge 26th Judicial C. Ill.

P. S. Since this memoranda was made, I have received the affidavits of twelve respectable citizens of Benton, among whom are several Black Republicans, (stating themselves to be such) who all swear that I was at home all day on the 10th of August, 1862.

I will also state that I am forty-two years old--was born in Bond county, Ill.—spent my life in that State. A lawyer by profession, was elected Circuit Judge of the 26th Judicial Circuit in said State on the first Monday in June, 1861. The Circuit is composed of the counties of Franklin, Williamson, Johnson and Saline. That I have a wife and four little children—have been married seventeen years—and served as a private soldier during the Mexican war in Col. E. W. B. Newby's Regiment of Illinois Volunteers. A. D. D.

The only parallel for the kidnapping of Judge Duff, of Illinois, in outrage to person and violation of law, was that of Judge Carmichael, of Maryland. Judge Duff relates as given above, the circumstances of his arrest and incarceration in the Old Capitol. When he arrived at that Bastile, he, with other gentlemen arrested at the same time, whom he names, were subjected to the worst treatment of the place. Among other outrages and indignities to which they had to submit or go hungry, was that of going with the throng of criminal prisoners, such as deserters, drunken soldiers, and soldiers under sentence of Court-Martial for offences committed, to feed at what was called the hog-pen—the place where several hundred prisoners rushed at meal time, to satisfy the cravings of hunger. The first interview between the writer and Judge Duff, and his companions from Illinois, was in the prison yard, where Judge Duff was standing with a piece of bread in one hand, and some meat in the other, the sickening atmosphere and disgusting sight of the hog-pen having compelled him to leave that place, and eat his rations in the open air.

Reader, if you be an American freeman, aye, or an American freewoman, picture to yourself the Judge of your Court kidnapped on the Bench of Justice by an arbitrary, illegal, tyrannical order, mayhap a telegraphic dispatch, from a drunken old scoundrel at Washington, directed to a satrap of the Administration, and executed by him in the most insolent and malignant manner, and follow this Judge, accompanied by the Clerk of his Court, the District Attorney, a Judge of another court who happened to be in attendance, and several other gentlemen, follow this crowd of victims of despotism, some of them manacled, to Washington, and see them thrust into that Bastile, and then subjected to the outrages, indignities, and hardships of that prison, for the long, weary, almost interminable months of suffering, and realize in the presence of this picture, if you can, that you are still living in the United States of America; in that country which boasts of its Constitutional Government, free and liberal institutions, and where personal rights are sacred in the eye of the law.

"But did Judge Duff and his companions commit no crime, at least some offense," the reader may inquire.

None, whatever, except that of being a Democrat in politics. Judge Duff, as he states in his narrative, offered to not only disprove the allegations of his accusers in Illinois, but to bear the expense himself of the examination of witnessess for that purpose. So far was he from having committed any offense and so self-convicted of wrong to Judge Duff and others, was the Secretary of War, and his man Friday, L. C. Turner, who was made Judge-Advocate for his servile and supple qualities, that an oath was exacted by them from Judge Duff, that on his being released, which occurred on the 11th of November, 1862, he would not prosecute them for having caused his arrest and imprisonment.

NARRATIVE OF THE ARRESTS OF J. BLANCHARD.

In May, 1861, whilst riding in my buggy in the streets of Carbondale, Jackson county, Illinois, I was arrested by a captain of the U. S. A. and four privates, and the first intimation I had of being arrested was the order to halt. Immediately five revolvers were cocked and presented to my breast, and I was commanded to surrender. I inquired by what authority I was arrested. The captain presented a cocked pistol to my breast, and replied, There is the authority. I was immediately taken to Cairo, where I was kept four days. At the end of that time, three or four witnesses arrived, who stated they had heard me make speeches against the war and against the Administration, and they therefore considered me disloyal. I was then sent to Springfield, Ill., to D. S. Philips, U. S. Marshal for the Southern District of Illinois. Mr. Phillips would not receive me, nor have anything to do with the matter, but advised the officer having me in custody to take me back to Cairo. I was immediately conveyed back to Cairo, where General Prentiss, commandant of the post, discharged me from custody; first requiring me to sign an agreement that I would not bear arms against the Government of the United States, nor give aid to the rebellion.

I then returned home, where I was peaceably engaged in the practice of the law until August, 1862, when I was again arrested by a captain and four privates of the United States army. The captain showed me an order from D. L. Phillips, Marshal for the Southern District of Illinois, to arrest me and deliver me to his deputy, at Centralia, the next day, at 12 o'clock. I was taken to Centralia, and delivered to the Deputy United States Marshal. Here I found nine other citizens of Southern Illinois—to wit.: Drs. Ross and Smith, of Tamaroa; Drs. McCarvier and Thermon; Mr. Newland, of Benton, Ill.; James Williams, of Spring Garden, Ill.; Mr. Haines, of Perry county, Ill.; and Mr. Hawkes, of Tamaroa, Ill.—under arrest. We remained at Centralia until midnight, when we were all handcuffed and put upon the train for Camp Butler. We were confined in Camp Butler twenty-four hours; at the end of which time, in charge of Marshal Philips, we were placed on board of a train bound for Washington City. When we arrived at Washington City, without any examination, or without knowing the reasons why, we were immediately locked up in the Old Capitol Prison.

I remained in the Old Capitol Prison about forty days. During this time, I wrote several letters to the Judge Advocate, the Provost Marshal, and the Secretary of War, asking them to inform me why I was arrested and confined in prison; to all of which no answer was ever returned. Finding inquiries to avail nothing, I then, in conjunction with several of my fellow-prisoners, sent a petition to the Judge Advocate, asking for an examination, or at least to be informed of the charges against us. The petition was as unsuccessful as my letters, and no answer to it was ever returned. At the end of forty days, I was taken before the Judge Advocate, where, by his Honor (?), I was asked the following questions:

Judge Advocate.—Do you now, or have you ever, belonged to the Knights of the Golden Circle?

Ans.—I am not acquainted with any such organization.

J. A.—Do you now, or have you ever, belonged to any secret organization?

Ans.—I once belonged to the Odd Fellows, and I once tried the Know Nothings a short time.

J. A.—I mean, do you belong to any secret organization now?

Ans.—I belong to a secret Democratic organization.

J. A.—Where do you meet?

Ans.—In the Court-House.

J. A.—Do you meet at night, or in the daytime?

Ans.—Just as it happens.

J. A.—What do you do when you meet?

Ans.—Nominate men that we vote for, and lay plans to beat the d—d Black Republicans.

After the above conversation, I was immediately discharged from prison, and sent home. Upon my arrival at home, there being a vacancy in my State Senatorial District, the people insisted upon my becoming a candidate for State Senator. I canvassed the counties composing my district, and was elected by almost the unanimous vote of the district.

THE KIDNAPPING OF REV. JUDSON D. BENEDICT—
CHRIST'S SERMON ON THE MOUNT REGARDED AS
TREASONABLE—MR. BENEDICT BROUGHT BEFORE
U. S. JUDGE HALL, OF BUFFALO, ON A WRIT OF
HABEAS CORPUS—DISCHARGED FROM CUSTODY
BY THE JUDGE, NO ONE APPEARING AGAINST
HIM—KIDNAPPED AGAIN, AND TAKEN TO THE
OLD CAPITOL.

Sept. 26th.—A reverend gentlemen was brought to the prison to-day, and quartered in our room, whose arrest and incarceration presents a grievous case, as it involves the most flagrant violation of the Constitution, and a conflict between the Executive and Judicial Branches of the Government. As this is an interesting case, involving the most serious questions affecting not only the personal rights of citizens, but the jurisdiction and authority of the Federal courts, I will give it in detail, as published in the Buffalo Courier of September 19th, as shown by the order of Judge Hall discharging the prisoner, Rev. Judson D. Benedict from arrest and imprisonment, and as related to me by himself in prison.

REV. MR. BENEDICT'S NARRATIVE.

I, J. D. Benedict, a minister of the Gospel, residing in East Aurora, Erie County, N. Y., was arrested by Deputy-Marshal Stevens, of Buffalo, N.

Y., on the morning of September 2d, 1862, and was committed to the "guard-house" in Fort Porter the same day.

I there found for companions in tribulation, a number of drunken soldiers together with three prisoners, so called, accused of "using language tending to prevent enlistment." One was a "Wild Irishman" of no possible utility but to cut bog and consume bad whiskey. The other, an old Dutchman of some seventy years of age, who could not speak three words of the English language, and the other, a crazy man by the name of Clark, whose business appeared to be selling "wooden nutmegs" and other New England indispensibles. This trinity with myself composed the sum of political prisoners in Erie County at the time of my incarceration.

I found the officers in the Fort extremely busy in having subscription papers circulated among the soldiers in order to procure their money just then paid them, that some "fuzzle-man" in the game might purchase as a present for said officers, a costly sword, horse, pistols, sash, etc., etc., that the trump of fame might be sounded through the papers of his "very high consideration." In vain did the poor soldier plead that he wished to send the money to his poor family at home. This otherwise potent plea was rendered wholly inefficacious by the more weighty argument that whatsoever was thus paid was insurance money for kind usage on the recipient's part towards the donor.

After staying some twenty-four hours in this filthy and vile place, with only one meal of victuals, we were transferred to the County Jail of the County, to await further orders. Our transit to the Jail was dignified, safe and orderly conducted; for the "*hand-cuffs*" were applied only to the "foreign citizens" with their rich "Irish and Dutch brogue," while Clark and myself being native born, were permitted to go without these official, ornamental jewels.

I feel a presentiment creeping over me that the native born citizen might notice this mark of deference paid the "adopted citizen," and take a note thereof in the coming election; I therefore assumed the carriage and airs of a "gentleman at large" for the especial benefit of the Republican party of Erie County.

The second week of my incarceration I was to have an examination at the United States Court Room in the city of Buffalo, at which time and place my friends attended. But instead of a public hearing, a private interview was had with the Marshal and his assistants, who expressed themselves satisfied that my arrest was not justifiable or necessary for the purpose of justice, and the Marshal wrote to that effect to the authorities in Washington.

I was hereupon returned to the jail to await the order of release from the Secretary, which I was assured by the Marshal I might expect within four days. After a week had expired I was informed by high authority that I was to be made a political prisoner in order to aid the Republicans in carrying Erie County, and that my release was to be postponed till after the fall election. I was further informed that a writ of *habeas corpus* might possibly be allowed by his honor Judge Hall, of the U. S. Court, and if so, that would release me and make a full end of this unpleasant affair, as no one could be induced to appear against me.

An application was accordingly made and the writ allowed, when upon the return thereof I was confronted by the Marshal and the District Attorney, Mr. Dart, who wished for an adjournment for a few days that they might examine the authorities; and in the meantime they desired the Court to place me in their hands for keeping. The adjournment asked for was readily granted to the prosecution, but the possession of the prisoner they could not have; and I thought that it was because the court lacked confidence in the claimants.

I was remanded to the custody of the Jailor, and his honor, Judge Hall, publicly observed that if any persons knew of any offense committed by the prisoner, at any time, it was their duty as good citizens to appear at the day of adjournment and then and there to make it known.

At the day of the last adjournment the Marshal came early in the morning, with his assistants, and made a formal demand of me from the Sheriff, the Jailor, and then from his assistants. Failing to obtain possession of me in this manner, the Marshal ordered up the soldiers from Fort Porter, and surrounded the jail, threatening that he would have me at the expense of blood.

At the hour appointed the Sheriff and Jailor went to the court room in order to advertise his honor of the threatened rescue, and to take his further order in the premises. The Marshal got possession of the Jailor's papers, and refused to give them up when demanded, upon which the court adjourned till 2 o'clock P. M., in order to give the Marshal time to return the papers to the Jailor, and for the Jailor to bring the body of the prisoner into court; and if the Marshal did not give up the papers, an order would be made committing him for contempt of court.

Before the hour of 2 o'clock P. M., the papers were given up to the Jailor by the Marshal, and the soldiers were withdrawn from around the jail, and the Sheriff, Jailor and myself walked down to the court room unmolested.

After I was discharged by his honor, Judge Hall, I was immediately rearrested by the Marshal and placed in a carriage with three Deputy Marshals as special guards, and the driver, and was thus conveyed to Lockport, in the County of Niagara, a distance of forty miles.

The cars for Lockport would have started out of Buffalo, (at the time I left), in about one hour. At about 9 o'clock P. M., we again started in a carriage through highways and byways, and at 3 o'clock next morning I found myself at *Batavia*, a few miles from Buffalo, on the Central railroad. At six o'clock we took the cars for Canandaigua, and from that to New York, thence to Baltimore and Washington.

The proceedings referred to by Mr. Benedict in his narrative were thus reported at the time by the Buffalo Courier.

THE HABEAS CORPUS VINDICATED—PROCEEDINGS OF THE
U. S. DISTRICT COURT.

U. S. DISTRICT COURT.—Judge Hall presiding.— September 18th.

The case of the writ of *habeas corpus* commanding A. G. Stephens, Deputy U. S. Marshal, and Wm. F. Best, jailor, of Erie County, to produce the body of Rev. Judson T. Benedict, in court was before the court.

A. Sawin made a statement of the service of the *habeas corpus* upon the Jailor of the Erie County Jail.

A. P. Nichols, Esq., the attorney for the Jailor, made a return stating that the Jailor had handed the writ of *habeas corpus* to U. S. Marshal Chase, by the advice of his attorney, and that Mr. Chase had refused to return it to him, and that it was impossible to return either the writ or the prisoner.

U. S. Marshal Chase claimed that the prisoner

was in his custody, having been arrested by order of the President, through the Secretary of War; that the Jailor was simply a machine, and that he was the proper custodian of the prisoner.

This was the position taken by U. S. District Attorney Dart.

Mr. Nichols claimed that the prisoner was now held by the Jailor by virtue of the writ of *habeas corpus*, and that he could not surrender him until that writ was vacated.

After a somewhat extended argument, Judge Hall made an order that Marshal Chase return the writ to the Jailor; and that he make a return at half past two o'clock, &c. The Court adjourned till that hour.

During the recess of the Court, Marshal Chase offered to deliver up the writ of *habeas corpus*, which he had withheld from Jailor Best, on the condition that the Jailor would deliver the prisoner into his custody. This the Jailor refused; and before two o'clock Marshal Chase surrendered the writ, evidently not wishing to disobey the order of the Court. The Jailor now being in possession of the writ, took the prisoner, in company with Sheriff Best, and escorted him to the Court Room, where we was cordially greeted by many of his friends from the country.

AFTERNOON SESSION.
Half past two o'clock.

U. S. Marshal Chase came into Court and delivered to the Judge a return to the writ of *habeas corpus*, setting forth by what authority his Deputy had arrested the prisoner, and that the writ of *habeas corpus* having been suspended, and he ordered to resist any attempt to execute it, he could not obey the order of the Court—This we understood to be the substance of the return.

Marshal Chase requested the Jailor to give him a copy of the order of the Court compelling him to return the writ.

The Judge said a copy would be furnished him.

A. P. Nichols, Esq., then made a proper return to the writ, and produced Rev. J. T. Benedict in Court.

U. S. District Attorney Dart said, that a turnkey had, in some way, obtained possession of a United States prisoner, arrested by order of the President of the United States, through the Secretary of War, for uttering seditious language, or language calculated to weaken the confidence of the people in the Government. In such cases, the President has suspended the writ of *habeas corpus*, and ordered that forcible resistance be made to its execution. He hoped that the occasion for arrests under this order had ceased, and that there would be no conflict of jurisdiction in this case. He asked the suspension of proceedings until Tuesday next, trusting that the matter might be satisfactorily arranged before that time.

Albert Sawin opposed the postponement. It was important that the great question of personal liberty in connection with the arbitrary arrests should be disposed of by a legal tribunal.

Judge Hall said the real question at issue was whether the President had the power to suspend the writ of *habeas corpus*, and if this was the question to be argued the time asked was not unreasonable. He was anxious that the matter should be fairly canvassed, and a conflict of authority avoided. He would, therefore, grant the request of the United States District Attorney, and adjourn the case to Tuesday next, at 11 A. M., meanwhile the prisoner to remain in the custody of the jailor, to be again produced in court at the time named.

The District Attorney desired the Judge simply to remand the prisoner, without naming the custodian.

Mr. Sawin opposed this. The Marshal wished to gain possession of the prisoner for the purpose of placing him in military custody, and beyond the jurisdiction of this Court. The rights of the prisoner were in jeopardy, and he appealed to the protection of the Court.

A. P. Nichols, Esq., asked the Court to make an order stating by what authority the jailor held the prisoner, whether by order of the Marshal, or under the writ of *habeas corpus* and the order of this Court. He wished the duty and the authority of the jailor clearly defined.

Mr. Dart desired that the Court would make no such order, but simply remand the prisoner. He thought the Court ought to have confidence in the Marshals, and believe they would respect the Court.

Judge Hall said the custody of the prisoner will continue with the Jailor as it is now. The prisoner is now held by virtue of the writ of *habeas corpus*. He is removed from the custody of the Marshal or Deputy Marshals, and neither of them can interfere with him until the hearing and determination of this writ.

Marshal Chase wished to know whether his authority in this case was at an end.

The Judge replied that he had as much and no more to do with it than any other citizen. If he or any other man knew of any crime the prisoner had committed, it was his duty to inform against him, that he might be punished according to law. It was especially the duty of the United States District Attorney to ascertain the facts and proceed against him, if he had been guilty of any violation of the laws of the land.

The following is a copy of the order of Judge Hall in the case:—

ON HABEAS CORPUS,
In the matter of
Judson T. Benedict.

The said Judson T. Benedict having this day been brought before me by W. F. Best, the keeper of the common jail of the County of Erie, in obedience to the annexed writ of *habeas corpus*, and the hearing under the said writ and the return made thereto having, at the request of Hon. Wm. A. Dart, U. S. District Attorney, been adjourned until Tuesday, the 23d day of September, at eleven o'clock in the forenoon, it is hereby ordered, on motion of the counsel for the defendant, that the said Judson T. Benedict be and he is hereby remanded and committed to the custody of William F. Best, as such jailor, to be kept and detained by him under the authority of such writ of *habeas corpus* and this order, until the time to which said hearing is so adjourned; and that said William F. Best produce and bring the body of the said Judson T. Benedict and the said writ of *habeas corpus* before the undersigned at the U. S. Court Room in the city of Buffalo on the said 23d day of September instant, at 11 o'clock A. M., then and there to do and receive what shall then and there be considered in that behalf.

N. K. HALL,
U. S. District Judge.

September 18, 1862.

The Courier commenting on the proceedings said: "The Marshal betrayed some uneasiness at the decision of the Judge; but remarked that he was a loyal man, and should respect the court.

After the necessary papers were made out, Rev. Mr. Benedict walked, in company with Mr. Best, back to his apartments at the jail. It was rumored that the Marshal would attempt the rescue of the prisoner, but this was unfounded."

But the Courier was mistaken. It did not know the character of the tyrants who ruled at Washington, nor of their minions in Buffalo and elsewhere. Notwithstanding the judicial order of Judge Hall discharging the prisoner, he was immediately afterwards, as he relates, kidnapped and hurried off to Washington and brought to this loathsome place, deprived not only of personal liberty, but of the necessaries of life.

Rev. Judson D. Benedict is an elderly gentleman of fine physical and intellectual appearance. He is of the Christian, or as it is commonly called the Campbellite persuasion. He had not voted for fifteen years, nor meddled in any way with politics. His offence is that he intimated in a sermon that it was sinful for brethren to be taking each others lives. This is construed by the powers that be into disloyalty, discouraging enlistments, and deserving of arbitrary arrest and imprisonment. Oh! could the people but perceive, properly appreciate and feel how they are outraged in their rights, liberties, Constitution and laws, by these arbitrary, outrageous and illegal arrests, how soon would our country be restored to her lost peace, happiness, prosperity and glory. But alas! they do not think of the condition of their fellow-citizens who have been made the victims of tyranny, for being loyal to their country and faithful to their duty as free Americans.

When the Majesty of the Despotism which ruled at Washington became appeased, Mr. Benedict was taken before one of the instruments of its tyranny, L. C. Turner, who is called Judge Advocate, who received the Rev. Gentleman with one of his most hypocritically bland smiles. After the usual interchange of courtesies, the Judge Advocate informed Mr. Benedict that he was discharged. Mr. Benedict ventured to enquire why he had been imprisoned. "Oh," said the Judge Advocate, "it was only to show the people that the military power is now above the civil power." What thinks the reader of this?

Preposterous as it may seem to the reader, especially if he be an intelligent freeman, Turner only said what was the truth, in fact no matter how different the theory may be understood in America at present. The military power *is* above the civil, just as it is in the despotism of the Old World, and just as it has been in all military despotisms. A detective of the lowest character armed with the power of the War Department, is above the whole Supreme Court of the United States and every other Civil Court in the United States. He can arrest whom he pleases without warrant of law or without any cause whatever, and it is not in the power of all the courts in the United States to wrest the victim from the clutches of this detective, backed as he is by all the Executive power. Such is the condition of poor America under the despotism of the existing administration, and such is the tenure on which freemen, as we were not long since, hold their liberty.

KIDNAPPING AND IMPRISONMENT OF GEO. W. WILSON, OF UPPER MARLBORO, MD.

The fifteenth of October had been designated as the day on which the draft for soldiers to fill the quota of Maryland in the Federal service should take place. In estimating the population from which the draft should be made, it was intentionally settled that the whole population, black and white, slave and free, should be taken as a basis—while of course the number required to be drafted could only be taken from the white inhabitants, capable and not exempt of bearing arms. This manifestly unjust and wicked course of the Administration was very properly rebuked by George W. Wilson, Esq. Editor of the Marlboro Gazette, who in his paper of the 15th of October, put the matter in the true light to his readers and the people of Maryland.

THE MILITIA DRAFT

In the State of Maryland will take place this day. It were useless to utter words of complaint against the unnatural call made upon this State, as the powers at Washington are deaf to all fair argument.—But we cannot forbear, though Federal bayonets and a dungeon were to threaten us, to proclaim the fact that the principles upon which the draft is to be made are unjust and oppressive to the Southern portion of the State. In making the apportionment federal numbers are taken as the basis of the levy, and the white and black population of the counties are added together. This process brings to Prince George's a quota far beyond what is equitable, for it compels her to furnish a much larger number than some other counties which have a greater free voting population.

This is not all—part of the very property upon which this basis is laid has been taken from us by the action of the authorities who now seek to tax it for both civil and military purposes. Such an outrage has never been perpetrated before upon a people whose only crime is that they do not approve the policy of an Administration whose principles and practises if carried out must result in the sacrifice of their rights of property under a plain written Constitution.

The whole sum and substance of this mode of raising troops from the militia of the State, is in fact, by making three-fifths of the slave and free colored population, *a part of the militia of the State,* when the bill of Rights, the Constitution, and the Acts of the Legislature of the State, distinctly declare the militia of the State shall consist only of that portion of her *free white citizens,* who are between the ages of 18 and 45 years. Was ever such oppression and tyranny practised on a free people."

No reasonable American freeman can find any fault with the doctrines or sentiments of the foregoing, nor, under the circumstances, with the manner in which these doctrines and sentiments are there expressed. None but an acquiescent servile minion of the despotism which rules our country will dissent from the position assumed by Mr. Wilson. Under the system adopted for drafting in Maryland, it so happened that in several counties there were not white men enough capable of bearing arms to fill the quota of these counties. No wonder that the course of the Administration towards that State inspired one of her children to exclaim,

"The despot's heel is on thy shore,
Maryland! My Maryland."

The wonder is that the people of that State suffered as they have done the outrages, the indignities, the oppressions, the despotism and the tyranny to which they have been wantonly subjected.

But we must not anticipate. In the same number of Mr. Wilson's paper which contained his strictures on the drafting system, another short articles was published, which reads as follows:

ARREST OF WALTER BOWIE.

The squad of soldiers belonging to the New York 141st, which has been recently stationed here, made an arrest on Saturday night last. WALTER BOWIE, formerly of this place, paid the town a visit on that evening, and not having the fear of the Sons of Abraham before his eyes, incautiously ventured out by the light of the moon. He was recognized by some sable promenader, who gave information to the soldiers, who forthwith proceeded to the house of Dr. BOYLE, where they made the arrest. He was confined in the Court House until yesterday morning, and then taken under an escort of thirty men to Washington city. We have no idea that the Government can prove anything against him, more than the fact that he left his native State to share the fortunes or misfortunes of our sister Southern States; and has imprudently ventured back to his old home. During his confinement he was treated with marked kindness by our citizens more especially by the gentler portion of this community, who provided him with better fare than he would have shared in a soldier's camp."

These were the newspaper articles which caused Mr. Wilson to be kidnapped and taken to the Old Capitol. Let us hear him give an account of the affair himself, for no one is better qualified than he, especially to make light of a serious matter. After his release from the Old Capitol, Mr. Wilson resumed his paper, and in the first issue after his return home, he gave his readers the following account of what had occurred to him:

RESUMPTION.

We resume to-day the publication of the Gazette, (temporarily suspended by reason of the involuntary absence of the captain and his crew,) and hope that no adverse winds or *drafts* may again throw it upon its beam ends.

On the morning of the 15th of October, a Government detective visited our villiage, and in our absence thoroughly searched our store house and premises, having been informed, as he said, that there were Government stores secreted about the building. He soon found out that he had been misled by his lying informer, who had, for some purpose, set him upon our track. His search was aided by a squad of soldiers, under the command of a Captain Bullock, and on our return to town, at noon, we reported to the captain, who at once put us under arrest. A private and informal examination of the case was held before the Provost-Marshal, of the the county, the detective and the captain, and after some discussion between these functionaries as to who had the greatest power over our case, a parole of two hours was given, when we were to report and hear our fate. At the hour appointed we found a horse in readiness, and were told that Washington was our destination — thither we were taken, and safely arrived at the Old Capitol, at 9 o'clock, P. M., — where we were lodged with ten or twelve genial, whole-souled Comstitutional Democrats, (among them two clever Western editors,) whose kindness and sympathies we shall long remember.

At the examination in Marlboro', the Marshal and detective acquitted us fully of the charge alleged, but the captain arraigned us upon the editorials published in the Gazette of that day. He read and re-read them, torturing our language into an "interference with the draft," and charging us with sarcasm in calling his soldiers "the sons of Abraham." The last we answered by reminding him that it was a cognomen of their own choosing, as their song announced that,

> "We're coming, father Abraham,
> Three hundred thousand more."

And if Abraham be their father, they were the "Sons of Abraham"—and we could not see why they should be ashamed of their father. We certainly meant no disrespect to them or the President, and no reasonable man could take exception to the use of the term. But our argument was "no go;" somebody had to be hurt—some feat was to be performed—and we were the victim.

The escape from the civil authorities (the Marshal and the Detective,) and the arrest by the military, brought to mind the situation of the Irishmen in 1798:—

> "Them were hard times for an honest gossoon;
> If he missed of the judges he met a dragoon,
> And whether the judges or soldiers gave sentence,
> The devil a short time they gave for repentence"

After remaining in the modern Bastile for six days our case was taken up, and we were discharged. Our respected Representative in Congress, Mr. CALVERT, was instrumental in obtaining a hearing for us, and we feel deeply indebted to him for his friendly offices in our behalf.

After our release we found work to do in obtaining substitutes in Baltimore for our drafted neighbors and employees, and for a week we were made a regular *draft*-horse in this business.

And now here we are again at our old desk, free to chat with our readers as of yore (except on the subject of a *military draft!*)"

During the few days which Mr. Wilson was an occupant of the Old Capitol and an inmate of No. 16 of the famous—infamous, rather—Bastile, he made his room-mates forget, most of the time, that they were victims of despotism. His *bon mots* and witticisms seemed inexhaustible, and for hours at a time the writer and several others of his companions in durance sat by him enjoying the pleasure which he seemed to delight in giving to his fellow-victims of tyranny.

Nor did his interest in the well-being of his fellow-prisoners cease with his separation from them. No sooner did he reach home, some twenty miles from Washington, than he dispatched a large box of provisions, which he knew, by his six days' experience of the treatment of prisoners of state by the Administration, that they much needed. Geo. W. Wilson, of Upper Marlboro', Md., will ever be held in grateful remembrance by his fellow-victims of despotism of No. 16, O. C. P.

THE CASE OF DR. ELLIS, A MEDICAL DIRECTOR IN THE ARMY.

I WILL next refer to the case of Dr. Ellis, of New York, who was arrested on the fifteenth of October, 1862, in his house, at night. Dr. Ellis is a British subject, and was surgeon in the British army in 1851. Dr. Ellis was requested by the military authorities to accept the office of Post-Surgeon, as they deemed him, from his military experience, peculiarly fitted for its duties. He relinquished a large and lucrative practice for this purpose, Secretary Cameron waiving the oath of allegiance in his case. He discharged the onerous and responsible duties of organizing the medical staffs of the volunteer regiments fitted out for the war, in New York. These duties ceased in the spring of 1862, when Mr. Stanton put a stop to recruiting. He then, by request of Surgeon-General Hammond, proceeded to the Peninsula, and ably discharged the duties of Acting Medical Director in the care of the wounded, after the several engagements of the army of the Potomac. His services were frequently commended by the heads of the Departments, and called forth from the newspapers of New York, Philadelphia, and Washington, and the Congressional Committee on the Conduct of the War, the warmest praises. He continued to fill this responsible office until his health, broken down by exposure and fatigue, obliged him, in September, 1862, to return to his home, from which he was kidnapped by detective Baker and his minions, the first day he left his bed of sickness, taken at night to Washington, incarcerated in the Old Capitol Prison, and kept there three months, one half of which he was kept in solitary confinement. The reader will ask, what was his alleged offense? He, to this day, has never had a charge preferred against him. His letters to his wife were suppressed, and his frequent demands for an investigation were treated with silence. His wife, who, after his arrest, was despoiled of her furniture and turned out of her house, not knowing whence he had been taken to, went to Washington, called on Judge Advocate Turner, who told her "he knew nothing of his arrest; had never heard of it; said it was an outrageous shame, and promised to look into it." The Secretary of War and his assistant also denied all knowledge of it, and made similar promises; and Detective Baker told her he would be discharged the following day, as there was no reason or cause for his detention. This Baker sent a man to her, who told her if she would pay $250 or $300, he would have him discharged from prison, which she properly refused to pay. Dr. Ellis, conscious of his innocence of any wrong, and anxious for an investigation, repeatedly wrote to Stanton, Turner, and several Senators and Members of Congress, claiming his right to a hearing. For this, and his denunciation of the wrongs inflicted on him, and his threatened exposure of Baker, he was put in solitary confinement. After some time, another victim was put in the room with him, and, as Baker and the Superintendent of the prison thought he learned from his fellow-prisoners some facts in connection with their cases, they again put him in solitary confinement, as he refused to become their spy and informer. This Baker admitted to Dr. Ellis that his arrest was caused by parties implicated in frauds on the Government, in New York, of which he had often expressed himself, and, to get him out of the way, had him arrested. The parties to these outrages were high army officials, some of whom had grown jealous of the well earned praise bestowed on Dr. Ellis by the most prominent members of both houses of Congress, and while in prison they suppressed his letters to these gentlemen and his friends. At length the British Minister, Lord Lyons was informed of his imprisonment, but as Dr. Ellis had worn the United States uniform he hesitated to interfere in his case. Thus the very services he had rendered the country were made a barrier to his obtaining redress. However, Lord Lyons, on becoming fully satisfied of the injustice done him, and on conferring with the English Government, made a formal demand on Secretary Seward for his release, which, as soon as Secretary Stanton learned, he ordered his discharge, and falsely assured him he never heard of, much less ordered, his arrest. Dr. Ellis is now through his minister seeking indemnity for wrongs and outrages committed on him, and the United State Government is still his debtor, not alone for those valuable services rendered to the wounded soldiers, but for money expended to purchase necessaries for the Hospital Transports which the ignorance and imbecility of the heads of the Medical Department had failed to provide. While he was in prison his wife was subjected to every imaginable kind of annoyance, followed by spies, insulted by Detective Baker, robbed of her house and furniture, and slandered to attempt to justify the cruel treatment she and her husband had received.

Among the numerous incidents and aggravating circumstances connected with Dr. Ellis' arrest and imprisonment, I will mention that when the detectives visited his house on the night of his arrest, they took forcible possession of all his private papers and brought them to Washington, and on Dr. E.'s release Dectective Baker admitted to Dr. E. that one of the persons implicated in these frauds on the Government had frequently tried to get possession of them, evidently for the purpose of destroying them, and thus prevent their being used as evidence to convict them in their gigantic swindling. Dr. E., on his papers being demanded, made no delay to surrender them, and freely showed the officers every part of his house. These officers, named Morse and Radford, freely admitted that they could not find anything to convict him, and expressed their censure of the injustice done him, and their conviction of his innocence, and for which Morse, the one in the employ of the War Department, was dismissed from his situation as Detective of the War Department.

Dr. Ellis, on his arrival in Washington in the custody of this Morse, was taken to the office of Chief Detective Baker. He demanded an investigation, or to be informed of the nature of the charges against him, if any, as he had, during the journey from New York, heard from Detective Morse that the statement he made him in New York of Dr. E.'s being only wanted as a witness in Washington, was false, this being the means usually adopted by them to make arrests, so as to prevent their victim being rescued. To his demand, a person acting as deputy for Detective Baker, named Lawrence, replied that he did not know the nature of the charge against him, and if he did he would not tell it, that his orders from the Secretary of War were to commit him to the Old Capitol prison. But ten weeks after this date the Secretary of War, his assistant, and the Judge-Advocate, as before stated, assured his wife that they had no knowledge of his arrest, and had not authorised it to be made. While Dr. Ellis was acting Medical Director in Virginia with the Army of the Potomac, he met Senator Chandler, Assistant Secretary of War Tucker, General Dix, and many other prominent supporters of the Lincoln administration, and as he had rendered valuable services to the government of which they expressed their approbation, and for which they offered their influence, he naturally appealed to them on his being sent to prison to use their influence to get him a trial or statement of the charge against him, but more than one of them informed his friends that such was the state of affairs in Washington, that they dare not interfere, no matter how aggravated the case might be, without jeopardising their own position and perhaps their own liberty.

After the battle of Fair Oaks, Dr. Ellis had the sole charge and care of the wounded amounting to four thousand Union soldiers and nearly five hunred rebels; for these he had to provide transports, clothing, medicines, food, and the necessary articles of nourishment, and such was the want of system in the Medical Department, that on his arrival at the White House the last day of the battle, there were nearly five hundred mutilated soldiers lying on the railroad track as they had been thrown out of the cars without any provision being made for their care or removal. He at once proceeded to get steamboats to the railroad wharf, got them on board, had their filthy and blood-stained uniforms removed, procured food and stimulants for them, as many had lain on the battle-field twenty hours without any care. He procured nurses, performed any necessary operations, and selected surgeons for each steamboat, which as soon as filled, he despatched to a Northern port. In the execution of these laborious duties he continued night and day with remission for a week, having gone three days without eating food and during the whole time he never lay down until he had despatched over four thousand. The last three hundred and sixty-four he put on board of the steamer Louisiana to Philadelphia, where citizens turned out *en masse* to welcome back her brave but unfortunate troops, and to manifest their appreciation for Dr. Ellis's unceasing devotion to their interests. On arrival at Philadelphia, Dr. Ellis on consultation with the Medical Director at that city, decided on giving furloughs to such of the wounded soldiers as were able to reach their homes, and this measure gave very general satisfaction; he also reformed the mode of using as hospital nurses the idle, lazy and dishonest men found in the ranks, believing that a soldier when suffering from wounds or sickness contracted in the discharge of his duties, should not be left at the mercy of the idle, vicious, or dishonest. These reforms, which have since been sanctioned by Congress, were at the time opposed by the head of the Medical Department, as being too progressive and ahead of his plans, and though at this time he informed Dr. Ellis that he had heard of his valuable services and "felt grateful for them," as they had "saved him and the country from disgrace," yet he never after lost an opportunity to make light of those services, and Dr. Ellis is of opinion that he was mainly instrumental in procuring his arrest, and prolonging his imprisonment, by causing the suppression of his communications to the authorities demanding an investigation. His release however was effected by the interposition of Lord Lyons and gentlemen of New York, who brought the matter to Mr. Stanton's notice, and obtaining an order for his unconditional discharge, on the 8th January last.

THE OTHER VICTIMS IN O. C. P.

ALTHOUGH but a few of the cases of victims of despotism in the Old Capitol Prison are given in this work, it is not because the others did not possess equal interest with those specially referred to. Every one of these cases has a history of its own; but the scope of this work will not enable the writer to give them all. To do so would put the book he designs to publish out of the reach of the millions for whose perusal it is specially designed. The time might come when every case of outrage to American freemen, by the sworn guardians of their persons and property, will be sought for by their fellow citizens, and when these victims of despotism will be vindicated, so far as their grievances were caused by devotion to the Constitution of their country, and by their efforts to preserve constitutional liberty in these United States; and when, too, appreciating their fidelity to the cause of their country, the names of these martyrs to liberty will be garnered and preserved as precious evidences that, even in the days of Abraham Lincoln, when the country was ruled by tyrants, and when the people were subjected to an odious and intolerable despotism, there were left a few who dared the worst penalties inflicted upon whoever presumed to exercise his God-given and constitutional rights.

ANOTHER APPEAL FOR A HEARING, OR TO BE RELEASED.

EVERY effort addressed to the President, Secretary of War, Judge Advocate Holt, Judge Advocate Turner and General Halleck, to be vouchsafed a hearing, trial, investigation, or any sort of an examination which would afford me an opportunity to prove that I was a faithful citizen of the United States, having failed of effect, I addressed a letter to Superintendent Wood of the Old Capitol, as he appeared to have more influence with our ruling powers than any one else, and as he manifested some good will for the unfortunate victims of despotism. The following is a copy of this letter which is published, as it states briefly what the relations of the writer were to the Government, even under the despotism to which I was subjected:

OLD CAPITOL PRISON,
WASHINGTON, D. C., Sept. 22nd, 1862.

Sup't. Wood:—For your information, and it may prove for your gratification, as well as for my own satisfaction, I make a brief statement of my relations to the Government, and request that you make use of it in my behalf, at the earliest favorable opportunity.

I acknowledge allegiance, loyalty, fidelity, and duty to the Government of the United States and to none other; nor have I ever violated, or intended to violate, nor contemplated the violation of my allegiance or loyalty, nor refused to perform any duty devolving on me as a true citizen of the U. S.

On the contrary, I have offered my personal service and my personal influence to raise among my friends and acquaintances a regiment of volunteers to maintain the supremacy and authority of of the Government, and to put down the existing Rebellion.

Although I feel that my personal rights have been outraged by an arbitrary and illegal order of the War Department, and myself and family — a wife and four children — subjected to grievous hardships, I would nevertheless maintain with my personal service, and my life, the Constitutional authority of the President of the United States, and any other Constitutional authority in the Government: and am ready and willing to resist by the same means and sacrifices, encroachments from any quarter on the rightful authority of the Government and on the integrity of the Constitution.

I am here the object of partizan malignity, or the victim of misapprehension of my position and relations to the Government, such misapprehension being caused by mistaking opposition to some acts of the Administration for hostility to the Government.

I have never opposed an act of the Administration which was designed to put down rebellion, though I have called in question the constitutionality of some of its acts, not for the purpose of embarrassing the Executive in the performance of its Constitutional duties, but on the contrary, for the purpose of preventing it from being subjected to the reprehension of violating the conditions on which it acquired the authority to administer the Government.

Such briefly, but sufficiently comprehensive to embrace it all, is my position and relation to the Government and the Administration. If I refuse to make any compromise short of an unconditional and unqualified discharge from imprisonment, it is not because I am wanting in loyalty to the Constitution, in allegiance to the Government, or in proper respect for those whom the people have chosen to be our rulers, but because I owe to myself and my family self-respect, and to my friends a duty which would be stigmatized in the former case and violated in the latter, were I to perform any act which by the most violent implication could be construed into an admission by me of the truth of the foul aspersions cast upon my loyalty, and of the malignant and false accusations of my personal and partizan enemies. Hence believing myself to be unjustly as well as illegally held here as a prisoner, I ask to be discharged unconditionally and unqualifiedly, or, if the Government has any evidence proving the contrary, I request a trial of the issue and shall submit in a proper spirit to such punishment as the laws prescribe.

Respectfully yours,
D. A. MAHONY.

This letter had no more effect than many others which had been addressed to other officials. The Superintendent was sent to Richmond about this time, ostensibly to effect an exchange of prisoners, but in reality to make propositions of peace to the Confederates.

Mr. Wood remained at Richmond some three weeks, and having failed to effect the real design contemplated by his mission to the condederate capitol, he was ordered home by the Secretary of War in apparent disgrace. This was done to cover the real object in view.

THE PEACE PROPOSITIONS.

The propositions which Mr. Wood was authorized to make were:

1st. That the Stave States should have a Congress of their own to regulate their domestic institutions.

2d. That the fugitive slave law should be enforced, or failing to do so, the State to which a fugitive escaped should pay his value and the costs made in an effort to reclaim him.

3d. That the representation in the Federal Congress should be based on white population only.

4th. That the debts of the confederacy incurred to carry on the war should be assumed and paid by the United States as restored to the Union.

5th. That slavery should be under the control of the respective States exclusively, but that no laws should be passed by Territories to exclude or permit the introduction of slaves.

Mr. Wood was not successful in his mission, because the Confederates had not enough confidence in the Administration to make any treaty with it, as then constituted.

It might be doubted by some that the Administration, or any member of it, authorized or directed these propositions to be made through Mr. Wood. It will be an objection in their minds that it is not such a person as Mr. Wood who would probably be selected for such a mission, but he was just the man for the *manner* of making such a proposition. He was to do it as if it were his own suggestion, and he was to make it to some of his old acquaintances in Richmond. If it took well it would not be difficult to consummate the arrangement through more respectable diplomatists. It will not be surprising if it should be denied that any such propositions as those above referred to were ever made or authorized to be made by any person in power at Washington, especially as the Administration has it in its power to crush the truth from being heard.

PRISONERS' HEALTH AFFECTED.

AFTER Mr. Wood's return from Richmond, he promised to have the Western prisoners, who had been under subjection for nearly three months, released. We were all suffering more or less from the confinement and bad treatment to which we had been compelled to submit. In my own case, my health was failing rapidly, so visibly so that two physicians who were in the room with me became alarmed at my situation. They voluntarily made an examination of me, and the following is the result:

PHYSICIAN'S CERTIFICATE.

This will certify that we, the undersigned, physicians and surgeons, having carefully examined Mr. Dennis A. Mahony, a prisoner of State, now confined in the Old Capitol Prison at Washington, D. C., do hereby affirm it as our professional opinion, that the bad health of Mr. Mahony is the result of continued confinement; and further, we believe the disease which he is now suffering from (namely, incipient paralysis) is aggravated by his imprisonment, and that a protraction of it will continue to affect him injuriously, and thereby endanger his life.

Thomas T. Ellis,
M. D. and M. R. C. L. S.
John I. Moran, M. D.

In presence of A. D. Duff.

This had no effect on the tyrants who held us in subjection. Indeed there is good reason to believe that they would have been glad had death taken us, out of their hands, instead of being obliged to let us go at large again. This presumption is more than warranted by the imposition of the conditions referred to in the following statement of these prisoners as the condition on which they were at last released.

CONDITIONS OF RELEASE OF SOME OF THE POLITICAL PRISONERS.

On the 10th of November Superintendent Wood, of the Old Capitol, presented to Messrs. Judge Duff, of Benton, Illinois, Judge Mulkey, of Cairo, Illinois, David Sheward, of Fairfield, Iowa, and D. A. Mahony, of Dubuque, Iowa, these being all who were left of the Prisoners of State, with a paper saying that he was directed by the Judge-Advocate, Turner, to say to those prisoners that they could not be released till they signed it, and agreed to comply with its requirements. After Mr. Wood left the prison, the paper was examined by the parties interested, and also by their fellow-prisoners. It was, as will be seen by the copy of it included in these observations, an oath, both of allegiance to the Government and an obligation not to prosecute the Federal or State officers concerned in the arrest and imprisonment of those four persons. The first impulse and determination of all was to refuse to take this or any other oath as a condition of their release, but on reflection and after a more considerate examination of the oath, proposed to be taken, and at the urgent solicitation of other prisoners who hoped by the discharge of the Prisoners of State to have the way opened for their early release, it was reluctantly decided to comply with the proposed terms. There was no other objection made to taking the proposed oath of allegiance than that it might be inferred from the taking of it that those who might do so, would be thereby admitting that they had violated the allegiance which was due from them to the Government, and that the taking of a new oath would be construed as a restoration of these persons to their condition of citizens, just as if they had done anything to forfeit their rights and condition as such. But on reflection they came to the conclusion that they would prefer to take an oath of allegiance, as by doing so the tyrants who had imprisoned them on the pretence of disloyalty, would have no good ground to stand on to justify their course.

So, too, did they come to the conclusion that, by taking an oath of allegiance, they would place themselves in a better condition to have damages for their illegal imprisonment, than if they went into court without that evidence of their loyalty. But the other portion of the obligation to prosecute the tyrants who had caused their arrest and imprisonment was a stumbling-block. What! swear away one's rights, and that, too, for the benefit of those who had injured us most outrageously, flagrantly, violently! But after this ebullition of indignation, Judgment said, will not the imposition of such an obligation on us be the best evidence that we have been here for three months the innocent and injured victims of Lincoln's despotism? and will it not also prove that the tyrants who are used to subject us to this despotism know themselves to be guilty of an offense for which we have redress against them? So said Common Sense. But admitting this to be so, how can we obtain any redress, if we forswear our rights to seek for it? The conclusion come to was, that if the Government protected its officers in the commission of crime, there would be still left the remedy which nature gave to every sentient being to protect and defend himself, and to obtain redress for injuries inflicted on him. With such conclusions, and being urged to it not only by their fellow-prisoners, but also by Superintendent Wood, who made a personal appeal to some of us, these four persons—Messrs. Duff, Mulkey, Sheward, and myself—took the obligation referred to.

Superintendent Wood told the prisoners, and the Judge Advocate reiterated the same thing, that this obligation was exacted because certain persons who had been released commenced suits for damages against the officers of the Government. Judge Turner went so far in this matter as to say to Judge Mason, counsel for Messrs. Mulkey and Sheward, that suits had been commenced in their behalf, and gave Judge Mason this as a pretext, lie as it was, that these prisoners should not be released. Nor did it appear that there was any foundation for the assertion that any one had commenced suits for redress, but even if they had done so, why should that fact affect the rights of others? If the officers sued were not amenable in any way, what harm could befall them from being sued by discharged prisoners? If guilty, why should they not suffer the consequences of their criminality and injustice?

But the fact was, that Judge Advocate Turner, the Secretary of War, and the other tyrants and villains who had been concerned in these arrests and imprisonments knew that they had done wrong, and they caught at any means which they thought would shield them from the consequences. Hence the imposition of the oath referred to on certain prisoners of state.

The following paper was drawn up by fellow-prisoners of the gentlemen referred to; appended to which is a copy of the obligation exacted of them on their being released.

OLD CAPITOL PRISON,
WASHINGTON, D. C., Nov. 11, 1862.

We, the undersigned persons, now confined in Room No. 16, Old Capitol Prison, hereby certify that on the evening of November 10, 1862, William P. Wood, Esq., Superintendent of said prison, did, in our presence and hearing, present to Dennis A. Mahony, of Dubuque, Iowa, Judge John H. Mulkey, of Cairo, Ill., Judge Andrew D. Duff, of Benton, Ill., and David Sheward, of Fairfield, Iowa, now confined in said prison, a form of oath and obligation of which a true copy is hereby annexed, requiring them to obligate themselves under oath not to prosecute any State or Federal officers who may have been instrumental or engaged in causing their arrest; and that unless they so obligate themselves they would not be released from imprisonment, and as they have, to our knowledge, made repeated but unsuccessful efforts to obtain from the authorities an examination or trial of the charges alleged to have been made against them, and as they have now suffered nearly three months' imprisonment, to the injury of their health and business, causing great family suffering, and in the case of the aforesaid Dennis A. Mahony, we are convinced that a continuance of the confinement would endanger his life.

Now we do certify that believing there is no hope for the aforesaid gentlemen to obtain justice or redress while they are imprisoned, we do recommend them to sign said obligation, although it is extorted from them as their only condition of release, and further we certify that the aforesaid gentlemen were unwilling to accede to this request and unjust condition, but at our solicitation they have been induced to comply.

THOMAS T. ELLIS, M. D.,
    late Post-Surgeon, New York.
THEO. T. EDGERTON, New York.
JOHN J. MORAN, M. D., Frederick, Md.

COPY OF OBLIGATION.

I ———— ——, of ———— ——, do solemnly ———— that I will support, protect, and defend the Constitution and Government of the United States against all enemies, whether domestic or foreign, and that I will bear true faith, allegiance and loyalty to the same, any ordinance, resolution, or law of any State convention or legislature to the contrary notwithstanding; and further, that I do this with a full determination, pledge and purpose, without any mental reservation or evasion whatever; and further, that I will neither enter any of the States now in insurrection against the authority of the Federal Government, or hold any correspondence whatever with them or with any persons in them during the rebellion, without permission of the Secretary of War, and that I will in all things deport myself as a good and loyal citizen of the United States, and that I will not cause or commence any action or suit against the officers of any loyal State or of the United States, for causing my arrest or imprisonment at any future time. So help me God.

Sworn to and subscribed before me this ———— day of ————.

A true copy.
J. J. MORAN.

RELEASED AT LAST.

On the 11th of November, Messrs. Judge Duff, of Benton, Illinois, Judge Mulkey, of Cairo, Illinois, David Sheward, of Fairfield, Iowa, and the writer, were taken before Judge Advocate Turner, and without any trial, hearing, investigation or examination farther than to enquire of us whether we belonged to the Knights of the Golden Circle, and requiring us to subscribe an oath to the effect that we did not, and to subscribe the oath that we would not prosecute Federal or State officers who had been concerned in our arrest, we were "honorably discharged." This discharge was in the following words:

(COPY OF DISCHARGE.)

OLD CAPITOL PRISON,
WASHINGTON, D. C., Nov. 11, 1862.

To all whom it may concern:

This will certify that the bearer, Dennis A. Mahony, a Prisoner of State, has been duly and honorably discharged from custody at this prison.

By order,
Secretary of War.
CAPT. B. L. HIGGINS,
Co. A. 86th N. Y. V.,
Commanding.

Similar discharges to this were given to Messrs. Duff, Mulkey, Sheward and Ross.

We returned to the Old Capitol to take leave of our fellow-victims of despotism, and to pack up the few pieces of clothing which remained with us after having passed through the ordeal of being worn in the filth of the prison. Our fellow-victims had managed to have a leave-taking supper prepared for us in room No. 16. The scene was affecting. The large room was lighted by two candles; the two tables used by the two messes in the room were placed together, and covered with such articles as the prisoners could procure. The Superintendent was invited to partake of the viands. He replied that it was against the rules for him to eat with the prisoners, but inasmuch as the four gentlemen who were about to leave were no longer prisoners, he would eat with them, and so he sat down, affected as much by our departure as was any one of our fellow-victims. There was not one among us all whose emotions did not overcome him. The four persons now about to leave were the longest under subjection. All the later arrivals looked up to us for counsel and sympathy, and now we were about to be separated from them. These and other reflections swelled their hearts with emotions which found vent in tears. We tore ourselves away, choking with emotions in the endeavor to say, good-bye.

DUPLICITY OF THE SECRETARY OF WAR—PUBLIC ORDER FOR THE RELEASE OF PRISONERS OF STATE—PRIVATE ORDER TO DISREGARD THE ONE PUBLICLY PROMULGATED.

The clamors of the people against the imprisonment of Political offenders wrung from the Secretary of War, an order from his department dated the 22nd of November, 1862, for the discharge of "all persons now in military custody" who had been arrested on the alleged ground of discouraging enlistments, &c.

The order was as follows:

WAR DEPARTMENT,
Washington, November 22, 1862.

Ordered—1. That all persons now in military custody who have been arrested for discouraging volunteer enlistments, opposing the draft, or for otherwise giving aid and comfort to the enemy in States where the draft has been made, or the quota of volunteers and militia has been furnished, shall be discharged from further military restraint.

2. That persons who, by authority of the military commander or Governor in rebel States, have been arrested and sent from such State for disloyalty or hostility to the Government of the United States, and are now in military custody, may also be discharged upon giving their parole to do no act of

hostility against the Government of the United States, nor render aid to its enemies. But all such persons shall remain subject to military surveillance and liable to arrest on breach of their parole. And if any such persons shall prefer to leave the loyal States on condition of their not returning again during the war, or until special leave for that purpose be obtained from the President, then such person shall, at his option, be released and depart from the United States, or be conveyed beyond the military lines of the United States forces.

3. This order shall not operate to discharge any person who has been in arms against the Government, or by force and arms has resisted, or attempted to resist the draft, nor relieve any person from liability to trial and punishment by civil tribunals, or by court-martial or military commission, who may be amenable to such tribunals for offenses committed.

By order of the Secretary of War:
E. D. TOWNSEND,
Assistant Adjutant-General.

While this order was promulgated to satisfy the public, a secret private order was issued at the same time to the commanders of the Bastiles not to release any political offenders under that order.

The following is a copy of this secret order:

WASHINGTON, Nov. 24, 11.50 A. M.
Commanding Officer, Fort ———:
None of the prisoners confined at your post will be released under orders of the War Department of the 22d inst. without special instructions from the Department.

By order of the Secretary of War,
E. D. TOWNSEND, A. A. G.

Thus is the Secretary of War convicted of duplicity, hypocrisy, treachery and deceit, as scarcely one, if any, prisoner was released under the order of the 22d November. On the contrary, most of the prisoners in Forts Lafayette and Delaware, if not in other Bastiles, were still kept in confinement until late in December, and some of them for a considerable time afterwards. The following-named prisoners were in Fort Delaware, and were not released under the published order of the Secretary of War:

Anthony Bender, Waynesborough, Chester county, Pa., arrested Nov. 4, 1862.

J. R. Ray, Mount Hope, Franklin county, Pa., arrested Sept. 11, 1862.

M. Y. Johnson, Esq., Galena, Illinois, arrested Aug. 28, 1862.

Dr. E. S. Sharp, Salem, New Jersey, arrested, Aug. 22, 1862.

S. H. Ford, Philadelphia, Pa., arrested Aug. 26, 1862.

T. T. Costello, Philadelphia, Pa., arrested Aug. 24, 1862.

W. Walton, Philadelphia, Pa., arrested Aug. 22, 1862.

J. C. Faber, Baltimore, Md., arrested July 26, 1862.

E. B. McClees, Baltimore, Md., arrested July 19, 1862.

J. T. Young, Martinsburg, Va., arrested July 14, 1862.

J. O. E. Sowers, Clarke county Va., arrested Aug. 13, 1862.

H. K. Gregg, Berryville, Clarke county, Va., arrested Aug. 13, 1862.

Dr. John Laws, Bridgeville, Susex county, Delaware, arrested Oct. 7; 1862.

W. W. Meredith, Willow Grove, Kent county, Delaware, arrested Oct. 7, 1862.

George Reynolds, Kent county, Delaware, arrested Oct. 3, 1862.

Thos. O'Keefe, Memphis, Tenn., arrested Sept. 27, 1862.

Patrick Ryan, Memphis, Tenn., arrested Sept. 27, 1862.

A. Parsons, Mayport, East Florida, arrested Oct. 2, 1862.

M. A. Crawford, Camden county, Georgia, arrested Oct. 12, 1862.

Captain William Sherman, England, arrested, Oct. 23, 1862.

George R. Waller, Charleston, S. C., arrested Oct. 7, 1862.

Daniel Campbell, Charleston, S, C., arrested Oct. 7, 1862.

Hiram Wentworth, Minnesota, arrested June 6, 1862.

Among the prisoners in Fort Lafayette who were still kept in confinement notwithstanding this public order of the Secretary were Dr. Olds of Ohio, and David Sheean, Esq., of Galena, Illinois, and there were doubtless many others whose names have not been given to the public.

Notwithstanding these well attested facts, Mr. Stanton in a report made by him on the 29th of November stated that,

" By a recent order all persons arrested for discouraging enlistments and disloyal practises in the States where the quotas of volunteers and militia are filled up, have been released. Other persons arrested by military commanders and sent from the d partments where their presence was deemed dangerous to the public safety, have been discharged upon parole to be of good behavior and do no act of hostility against the Government of the United States."

This Mr. Stanton knew was a barefaced wilful and premeditated falsehood, uttered to mislead and deceive the public.

It is also alleged and is no doubt true, judging the circumstances by the other acts of duplicity of Mr. Stanton, Secretary of War, that on the application of Hon. Reverdy Johnson, an order was issued from the War Department for the release and discharge of Judge Carmichael of Maryland, and that a private order was sent simultaneously to the commandant of Fort Delaware *not* to release Judge Carmichael on the presentation of the order to that effect.

If anything more than this be wanting to convict the Secretary of War, the tool of the Administration, of duplicity, deceit, hypocrisy and treachery, besides being a tyrant of the meanest and most despicable character, what is it that is necessary to complete the proof? Do the American people, does the world at large, need more evidence of the truth of the charge?

CONCLUSION.

I AM obliged to bring this book to a conclusion at this point, because, having limited the price of it to such an amount as will place it within the reach of most persons who desire to read a book of this kind, my publisher has been obliged to limit me to the number of pages to which the work is now extended. I had designed to introduce in this book the result of many interviews I had with Confederate prisoners in the Old Capitol, in relation to the restoration or reconstruction of the Union, and I may say here that it is quite feasible, not only in my opinion, but in that of most Southern men, to restore or reconstruct the Union on a solid and lasting foundation. It needs only that peace be restored to effect this object. War will never accomplish it, as war keeps the people of both sections at enmity with each other. There are many in the South, as well as in the North, who attach themselves to the war party who were originally opposed to the war. Some are influenced by what they believe to be patriotic motives, others by self-interest, and others because it appears to be the most popular position. But whatever the motive or the influence, certain it is that while the North wars against the South, the people of the South will be united in the effort to resist what appears to them to be an aggression upon their rights of person and of States.

I had also designed to give the result of my reflections on the arbitrary course of the Administration in relation to those citizens of the Northern States who, like myself, differed with it in opinion as to the best means of putting down the rebellion and restoring the Union, or failing to restore it, as I think we shall fail, of reconstructing it, on such a basis as will bring all the States back under one Government which will give security and protection to every individual citizen, and to each sovereign State, and be supported in the exercise of its legitimate functions by both States and People.

It has also disappointed me, that I have not been able, for want of space, to include in this work the cases of many of my fellow-victims of despotism in the Old Capitol, and in the various other Bastiles used by our tyrant rulers for the oppression of hundreds of American freemen whose offense, in the eye of the Administration, was a virtue in the estimation of Patriotism. But I console myself, and will endeavor to satisfy the reader, by the prospect that if this work should be appreciated by the few freemen who have not been corrupted by the favors of the Administration, or overawed by its powers, I shall publish a sequel to the Prisoner of State, which will include all that I have been obliged to leave out of this work.

Meantime I commit the "Prisoner of State" to the consideration of my fellow citizens, trusting that its perusal may confirm those who have remained faithful to the Constitution, in the principles of free Government embraced in that inestimable charter of our liberties, and that it might restore to the truth many who have been led away by partisan zeal or by impulses which they felt to be patriotic.

The majority of mankind seem to be affected and

influenced more by sentiment than by principle.—The founders of the Federal Government presumed that their descendants would be like themselves—men of principle—and that in a conflict of sensibilities with truth, right and judgment, there would be no doubt that a sacrifice would be made by those of mere feeling in preference of a surrender of that which was most dear to them as men and citizens of a free Government. The best test of patriotism, according to the standard of our ancestors was to live up to the restraints of the Constitution, and in rulers, its vigorous enforcement. In our days patriotism consists in disregarding the Constitution altogether, and those who ought to be the foremost in submitting to its restraints, conforming to its obligations, and in preserving it from violation, are the first to act in utter disregard of its provisions, and to set an example of faithlessness to the people at large. This is manifested by almost every act of the Federal Administration, and by, apparently, a majority of the people who sustain it in its arbitrary and despotic course, and in its imbecile and vacillating policy.

And now, if I could influence the reader to draw any conclusions from this book worthy of the cause to which it is devoted, and of service to our unfortunate country, I would make that conclusion be: THIS WAR MUST END. PEACE IS UNION. War is not the best means to restore the Union. War cannot make the people of the North and South love each other; on the contrary, the longer it is waged, the more alienated from each other will the people of these two sections become to one another. Peace might restore friendly relations between the North and South, if the people of both sections will only repress those feelings of hostility towards each other which have resulted, by their manifestation, in war; and these relations of amity being once restored, reunion must be the inevitable consequence. To effect this, let every American who would transmit to posterity the heritage bequeathed to him by his fathers, emulate the patriotism of his ancestors, and take a lesson from their self-sacrifice, their self-immolation, and let history record it of us, as it does of them, that we preserved from the destruction of partisan fanaticism, and from the subjection of domestic tyrants that precious legacy of free Government, wrested by them from foreign tyrants and embraced in State Sovereignties incorporated in a Federal Union. It is the hope, as it is the prayer of the author, that such may be the happiness of the American People.

THE END.

www.ingramcontent.com/pod-product-compliance
Lightning Source LLC
Chambersburg PA
CBHW050847300426
44111CB00010B/1166